Suzy Gershman's

BORN TO SHOP

ITALY

*The Ultimate Guide for
Travelers Who Love to Shop*

10th Edition

WILEY

Wiley Publishing, Inc.

For Aaron and Jenny—my kids, and the new kids on the block in these pages—who have brought new life to Italy and extra sunshine to my life.

Published by:

Wiley Publishing, Inc.
111 River St.
Hoboken, NJ 07030-5744

ISBN 0-7645-2561-1
ISSN 1066-2804

Editor: Paul Prince
Production Editor: Heather Wilcox
Photo Editor: Richard Fox
Cartographer: John Decamillis
Production by Wiley Indianapolis Composition Services

For information on our other products and services or to obtain technical support, please contact our Customer Care Department within the U.S. at 800/762-2974, outside the U.S. at 317/572-3993 or fax 317/572-4002.

Wiley also publishes its books in a variety of electronic formats. Some content that appears in print may not be available in electronic formats.

Manufactured in the United States of America

5   4   3   2   1

CONTENTS

MAP LIST

ABOUT THE AUTHORS

Suzy Gershman is an author and a journalist who has worked in the fiber and fashion industry since 1969 in both New York and Los Angeles, and has held editorial positions at *California Apparel News, Mademoiselle, Gentleman's Quarterly,* and *People* magazine, where she was West Coast Style editor. She writes regularly for various magazines; her essays on retailing are text for Harvard Business School. She frequently appears on network and local television; she is a contributor to *National Geographic Traveler* and *Where Paris*.

Suzy lives part time in Paris, part time in Provence, and part time at the nearest airport.

Jennifer McCormick is a graduate student and part-time editorial assistant for *Born to Shop*.

Aaron Gershman is a singer-songwriter who lives in Brooklyn, New York, and is a contributing editor to *Born to Shop*. He has been on the *Born to Shop* team since he was 4 years old, but has only recently begun serious research responsibilities.

TO START WITH

Now that I live in Paris, I am a little more jaded about travel to neighboring Italy—the things that once seemed such good buys are now being reevaluated, either because prices have changed with the arrival of the euro, the fall of the dollar, and the way the world is whirling . . . or simply because I now live in Europe and have more access to this kind of merchandise, so it doesn't seem so special.

For this reason—and many others—I have two full-time Americans helping me out to give you a different perspective, as well as their version of reality—as seen from the young person's point of view. Okay, okay, they are family; this is Italy—we believe in nepotism. Besides, did I know what Golas were? Not before Aaron and Jenny explained. (See "Sneakers," p. 59.)

This book has always been different from other titles in the series, because Italy has so many primary shopping cities. This edition is packed with even more destinations . . . with luck, someday we'll go to two books and even more details. I feel like more and more people are interested in driving around, in renting a summer home, and maybe even purchasing a second or retirement home.

The fall of the dollar has made me especially sensitive to prices. Besides, with prices as high as they are, I think more and more people are interested in outlets and local sources, which tend to be out of major cities. Besides, I found Florence so filled with tourists (and it wasn't even "in-season") that I can't imagine anyone thinking this would be fun.

I hope some of my extra side trips have inspired you to reach out past the big cities and to slow down, smell the slow food, and buy a little olive oil. There are more and more factory outlets in this edition, and also more information about arranging for someone to drive you into the countryside if you do not want to drive yourself.

Many thanks to the guys who help me do my job: Karen Preston at Leading Hotels of the World, who helps me organize a lot of my travel; the team at Boscolo; Guiseppe Mazza at Bagnioli; and, of course, Logan Bentley and Maria Teresa, who runs Tuscany by Tuscans and can arrange anything and make it seem simple. *Grazie mille* to Rolando Fallani, general manager of the Grand Hotel Villa Medici, Vincenzo Pagano from Naples, the Sersale family of Positano and Naples, and most importantly the guys at Delta Air Lines. To one and all, my heartfelt thanks. Thanks also to my personal team, generous with information and secrets: Alan Heller (Milan) and his sister Faith Heller Willinger (Florence and Rome).

Big *baci* to all; the next pizza is on me.

Chapter One

....

THE BEST OF ITALY IN AN INSTANT

Italy has more style per square mile than you can shake a *for-maggio* at, especially in the northern regions. The south has more *limoncello,* that delectable lemon vodka brew that makes me tipsy after one thimbleful . . . so wherever your travels take you, I know you'll find a lot to buy and a lot more to enjoy. Prices have gone up now that Italy has switched to euros, but there's still plenty to buy . . . and even a few bargains to be had. Even if you're on a cruise and don't get to do much shopping, you'll still find specialty items to put a smile on your face— and your wallet. Welcome ashore, mates.

If you're in a hurry, you may want to breeze through what I consider some of the highlights of the whole country, crammed into these up-front pages, so when you stop by these places, you can worship and shop and feel like you've indulged. By no means is my list comprehensive; it will take years for me to perfect it, so bear with me while I shop, shop, shop.

The Best Store in Italy

10 CORSO COMO
10 Corso Como, Milan.

No, that's not a typo; the store's name is its address.

There's much more written about this store in the Milan chapter (see chapter 8), but suffice it to say that this is a bazaar, a magic act created by one of Italy's most famous fashion editors and stylists who turned to retail and hasn't looked back.

The store is well stocked, but for people who shop a lot, there are no surprises in terms of merchandise. What's yummy is the way it's laid out and presented and served on your platter. You can gawk and enjoy and not buy a thing, but don't miss it. Note the cafe (speaking of served on a platter), the furniture in the garden, and the upstairs bookstore.

The Second-Best Store in Italy

VENETIA STVDIVM
Calle Larga XXII Marco, San Marco 2403, Venice;
Mercerie, San Marco 723, Venice.

Fortuny-inspired pleated silks made into wraps, bags, tassels, and treasures . . . a wonderland of fairy tales and dreams in colors that will make you swoon. Two shops in Venice and one in London (go figure).

The Best Grand-Scale Shopping City

MILAN

Milan may not be adorable or overwhelmingly charming or flashy, but the shopping is divine. One reason is that Milan offers high-quality goods in many different price ranges. Milan has excellent alternative retail—street markets, jobbers who sell discounted designer clothing, and more.

The Best Small Shopping City

DERUTA

Italy is filled with tiny cities devoted to craftspeople and artists where shopping has been elevated to an art form. But the best of them all is the city of Deruta, in Umbria, where every store sells hand-painted faience. Deruta is about an hour from Rome.

The Best Port City for a Quick Spree

VENICE

Venice is not included on every Mediterranean cruise, but if you can get here, even if only for 1 day, do—it is magic. The shopping isn't bad, either.

The Best Factory Town, North

COMO

Perhaps because Como is ever so much more than a factory town, it wins my vote for the best factory town in Italy. It's gorgeous, it's upscale, it's got a lake, it's got Switzerland nearby, and it's got silk factories galore. Prices are laughably low on the biggest names in designer fashion fabrics, including French names. Go home with fabric by the yard or ties, scarves, and shawls for at least half their regular retail price. The best factory in town? Ratti.

Como is about 30 minutes from Milan by train. **FoxTown**, one of the many outlet malls selling designer things at a discount, is located across the Swiss border between Como and Lugano (see chapter 8), but note that Switzerland does not use euros and prices there tend to be high.

Best Factory Area, South

The area between Florence and the sea is filled with factories, whether you go south toward Arezzo and the Prada outlet or north, toward Lucca and the Pratesi outlet. Florence is so touristy these days—and expensive—that you may well want to take in all of Tuscany and enjoy your drive under the Tuscan sun with punctuation marks at various factories and outlet stores. Many are even in real factories, not in fancy malls. The Mall, however, does include a handful of big-name designer outlets where once a mere Gucci outlet stood tall.

The Best Outlet Mall

Eeeny, meeny, miney, moe . . . I'm going with Serravalle here, mostly because the other malls are new and just getting it together. Watch this space. *Note:* This mall is an hour's drive south of Milan or 45 minutes north of Genoa; do not attempt it on the train from Milan—the connections are difficult and near to impossible.

The Best Airport Shopping

LEONARDO DA VINCI INTERNATIONAL AIRPORT
Rome.

It's virtually a shopping mall, with all major designers represented. Furthermore, a guide to its shops, which lists prices, is made available once a year. Use it to comparison-shop. Not everything is a bargain, but you'll have a great time finding out which items are well priced.

The Best Sales

FENDI
Via Borgognona 39, Rome.

You haven't lived until you've wandered into the Fendi store in Rome at sale time (twice a year, Jan and July). There are mounds of goodies (some of them a few seasons old) selling at a fraction of their regular price. Affordable luxury goods!

While Fendi sales are good at all Fendi shops, the best sale is in the Rome store. From a design perspective, it is the most fun-to-look-at shop in the Spanish Steps luxury shopping district; to get a sale and an eyeful of glamour at one time is indeed to see the face of bliss.

The Best Department Store

LA RINASCENTE
Piazza del Duomo, Milan.

In response to competition, La Rinascente has redone its image in recent years. The store is a lot like an American department store and may not impress you at first. Wait until you experience its details—that's where its greatness lies. The store offers non-Italian-passport holders a flat 10% discount on health, beauty, and makeup treatments on the first floor. And there's a tax-free office upstairs, as well as a travel agency, hair salon, and full-service bank. Its cafe overlooks the Duomo and will drench you with magic and memories.

The Best Historical Shopping Experience

ANTICO SETIFICIO FIORENTINO
Via Bartolini 4, Florence.

You will step back in time when you enter this 18th-century silk factory that was renovated by the Pucci family. It still produces damasks, silks, and cottons on looms that have hummed for hundreds of years.

The Best Street Market

SAN AGOSTINO MARKET
Viale Papiniano, Milan.

Fun? It just doesn't get much better than this! On Tuesday and Saturday, you can enjoy this fabulous street market, which sells fruits and vegetables in one part and designer goods in the other. Arrange your visit to Milan so that you're in town for one of the market days!

Best Weekly Market
(Runner-Up to Best Street Market)

SIENA, EVERY WEDNESDAY

I have been to a fair number of markets in my life and celebrated market day in a large number of cities all over the world, so when I say this is one of the best, I really mean it. It helps if the sky is blue, the sun is shining, the temperature is not too high, and the crowds aren't too great—but any way you slice it, this is a market for locals, filled to overflowing with everything from shoes to tractors. Thoughtfully organized by category of goods—with foodstuffs to one side and dry goods on the other—this market takes up a half-moon area at the top of town.

The Best Museum Shop

THE VATICAN
Vatican City, Rome.

No cheap pope scopes, but beautiful reproductions of precious treasures. Puzzles of the Sistine Chapel ceiling . . . and more.

The Best Free Postcards

HOTEL EDEN
Via Ludovisi 49, Rome.

Postcards from Il Papiro created in medieval style with a bright blue background, lots of gold stars, flowing borders, detailed insets, and design-school whoop-de-do.

The Second-Best Free Postcards

LISA CORTI
Via Conchetta 6, Milan;
Via del Bardi 58, Florence.

This artist, known for her splash of vibrant colors on cotton, gives away free postcards created from several of her prints.

The Best Gifts for $10 or Less

- Designer pasta in fashion colors. Find it in all sorts of brand names, in all Italian cities in grocery stores, *entocas* (wine/food shops), and TTs (tourist traps); 5.45€ to 9€ ($6–$10) a package.
- For an alternative to designer pasta, look for regional pasta specialties. Barilla, Italy's largest pasta maker, creates specific "designs" for specific markets. In Venice, I bought

Casarecce, a style only available there. Go figure. For less than 1.80€ ($2), I look like a genius to a foodie.

- Caldo Caldo brand of coffee—even coffee with grappa—or hot chocolate in a "magic" cup that heats itself when you employ (or deploy) the push-in bottom, about .90€ ($1) per cup. *Note:* These are hard to find. Best source—Milan Centrale train station grocery store.

- Chocolate postcards. I wouldn't try mailing these, but they are darn cute gifties. Caffarel, a mass maker of chocolates, offers the Italy's Treasures Collection—a series of postcards that picture famous historical sites. In the main Milan train station, I found a selection of "cards" representing five different cities.

- Soap. Try the Weekend soap from Farmaceutica di Santa Maria Novella or any of Rancé's soaps sold at the freestanding Rancé store in Rome at Piazza Navona. The Weekend soap, available at the Farmaceutica di Santa Maria Novella stores in Florence and Rome, costs 9€ ($10) for a package containing three soap bars, one each for Friday, Saturday, and Sunday. You can also buy Italian soaps in grocery stores or at any of the *erbolistas*.

- Limoncello liquor. Sold most readily in southern Italy below Florence and in most supermarkets and airports, limoncello is like lemon vodka with a pucker. This is a wonderful souvenir; serve chilled.

- Lush gifties. Yes, Lush is a British firm famous for its bath and beauty products; and, yes, there are now Lush stores in the U.S. (1st one is in San Francisco), but the Italian Lush products are made with local ingredients, so you can buy limoncello soap or shampoo.

- Cardinals' socks. Sold only in Rome, at about 9€ ($10) a pair. Fine cotton knits, they come only in red, of course.

- Milk-frothing machine. It's a battery-operated job that looks like a small wand and makes the milk in your cappuccino stand up and smile. I found the old-fashioned ones in a market in Rome for 5.45€ ($6) and in an appliance store in Florence for 7.30€ ($8).

The Best Extravagant Gifts

- Mantero scarf, in the shawl size; printed with so many screens of gorgeous color that you will weep for its beauty and finesse. Come to think of it, anything from Mantero will tickle any extravagance bone. Buy yours at the outlet store in Como for savings.
- Important art glass. Venice or Murano.
- Gucci dog collar. Hmm, Gucci anything. Gucci outlet, anyone? It's outside Florence.
- Etro paisleys. Silk or cashmere; in all Etro stores, in most major cities . . . but then, maybe you can find them at the Etro outlet in beautiful downtown Milan.

Jenny's Five Best Buys in Italy

- Black squid-ink pasta (2.70€/$3), available at the Free Store in Milan's Centrale train station.
- Caldo Caldo self-heating "Magic Coffee" cup (.90€/$1), at the Free Store in Milan's Centrale train station.
- Necklaces and other items (14€–36€/$15–$40 each) sold at the Kalos jewelry store in Milan.
- Venetian-glass necklace (5.45€/$6) found at various shops in Venice.
- Pratesi beachwear and shoes (18€–46€/$20–$50) sold at the Pratesi factory outlet, in Pistoia, near Florence.

Aaron's Five Best Buys in Italy

- Fedora hat (10€/$15) sold by street vendors in Florence.
- Diesel (36€/$40) and H&M (14€/$15) jeans at the Mercato delle Cascine, in Florence.
- Prada suit (182€/$200), sold at the Prada outlet store near Florence.
- Ruggeri notebooks (under 9€/$10), available at the Free Store in Milan's Centrale train station.
- A pair of Gola sneakers (27€/$30) at the Mercato delle Cascine in Florence.

Chapter Two

....

DETAILS

WELCOME TO ITALY

I'm not sure when you were last in Italy, but my heavens, *madonna mia,* have things changed. Not just the fact that Italy uses the euro (€), but the fact that while trying to merge into the whole of Europe—and maybe take some hints from the U.S.—Italy has all sorts of new ideas. Colosseum meets Rose Bowl; Milanese move into Rome and turn up the heat; Bulgari family goes into hotel business as a line extension . . . teaming up with Marriott International (the 1st hotel has opened in Milan). Ah, those family jewels.

Italian prices have gone up, up, and then up again, so that locals complain about their cost of living and the government complains that it can't afford the maintenance on the landmarks. Seriously, folks. There's the possibility that the Italian national monuments will be leased out or sold to private firms. So along with the Rose Bowl and the Orange Bowl being sponsored events, or corporate stadiums, you'd have the Enron Leaning Tower of Pisa . . . or maybe the Pizza Hut Leaning Tower of Pisa. I kinda like that one.

When lire were converted into euros, the official exchange rate was essentially 2,000 lire to 1€, but the talk of the town is that prices are now so high that things cost in euros what they cost in lire. That means prices are perceived as being twice as high. Not just prices paid by tourists, mind you, but prices for everything and everyone, even the government.

Meanwhile, in legal matters, in March 2003, the *Times* of London announced that new laws in Italy not only make divorce easier, but now allow one to cite an overbearing mother-in-law as grounds. *Mamma mia!* What is Italy without mama to butt in?

The Slow Food movement has become so popular that people brag about their membership in this club. Yet everyone is talking on a cell phone with an earphone so he can still wave his arms while shouting. I mean, talking. Of course, Slow Food somewhat makes sense, even though the first time I heard about it, I burst out laughing. Slow Food is also old news. The new food chatter is about the addition of a Fruit Sommelier at various tony hotels.

The more things change, the more they stay the same. And the beat goes on. You're gonna love it. Spaghetti is still cheap, so even with high prices, careful shoppers will rejoice.

Lo Shopping

It's possible the Italians invented modern shopping—maybe not trade, but certainly browsing, finding the newest new thing, and most aspects of the current art form of shopping—from markets to malls. Some of it was borrowed from the Chinese when Marco Polo brought magic from China to Europe, but Marco's fine eye and curious shopping skills only created the foundation to the Italy we love, and set the pace for generations to come. There have been other influences, especially lately.

Meanwhile, the French are making a contribution to Italian style. French designers have, for years, produced their clothing in Italy. Everyone knows that Karl Lagerfeld (a German Frenchman at that) has designed the Fendi furs for decades. Now the French are getting into an Italian mood with some serious spin—French architect cum designer Philippe Starck has created a New Age lion for the gates of Venice; Christian Lacroix has taken over designing Pucci. Sephora—the French-born makeup and beauty supermarket that's now international in scope—has a huge store in the Rome train station and stores dotted all over Italy. Sofitel, a division of Accor, has opened a hotel on a private island in Venice that will surely make you sigh *ohlala*. In fact, Sofitel has taken several old hotels and turned them around and offers a lot of bang for the euro.

But then, so do many Italian firms. In fact, the new hotels in Italy alone are reason enough to check it out, or just check in and sigh. At last you can afford to give Bulgari your business.

The Italian ability to set aside the traditional and adapt to the new is mind-boggling. The new Euro dynamic of a single currency and a fluidity of design borders makes shopping a little more expensive than in past years, but more fun than ever. Giorgio Armani is making chocolates while Gucci is doing custom wares. Bulgari isn't the only luxury-goods firm in the hotel business; there's also Ferragamo. Benetton owns the Autogrill, a series of fast-food restaurants on the highways, but they too have now gone into hotels—and not auto-route hotels, but fancy-schmancy hotels. Shopping, seeing, and sleeping in Italy has never been so rewarding.

Italian Contrasts

An Italian wedding-ring company has been running an advertisement for platinum wedding bands in all the fashion magazines. The selling image is a bride in traditional white gown and veil, holding not a bouquet of flowers but a bouncy little infant—the latest in wedding accessories. Is this old-fashioned country a place of contrasts or what?

As you shop in Italy, you can appreciate views of hills as old as the ages, peeling palazzi with tile roofs and handmade wrought-iron gates and window grills, masterful antiques, and then whammo—smack in the middle of it all, tables perched precariously on bent triangles, clothes in medieval colors, shoes and bags in styles you've never thought of, and a pride of craftsmanship in absolutely everything.

At the same time, in today's Italy you'll find that flea markets and antiques fairs are bigger than ever, and that Italians have taken seriously to resale and to outlet shopping—several new outlets and even outlet malls have opened recently. *Veni, vici, ya'll.* I came, I saw, I shopped. Now it's your turn.

GETTING THERE

From the U.S.

You'll get the best fares for direct flights from the U.S. to Italy if you latch onto a new gate or a promotional rate, or even the launch of a code share . . . so watch local papers closely. (A code share is an airline deal whereby you book your tickets, pay for them, and are ticketed by one airline—say, Delta—but find yourself flying on another carrier, such as Air Singapore.)

It may even pay to make a domestic hop to a nearby city if direct flights to Italy have just begun to be offered from there. Ask your travel agent. You can always go via New York; explore other options if you are looking for a price break. Note that deregulation of intra-European flights has brought on all sorts of new choices and that many low-cost European carriers specialize in getting you to Italy.

You might also want to remember that Italians still have a tendency to declare a strike—or even threaten a strike—every time someone gets PMS. Back-up plans (and planes) are a good idea; also stay away from those carriers that are more prone to strikes than others. Always check your trains before you go to the station. Strikes are usually posted in the *International Herald Tribune.*

Alitalia, the Italian national carrier, has various flights and connections from the U.S. to Italy, but doesn't play by the same promotional rules as U.S. carriers. It is also scheduled to become privatized, so it may get competitive in new ways.

I usually fly **Delta Air Lines,** partly because I can go into Milan and come out of Rome without much ado. Delta also has a great nonstop from New York to Nice; this is a super way to get into Italy. Delta also has a code-share program with Alitalia, so I can get miles and use Alitalia for local connections as needed. Seamless, *uomo,* seamless.

Best Deals

- **Book online.** Or at least check it out. Look at regular carriers as well as brokers for discount tickets. I was amazed (maybe because I am unsophisticated in these things) that many airlines have two different sites with different kinds of deals. So if you check out www.alitaliausa.com, you get deals created just for the American market. There's another site (in another language) for other deals.
- **Book off-season.** Off-season travel always offers better value; sometimes packages do too. Use up your miles, buy into promotional rates, and check out websites that offer deals. Be sure to compare packages, which may offer the best prices.
- **Book specialty tours** that include everything and are prepaid in dollars. The way the dollar is going, you don't want any nasty surprises or escalating costs.

Delta also has code shares with several other airlines; this allows me to use Paris as a hub (traveling onward with Air France). Also note that Delta is one of the airlines that did away with regular first class and instead installed "business first," which is much more first class at a business-class price than any other business-class seat on other airlines. If value is related to the size of your seat, and you splurge on business-class or upgrade travel, this is the way to go.

American Airlines flies through Chicago to Milan and has just launched New York to Rome service. Note that American still has three classes of service. As we go to press, American Airlines is having its own share of woes, so who knows what will happen with their international routes.

Most airlines offer special deals when you book online.

From London & Continental Europe

Low-cost airlines have made a huge dent in the Italian tourism business, especially flights from the United Kingdom. Sometimes

British Airways, Air France, and **Alitalia** get so annoyed at these discounters that they go to war with low, low fares. The big names tend to serve the well-known airports; the lesser-priced airlines use less-frequented airports—but in Italy, that may work just great.

Many of the low-cost airlines have gone out of business or merged with others, so I can't promise this will be around when you are ready to travel, but you might want to look into **Volare,** a newish Italian airline that serves Paris from the Beauvais airport and flies to Milan's Malpensa, Venice (Marco Polo), and also to Bari. When it has promotional deals, one way of a round-trip ticket can cost as little as 1€ ($1.10) . . . with a 3€ ($3.30) supplement for security. From Paris, call toll free © 0800/047-290, or go to www.volareweb.com.

Sometimes you'll save money by flying into a European city and getting a low-cost flight from there. Do make sure you know which airport you are using, however; many low-cost airlines use alternative airports. This can be especially important when you think you are flying to Venice since the regular airport (Marco Polo) is slightly out of town and the alternative airport is significantly out of town.

Some thoughts: **Air Berlin** flies to Milan from many German cities (not just Berlin); **RyanAir** (www.ryanair.com) flies from London Stansted to Turin, Milan, Treviso, Trieste, Genoa, Pisa, Ancona, and Rome. If you don't know where some of these cities are, look at a map. Also check to see if new destinations or changes in airports are available. RyanAir also has flights from Brussels and Frankfurt to a handful of different Italian cities.

You can also cross the channel and connect with sleeper trains, which are usually routed through Paris. At certain times of the year, British Airways does a promotion that offers a free layover in London to passengers with ongoing outbound flights. These fares are dramatically priced and should be considered, even if you hadn't at first thought about adding on a British stopover.

Secret Cities

If you are coming from another European country via train, try combining your U.S.–bought train passes. A complete Eurailpass may be a wasted value, especially if you are just visiting two countries (say, France and Italy). Nowadays there are so many different types of rail passes that it pays to figure out which kind is best for you.

If you are flying between connecting European cities, price your tickets carefully. I needed to go to Rome and priced the airfare from Zurich and from Nice, and found Nice offered me a 455€ ($500) savings. If I had the Swissair pass program, it would have been less money, but since I didn't, I could just call my travel agent and pray. French prayers were answered.

For Americans, the various air-pass systems offered by different carriers can be a lifesaver, surely a fare saver. But they do have restrictions and must be bought in the U.S. before you depart.

Also note, the city of Nice (France) is only 229 miles from Milan. If you are a Delta customer, as I am, note that you can fly into Italy through Nice, Milan, or Rome—the Nice International Airport is only about an hour's drive from the Italian border. If you are driving around northern Italy, or combining the two Rivieras (Italian and French), this is even better—as you'll be in Torino in no time at all.

To depart from Italy through Nice, you can take the train from Milan to Nice, or even from Venice to Nice (this is an overnight journey and saves on a hotel room). Or you can fly (it's a 1-hr. flight).

Also note that since Nice is the turnaround point on the train lines, you may want to simply pop on the overnight train to Rome, or points south. This involves a transfer from the Nice airport to the Nice train station, which can be done by bus or taxi.

Specialty Shopping Tours

I've been seeing ads for two companies that offer trips to various Euro cities that include airfare, hotel accommodations, and an antiques dealer to help you: **Antiques Abroad, Ltd.** (© 704/332-5577; www.antiqueslimited.com) or **Through the Looking Glass** (© 800/640-2269; www.throughthelooking glass.com). Both companies have Italian antiques-shopping packages for about $2,500; their expert goes with you and helps with shipping and shopping, and you travel with like-minded people who are intent on serious shopping.

GETTING AROUND ITALY

By Plane

Most intra-European flights are outrageously expensive. However, as European skies deregulate, new local services are popping up. There are now air wars over business travelers flying between Rome and Milan, a 20-minute flight. **Alitalia** flies this corridor, of course, but so do some upstarts, and now **Lufthansa** has gotten into the action by going into partnership with **Air One.** Check with your travel agent.

Note that prices may vary based on the time of day. Usually, flights between 11am and 3pm are 40% cheaper than early-morning and late-afternoon flights.

Alitalia also has a deal where if you buy your tickets 7 days in advance, you get a 40% discount; 14 days, 50%; and 21 days, 55% off. Not bad.

As we go to press, several firms are trying to cook up a low-cost airline to serve these popular intra-Italian routes. Stay tuned.

By Train

I just can't imagine driving around Italy when you can take a train to the big cities and then rent a car to explore the countryside for a day or two. While train fares from city to city are not expensive (especially in 2nd class), your best buy is an Italian Rail Pass, which can be bought from a travel agent or Rail Europe in the U.S. before you leave the U.S. (© 800/361-RAIL or 888/382-7245). Or visit Rail Europe's website

Traveling with Fido

My dog, Samantha Joe Cocker, is an American expat living in France, where she goes everywhere because the French love dogs. She recently accompanied me throughout Italy and had various bitchy experiences because the Italian rail officials are not as friendly as the French.

In some cases, Sam was warmly welcomed. In two cases, a bribe was required, even though she had her own doggy ticket (about 50€/$55 from Paris to Milan). In one case, the conductor threw us off the train, tore my tickets in two, and said dogs were not allowed on the Eurostar.

I was given a new ticket and told that dogs are indeed allowed, but they should be in their containers. Although I had Sam's container with me, Mr. Stronzo train conductor never said anything about that.

If you are traveling on the train with a dog, have lots of cash and patience on hand.

Note: At no time did anyone ask to see Sam's doggy passport.

Oh yes, Sam could have flown in her kennel from any Euro city—or from the U.S.—as long as she had her papers. Cost from Paris to Rome is 7€ per kilo of doggy weight.

(www.raileurope.com), where you can not only book online and compare products, but also get promotional offers.

The price of this pass depends on many factors, including the class you choose and the number of days you actually want to travel within a given 2-month period. The kids—aged 22 and 23 for this research trip—bought passes for those aged 12 to 26, which offer second-class travel at a low rate.

On my first trips to Italy, I purchased first-class passes; thereafter, I switched to second class. I usually pay about 136€ ($150) for a 5-day second-class pass, and it's good for unlimited travel on all trains, including the luxury Eurostar, the faster IC (Inter-City) trains, and the *rapido*.

Curious You

Do note that some trains are called **Eurostar Italia.** These trains do not go through the Chunnel, but they are new, fast, and deluxe. And expensive. They even come with a cute little boxed snack. Such trains are marked "ES" on the schedule or the big board.

To revise this book 2 years ago, I bought a three-country Eurailpass and splurged on first-class seats. I flew into Milan and out of Nice, and used the Eurailpass to connect me to Venice, Geneva, and Monte Carlo before returning to Nice. I got five train rides for about 273€ ($300), which I thought was a fabulous bargain.

If you have a first-class ticket and a reservation, which are two completely different things (and are even purchased separately), you will not have to worry about finding a seat on a crowded train—which can be hairy, especially if you are schlepping some luggage with you. Even with the train pass, you do not have a specific reservation—so plan ahead and book one if you will need it. *Note:* Reservations in Italy are one of the items that have gone sky high, price-wise. They cost 8€ each, which for me was enough of a reason to not book one and to take my chances.

There are extra *supplementos* for some trains and reservations are required—even with the train pass—for others. I suggested that Aaron and Jenny save the cost of reservations, but they ended up paying a fine (32€ each) when they got onboard. *Mea culpa!*

By Car

If you want to drive around Italy, reserve your car in the U.S. before departure, using a prepaid plan. It'll be half the price you'll be charged in Italy—even if you reserve through an American rental agency, such as **Avis** (© 800/331-1084) or **Hertz**

(© 800/654-3001). **Thrifty By Car,** the Italian division of Thrifty, has beefed up promotions with fair daily rates and special 2-day weekend rates.

Fly-drive packages may offer the best prices; check to see if your airline has a fly-drive affiliation with a car-rental agency.

The best deal I've ever used came from **Kemwel** (© 800/678-0678); our car rental in Italy went smoothly . . . and inexpensively. Before I wax on about the glories and low prices of Kemwel, let me first remind you that because of the crime rate in Italy, car rentals there are far more expensive than in other European countries, and various insurance plans are mandatory. You have no choice. Furthermore, American Express and credit and bank card firms that offer car insurance automatically with your membership have now waived coverage in Italy. *Do not assume you are covered by your credit card.*

European rental rates are usually more expensive than those offered in the U.S. for use in Europe, although a package plan will always be less expensive than a daily rate. In Italy, Avis offers a 3-day winter promotional package for around 145€ ($160) and a 7-day package for 309€ ($340)—these include unlimited mileage—if you can read Italian, go online to www.avisautonoleggio.it.

Shopper's trick: If you want a car at the last minute, you can reserve by making a long-distance call to the U.S., paying by phone, and receiving a faxed prepaid voucher with U.S. prices.

DRIVING AROUND

I bought the Michelin spiral-bound map book to Italy (18€) for a proposed driving trip. This book also has a handy mileage chart so you can plan just how far you want to drive.

CAR & DRIVER

If you can afford it or you want to splurge, a car and driver are a wonderful way to do a day trip or to connect to other parts of Italy. I certainly wouldn't want to be driving the

---

I Have Gas

The cost of gas in Europe is four times what you'd pay in the U.S.; you will also pay high fees for the use of highways. Both highways and gas stations do take credit cards. Gas in Italy is slightly less expensive than in France. Go figure.

Amalfi Pass on my own. And sometimes I have so much luggage that a trek through a train station could be a nightmare.

However, try to make sure in advance that your driver will meet your needs. I recently used a service to drive me to Como and to outlets along the way. Not only did the driver not know where anything was, but he didn't speak English, refused to call the factories for directions, and wouldn't cross the border into Switzerland to get to FoxTown. *Urrrrrgggh.* To avoid problems like this, consider taking a train to the destination city and then hiring a local taxi driver for a flat rate.

SLEEPING IN ITALY

Hotel Chains

While there is specific hotel information in each of the following city chapters, for those who like to make all or most of their reservations with one hotel chain or one phone call, there are a few firms that can help you out. Ask each if it has promotional deals.

Baglioni   This is a small chain, still owned by a real family and offering up four- and five-star hotels in major cities. The top of the line is their hotel in Milan (member Leading Hotels of the World), but my fave is the nugget in Florence, the Bernini Palace. A member of the Sterling Hotel & Resort booking group, online it's www.baglionihotels.com; there is no toll-free reservation number in the U.S.

Boscolo   Be still my heart! The new Exedra Hotel is part of my love affair with Rome, but the Aleph Hotel ain't bad, either. I first met this chain when they took over one of my regular hotels in Nice. They do have a handful of hotels in France, although there are over a dozen properties in Italy. Some of the hotels are normal four-stars that are good finds; a few are to-die-for places worthy of a spread in *Architectural Digest*. So go to www.boscolohotels.com.

Concorde   This French hotel chain owns the Crillon in Paris and also has a few hotels in Italy in main destinations such as Rome, Milan, Florence, and Como (© 800/888-4747; www. concorde-hotels.com).

InterContinental   This chain is changing its image and renovating many hotels. While their showcase hotels are in Hong Kong, London, and Paris, there is a hotel in Rome in a great location. Call © 800/327-0200, or go to www. intercontinental.com.

Jolly Hotels   This leading four-star hotel chain in Italy also operates some spas and also has hotels in other European cities (© 800/247-1277; www.jollyhotels.com). Many of the hotels are modern and may look like they are stuck in the 1960s from the outside, but inside they are great. Some are rehabbed grande dames. They have special weekend promotions—you can luck into a very good hotel for 64€ ($70) per night per person. Trust me on this; it's a great find and you can make all your Italian bookings with one chain.

Leading Hotels of the World   This organization also represents Leading Small Hotels of the World, with a wide selection of the fanciest hotels in the world, sometimes multiple choices in the same city (three hotels in Florence, three in Milan, and five in Rome). Note that most of the hotels have their own websites, posted in the annual Leading Hotels catalog. To contact Leading Hotels, call © 800/223-6800, or visit www.lhw.com. Also check out www.luxury-alliance.com, which is the combined website for Leading Hotels and Relais & Châteaux.

Meridien & Trust House Forte These chains have merged; they have several luxury hotels around Italy (© 800/543-4300; www.lemeridien.com), including the over-the-top Savoy in Florence and De La Russie in Rome.

Orient Express Although Orient Express (© 800/237-1236; www.orient-expresshotels.com) has only three hotels in Italy, they are winners, and its famous train ain't bad, either. Note that most of the hotels are also members of Leading Hotels of the World.

Relais & Châteaux Stay at any of its 30 or so properties all over Italy, and you'll rest in luxury and eat awfully well (© 800/735-2478; www.relaischateaux.fr); note a newish partnership with Leading Hotels of the World called Luxury Alliance, www.luxury-alliance.com.

Sofitel Part of France's Accor Group, this chain has hotels in Venice, Bologna, Florence, and Sardinia (© 800/763-4835; www.sofitel.com). The new hotel Isola in Venice is a knockout . . . more like a resort than a hotel, a destination unto itself. Most of the other hotels (worldwide) are less extravagant. The company also has a weekend promotional deal that takes 30% off the room rate and includes complimentary breakfast in most of its European hotels.

Westin Westin ended up with some of the old CIGA hotels through Starwood, so it does have several luxury hotels in key cities and can take care of your needs with one swift phone call (© 888/625-5144; www.westin.com). For Starwood's Luxury Collection hotels and resorts, call © 800/325-3589 or go to www.starwood.com/luxury.

Sleeping Promotions

When business is slow, promotional rates get better. Airlines do 'em, hotels do 'em, and even credit card companies will play ball. Check with the travel service division of all the cards you hold to find what's on offer. Also go to hotel and airline websites; very often there are special deals offered only online.

Electronically Yours

The Internet is a great source for tourism information. Here are unusual addresses you might want to check out before you begin your Italian adventures:

Arts & Events	www.enit.it
Furniture	www.italydesign.com California firm that can help you learn and price Italian furniture and design, which may be cheaper in the U.S.
Made in Italy	www.made-in-italy.com Made in Italy online is Logan Bentley's fashion and design–related site, with information on wine and food, travel, and shopping. You can also book Roman shopping tours with Barbara Lessona.
Tourism Office	www.italiantourism.com This is the Italian National Tourist office's official online source for information—find a hotel or look up a train schedule.
Faith Heller Willinger	www.faithwillinger.com Not just for foodies, this site offers all sorts of info, but it's internationally famous for info on Willinger's food, restaurant, and recipes. She holds cooking classes in her home.

I recently found a deal through Visa that offered 2 nights for the price of 1 at Le Meridien Hotels. To get the deal, you had to know the code word (in this case, "2 pour 1"). There were also restrictions in terms of the length of stay, etc. Still, it's worth checking out: Call ☏ **800/543-4300**, or go to www. lemeridien.com. You may also want to look at www.visa destinations.com for all its deals.

If you have an American Express Platinum Card, you can buy two-for-one airline tickets and get various hotel amenities. I also found an offer for a free night at the ultra-fancy Hotel Eden in Rome.

Most hotel chains also have deals, either with partners or just to sell rooms in odd seasons or on weekends. Jolly Hotels in partnership with Sixt car rental and Lufthansa also has online promotions (www.jollyhotels.com).

Don't be shy about calling a hotel directly and making a deal. Just don't be rude or pushy. Sometimes a nice fax to the hotel's general manager can get you a good rate plus added perks. Write to the affect of "I love your hotel, have stayed there for years, but prices are too high now; can you cut a deal for me?"

Home Suite Home

If you'd rather rent an apartment or even a villa, there are several services that will help you. Many of the websites and professional shoppers listed below can help (not the Vatican, however). If you are looking for something very high-end, there's a rental division of tour masters **Abercrombie & Kent,** but a castle may well cost you 27,272€ ($30,000) a week. Call toll-free ☏ **800/323-7308;** www.abercrombiekent.com. **Best In Italy** handles properties that begin around 9,090€ ($10,000) a week: www.thebestinitaly.com. If your budget is far below that, try **Custom Italy** (www.customitaly.com)—prices there begin around 3,636€ ($4,000) per week.

PROFESSIONAL HELP

If you are looking for guidance in making travel plans, there are a few organizations that specialize in showing you the insider's Italy. The good ones are usually regional. They charge by the day or half day, but sometimes you have to spend money to save money. Try contacting these people, whom I know, trust, and have, in most cases, worked with:

In Venice: Samantha Durrell
fax: 041/523-23-79

In Tuscany: Maria Teresa Berdondini
Tuscany by Tuscans (see www.tuscanybytuscans.it)
Villa L. Galvani 13B
51016 Montecatini Terme Italy
℡ and fax **0572/70-467;**
tuscany@italway.it

In Rome: Barbara Lessona
℡ **06/44-23-72-25;** cellphone: 348/450-3655;
info@personalshoppersinitaly.com

In Rome and Florence: Elisa Rossi
With Style
Via Monte Santo 2
℡ **06/481-9091**

PHONE HOME

Please remember:

- International phone calls made from the U.S. to Europe are far less expensive than those made from Europe to the U.S. If you are in Italy and want to call home, your cheapest solution is to call family and friends on the hotel phone and ask them to call you back.
- An international call from Italy to the U.S. on your cellphone may be less expensive than calling from a hotel. Check it out. This may be especially advantageous if you have a U.S. cellphone and an international calling plan.
- Hotels usually charge a flat rate for a fax—it often comes to 9€ or 14€ ($10–$15) per page. This rate is often less

expensive than a phone call, but it is still outrageous. However, consider sending a fax home. Ask rates so you can compare.

Phone cards can be the cheapest way to call home, if you don't mind making phone calls from a phone booth. I buy a SIPS card at any *tabacchi* (tobacco shop) in Italy and use it in Italian pay phones. With the 6–9 hour time difference between the U.S. and Italy, this is often a pain (who wants to schlep to a phone booth in the middle of the night?).

If you prefer to dial direct using the services of a U.S. long-distance carrier, the access phone numbers for the major carriers in Italy are **AT&T** (© **800/172-444**), **MCI** (© **800/172-1022**), and **Sprint** (© **800/825-8745**).

CODES

For calling Italy from abroad, the **country code** is **39**. The access codes (area codes) for the major cities are **Florence,** 055; **Milan,** 02; **Venice,** 041; **Rome,** 06; and **Naples,** 081. For example, to call Rome from the U.S., you would dial 011 plus 39 plus 06 (the access code for Rome) plus the number.

If you need an Internet connection for your laptop computer to access e-mail, work with your hotel front desk or business center directly. If your laptop uses a dial-up modem, it won't work if it's plugged into a digital phone line (common in Europe instead of the analog phone line found back home). More modern hotels often have better facilities for getting connected; Four Seasons Hotels & Resorts even have 110-volt electricity and direct dataports in all rooms.

Most hotels have a business center where you can find Internet connections, or offer Internet access through your room's television. Luxury hotels usually have a dataport in each guest room. There are Internet cafes all over Italy. My favorite one in Rome is easyInternet Café, at Piazza Barberini right next to the cinema.

SHOPPING HOURS

Shops open at 9 or 9:30am and usually close at 1:30pm for lunch. They reopen at 3 or 3:30pm (or even 4pm) and stay open until 7:30pm.

Some stores close on Saturday from 1 to 4pm. Stores are open on Saturday afternoon in winter and are closed Saturday afternoon in summer.

Some stores do whatever they please.

The notion of staying open all day is catching on in big cities, but not the countryside. You never find shops open all day in the south, where it is too hot to think in the afternoon, let alone shop.

Stores that do not close for lunch write their hours as "nonstop" or "continual hours," which is usually spelled out in Italian. In all cities, major department stores stay open at lunchtime. Unless it's Monday, which has its own rules; see below.

Surviving Monday

Monday mornings are a total write-off for most retail shopping in Italy. With the rare exception, most stores open at 3:30pm on Monday.

But wait, that's why God invented factories. Because factories are open on Monday mornings, most factory stores are also open. Not all, just most. Call and ask, or have your hotel's concierge call. Also note that food shops are open.

If you are in Milan on a Monday, fret no more, my lady—you are off to Como (see chapter 8).

Sunday Shopping

Laws have changed, and most of Italy's big cities have some Sunday shopping now; often big department stores are open even if mom-and-pop stores are not. If you want to shop on a Sunday in a town that has no regular retail, try for a flea market.

- Venice is wide, wide, wide open on Sunday.
- Milan is far more dead on Sunday than other communities, but you can get lucky—at certain times of the year, things are popping on Sunday. During fashion weeks, stores in the Montenapo district often open on Sunday; they also have specific Sundays when they open, beginning in October and going on until Christmas. Some stores in the Navigli area are also open on Sunday. The regular Sunday stores are **Corso Como 10** and **Virgin Megastore.** Sunday hours are most often noon to 5pm.
- Florence has a lot of street action on Sundays, and department stores and chains are usually open.
- Rome has special Sundays when stores are open.

Sale Shopping

Each city in Italy has the right to decide when the twice-a-year official sales will begin—and it does vary from city to city by as much as a week. Good luck.

Exceptional Hours

Summer Hours   Summer hours begin in the middle of July for many retail businesses; August is a total loss from a shopping point of view because most stores are closed in major cities. Sophisticated people wouldn't be caught dead in Milan in August; shoppers beware.

When stores are open in August, they close at lunch on Saturday and do not reopen until 3:30 or 4pm on Monday.

Holiday Hours   The period between Christmas and New Year's Day can be tricky. Stores will close early a few days before a major holiday and use any excuse to stay closed during a holiday. Sales begin in the first week of January (usually after Epiphany), but store hours are erratic before then. But then, the first half of January can be erratic; see below.

Early January   The first week to 10 days of January are slow to slower—all factories are closed until after Epiphany, as are many stores. Others decide to close for inventory. Do not assume that shopping life returns to normal on the first day of business after New Year's Day.

Night Hours   Stores usually close for the day somewhere between 7:30 and 8pm. Should you need an all-night pharmacy, there is usually one at the train station in a large city.

Surviving Summer

Summers in Italy have two problems: It can be too hot to shop, and stores can be closed.

Also, August is the official summer-vacation season, especially in northern Italy. Most shops in Milan and many in Rome close between August 1 and September 1. Shockingly, some stores close for a longer time.

In southern climates, especially in summer, expect stores to close from 1 until 5pm, during the heat of the day, but to be open until late in the evening.

Holidays

Keep track of local holidays (when you check into a hotel, always ask the concierge immediately if there are any holidays approaching and how they will affect the banks and stores!), since shops will close then. Cities celebrate religious holidays with differing amounts of piety. Shops that are closed in Rome may be open in Milan. (Dec 8 is a big holiday in some towns, a medium holiday in others.) August 15 is a big religious holiday (one of the feasts of the Virgin), and all stores are closed.

SCAMS

Despite the arrival of the euro, or maybe because of it, there are still plenty of locals and immigrants who are ready to take advantage of tourists, and especially consider Americans as fair game. Most of them are small-time shopping scams, but they are annoying nonetheless and can be expensive if you get taken. Scams exist in stores, on the streets, and especially in taxis, which are the most difficult to nail when you don't know your way around or when one-way streets make routes seem unnecessarily convoluted.

I just heard from a reader about a really sophisticated scam. A store in Venice had changed its name. The store next door had someone standing out in front saying the store with the changed name had been bought and shut down. Guess what? It was bought, thus the name change, but it was open.

Reputable shops (and hotels) usually safe. But even in classy establishments, be careful when you talk to strangers. I've met some wonderful people in hotels and on airplanes around the world, but there is a rather well-known scam in which the con artist pretends to be just the kind of person you'd like to know and then—whammo—takes you for a ride.

Remember:

- Merchandise, especially name merchandise, selling at a price that is too good to be true is usually too fake to be true. I don't care how fancy the store. I don't care how good the sob story about why they are taking a loss.
- If a person volunteers to go shopping with you, to steer you to some real "finds," to help you find some long-lost family members of yours, or whatever—don't trust him or her! There are more tourist scams of this nature in Italy than anyplace else, except maybe Hong Kong. Be safe—not sorry.
- No matter how well dressed the person is, no matter how friendly the person is, no matter how helpful and endearing—the answer is still "No." If such a person is following you or becomes a real nuisance, call the police, duck into a prestigious hotel and ask the concierge for help, or walk right into the American embassy.
- Likewise, if a person volunteers to take your money and buy an item for you cheaper than you could get it because you are an "Ugly American," forget it. If you want the concierge of a reputable hotel to handle some shopping for you and you know the hotel well enough to trust the concierge, by

all means, do so. (Don't forget to tip for such a favor.) Otherwise, you are taking a risk.

- Always check your purchases while they are being packed by the store. When you return to your hotel, unwrap them to make sure you got what you thought you were getting. Mistakes occur, but occasionally someone will switch merchandise on you. Return to the shop the next day if an error has been made. Bring your sales slip. If you anticipate a language problem, have the concierge call the shop for you and explain the situation, then have him tell the shop when you will be in for the proper merchandise.

- And then there's the old *O Sole Mio* scam. You are involved in a transaction being conducted in Italian, which you barely speak. If you question the mathematics, the vendor rolls his eyes, waves his arms, and screams at you. You feel like an idiot and leave, not wanting to cause a scene. You have just been cheated out of 45€ ($50) in correct change. (This actually happened to me.)

- And then there's the mail trick, which is a hotel scam. You ask the front desk to mail postcards or letters. You are charged a mark-up on the stamps, or are even charged the U.S. rate for mail within the EU.

- My favorite (this also happened to me): You give the taxi an address that is slightly off the beaten track. He pulls up to a door and says something to the affect of "here you go." You say "no" because you know this isn't it. He insists on getting out of the cab, going to the front door, and verifying the fact that this is not the place you want. Meanwhile, the meter is running . . . and running.

IT'S A CRIME

I don't want to put a damper on your shopping spree before you even start out, but I do feel compelled to point out that the hard times in Italy have brought more and more criminal elements to the front. They are in front of, and behind, your handbag. And your rental car.

I was accosted not once but several times by thieving bands in Milan. Two incidents occurred on different days, but in full daylight, in the area immediately surrounding the Duomo. In one case, it was a Saturday, and I was surrounded by a throng of shoppers. When I screamed out, none of the other shoppers even gazed in my direction.

- Keep handbags close to your body and under your coat or sweater. Don't put valuables in a backpack or fanny pack that is beyond your watchful eye. Don't sling shopping bags across a shoulder and away from your body so that their contents can be lifted from the rear. Leave nothing in your rented car, and be careful where you park it. Last time I rented a car in Italy, I was told which cities, such as Naples, were considered unsafe for parking a car on the street or in an unattended lot. If you're given a similar warning, heed it.

- Don't forget the old newspaper scam. A street person (or two or three) spots you with an attractive shopping bag. He or she is reading or holding a newspaper as he passes you on a crowded street—or worse, on a bridge. The newspaper passes over your shopping bag while the thief's hand goes into your bag for the goodies. The person reading the newspaper may or may not be the actual thief—this scam is worked by mothers with three or four children in tow. We've also heard it worked so that the person reading the newspaper passes you, grabs your glasses, and then runs off while several children pounce on you, take your shopping bags and handbag, and dash away while you are left wondering what hit you.

- Watch out for the old subway trick. You know the one, where some "boys" pick a fight among themselves between subway stops, and your pocket is picked, and they are out the door before you know what has happened.

- There is a variation of this one that I call the "Ice-Cream Trick." Someone bumps into you and knocks his ice-cream cone all over you. He's very apologetic and helps clean you up. He also cleans you out.

BUYING FROM DUTY-FREES

While intra-European duty-free has been outlawed, this does not affect travelers leaving the EU through Italy and may not affect those traveling within the EU, depending on airport policy. On my recent departure from Paris to Milan, one of the French duty-free shops was allowing the discount for EU travel, and the other one was not. Go figure.

It's easier upon departure from Italy, especially if you are indeed flying back to the U.S. or out of the EU. The Rome airport is virtually one giant shopping mall once you pass through immigration. While there are tons of stores and the selection can be huge, the savings are not a sure bet. Perfume and cosmetics may be cheaper at the duty-free you left behind in the U.S. or London, or in the in-flight magazine. Not every shop in an airport selling area is duty-free (or, more accurately, tax-free; you may pay duty on what you buy in a "duty-free" shop when you take it home). Many of the designer shops are not duty-free shops. Ask! Not every shop offers a bargain—many are outrageously expensive; some just charge the going rate.

You may get a flat 19% discount off regular Italian retail on Trussardi, Enrico Coveri, and Ferragamo shoes as well as many other things. The catch here is that the Italian retail price might be so inflated that a discount of 19% is meaningless. If you buy at the Ferragamo sale, you'll do better than at the airport.

Don't forget that whatever you buy at the duty-free shop must be declared when you return to the United States. Unless you eat it on the plane. And never forget that duty-free shopping no longer ends when you leave the airport. All airlines now have duty-free shopping on the plane. The price list should be inside the in-flight magazine. *Buon viaggio.*

MAILING & SHIPPING FROM ITALY

Shipping anything from Italy begins before you get there. If you are smart, or serious, you will do some homework before you leave and have your shipping arrangements partly made before you even arrive. You'll complete the transaction once you arrive in Italy with a preselected and guaranteed broker.

Contact a shipper in your hometown, or in New York, London, or your chosen port of entry for your goods, and work with them to make sure all your shipping days are pleasant ones. The shipper should be able to act as your agent—the buying game will be much less tense once you have someone to take care of you.

Find out if you need a customhouse broker to meet your goods and clear them, or if the shipping agent does this, and if so, is it included in the shipping cost, or is there an additional fee? Likewise, make sure you pay for adequate insurance and do not assume that it is included in the freight price.

Small items should be shipped via Federal Express, DHL, or another courier service you know and trust. Italy does have a service called "express mail," but don't trust it.

Before I totally pooh-pooh the Italian mail system, I want you to know that all the postcards I've ever sent from Italy have been delivered home and abroad, sometimes in less than a week. I've also noticed that concierges have charged differing rates for a simple postcard stamp. Actual postal rates are posted at the post office. I have mailed items in jiffy bags from large city post offices and gifts have arrived—always mark an item sent to the U.S. with the words UNSOLICITED GIFT, UNDER $50.

THE MOSCOW RULE OF SHOPPING

The Moscow Rule of Shopping is one of my most basic shopping rules and has nothing to do with shopping in Moscow, so please pay attention. Now: Average shoppers, in pursuit of the ideal bargain, do not buy an item they want when they first see it, because they're not convinced that they won't find it elsewhere for less money. They want to see everything available, then return for the purchase of choice. This is a rather normal thought process. However, if you live in Russia, for instance, you know that you must buy something the minute you see it, because if you hesitate, it will be gone. Hence this international law: the Moscow Rule of Shopping.

When you are on a trip, you probably will not have the time to compare prices and then return to a certain shop. You will never be able to backtrack to cities, and even if you can, the item might be gone by the time you get back, anyway. What to do? The same thing they do in Moscow: Buy it when you see it, understanding that you may never see it again. But since you are not shopping in Moscow and you *may* see it again, weigh these questions carefully before you go ahead:

- Is this a touristy type of item that I am bound to find all over town?
- Is this an item I can't live without, even if I am overpaying?
- Is this a reputable shop, and can I trust what they tell me about the availability of such items?
- Is the quality of this particular item so spectacular that it is unlikely it could be matched at this price?

If you have good reason to buy it when you see it, do so.

Now hear my tale of warning. I bought a pair of trousers at Marina Rinaldi in Rome that turned out to be great for me. They were also available in navy in Rome, but by then it was Sunday and I couldn't go back to the store. When I got to Florence, I went to the Marina Rinaldi store, wearing the trousers and asked for them in navy. The sales woman swore they weren't from Marina Rinaldi. Then she swaggered that they came from Marina Rinaldi in the U.S., a different kettle of pants. When I told her they came from Rome, she simply shrugged. Buy it when you see it and don't expect the same brand to have the same stock.

Caveat: The Moscow Rule of Shopping breaks down if you are an antiques or bric-a-brac shopper or if you are shopping in a factory outlet. You never know if you can find another such item, or if it will be in the same condition, or if the price will be higher or lower. It's very hard to price collectibles and bargains, so consider doing a lot of shopping for an item before you buy anything.

ITALIAN CITY PLANNING

If you are going to a variety of Italian cities, you probably are wondering which one offers the best price, the best selection, and the best value. There are no firm rules—the Moscow Rule of Shopping really applies—but I do have a couple of loose rules to guide you.

The City of Origin Axiom   An item usually is cheapest in the city where it's made or where the firm's headquarters are. That's because the trucking and distribution costs are less. According to this rule, **Pratesi** linens should be bought at the factory store in Pistoia; **Fendi** goodies should come from the mother store in Rome; and **Etro** should come from the factory near Como, or, at least, Milan.

The Milan Rule of Supply and Demand   If you don't know the city of origin for an item, or want to be safe, use the Milan Rule of Supply and Demand. Because Milan is the center of the fashion and furnishings business, it should have the best selection of big-name merchandise. If you are shopping in only one city or creating a schedule that allows only a 1-day spree, Milan is the city for you.

Milan is far more industrial than the other big cities. Its entire psychology is one of moving and selling goods and services. Furthermore, while in Milan you have the opportunity to shop at factories that are just outside of town or at flea markets that sell leftovers from factories (you mean those ties didn't just fall off a truck?), or you can luck into very good sales that are created to move merchandise.

The Roman Holiday Rule of Shopping   If you just want designer merchandise and a good time, forget about the rest of Italy and just do Rome. You won't get the faience, the souvenirs, or the gilded wood trays, but you will find all the big names in one easy-to-shop neighborhood.

Venice and Florence are crammed with tourists, especially in the spring and summer months, and the shopkeepers know you are a tourist. Prices in Venice are high to begin with and soar in season. Florence has changed dramatically in the last couple of years: The merchandise in the streets and stalls has gotten junkier and junkier, but prices here for clothing are often less than in nearby cities because of the turnover.

If you're going on a cruise of Italy, please note that chapter 10 in this book has information on shopping in various Italian port cities. Unless you have a pre- or post-cruise layover in Rome or Venice, you will not have an opportunity to do much traditional Italian-designer shopping.

The Coca-Cola Price Index   To find out how prices fare in any destination, ask for the price of a Coca-Cola. Just so you know, the average price of a single can of Coke in a grocery store is about .45€ (50¢), and a six-pack costs about 2.30€ ($2.50). The average can of Coke on the street costs 1.80€ ($2); it is expensive if it costs 3€ ($3.30), and it is a crime if it costs 7.30€ ($8).

SHOPPING FOR FAKES

In years gone by, some of the best buys in Italy were on fake designer leather goods and scarves. These items are harder to find, and once found, are often so inferior to the real thing that the game is no fun to play at all. Although there is that pesky little rumor that Prada makes their own fakes . . .

The bigger question is, why buy a fake when you can have the real thing through an outlet store or a sale? Fendi key chains were going for 15€ ($16) at the sale in Rome. I mean, *really* . . . get real, buy real.

IN THE BAG

Shopping bags are freely given out at boutiques and department stores when you make a purchase. Not so in grocery stores. Either bring your own or expect to pay about 50¢ per plastic sack. The large can of olive oil that you came to buy comes with a handle, so you might not even need a bag.

If you score at a sale in a designer shop, you can ask for gift wrap and a designer bag, but you may not get them. Pucci gave me tons of attention and free wrap; Fendi settled on tissue and Fendi bags—no wrap or ribbon. Best of all was Armani when all I bought was a blush, but they gave me a canvas tote bag.

BAR NONE

This is not strictly a shopping secret, but is nonetheless a strategy: Next time you belly up to the bar, consider how much money you've just saved. That's right—eating at the bar (while standing) is a money-saving tactic.

If you see a bar you'd like to wander into for a coffee or a snack, remember that all bars in Italy have two systems: Either you order at the bar and stand and drink at the bar, or you order at the bar or a table and then sit down. To eat at a table will cost just about double the price of a meal at the bar. It is rude to order at the bar, pay at the bar, and then wander to a chair with your snack and sit down.

TO MARKET, TO MARKET

One of the difficulties of shopping in Italy is deciding which markets to visit and which to pass up. Italy is crawling with good markets, for food and for fleas. There are dozens of them, and it's impossible to get to them all unless you spend a month doing little else. Maybe a year . . . or two.

Remember:

- Dress simply; the richer you look, the higher the price. If you have an engagement ring or one of those wedding bands that spells out "Rich American" in pavé diamonds, leave it in the hotel safe. Do not carry a $700 designer handbag.
- Check with your hotel's concierge about the neighborhood where the market is located. It may not be considered safe to go there alone, or after dark. Beware Rome. Beware the Ides of March.
- Have a lot of change with you. It's difficult to bargain and then offer a large bill and ask for change. As a bargaining point, be able to say you have only so much cash on hand.
- You do not need to speak any specific language to make a good deal. Bargaining is an international language of emotion, hand signs, facial expressions, etc. If you feel like you are being taken, walk away.
- Branded merchandise sold on the street may be hot or counterfeit. If the deal seems an exceptionally fine one, suspect fraud.
- Go early if you want to find the best selection. Go late if you want to make the best deals price-wise.
- Never trust anyone (except a qualified shipping agent) to mail anything for you.
- In Florence and Rome, most market areas are so famous that they have no specific street address. Usually it's enough to give the cabbie the name of the market: Ask your concierge if you need more in the way of directions. Usually buses service market areas. Expect markets to be closed on Monday morning.

OUTLET SHOPPING

Italian factories have had outlet shops for their employees or the local community for years; these addresses used to be secrets. Not anymore. They say the second-most-visited sight in Florence, after the Uffizzi, is the Prada outlet store.

Outlets are so popular to locals and tourists alike that there are locally published guides to outlets. I often use a book called *Lo Scopriaoccasioni (Bargain Hunting in Italy)*, written in Italian, which is a listing of over 1,400 outlets, according to the cover. This book costs about 23€ ($25).

Note:

- There is another edition of the same book *(Designer Bargains in Italy)* that costs as much, is in English, and isn't revised as often or as comprehensive. Beware.
- Check the copyright page before you buy. I once grabbed the display copy only to find I had mistakenly bought the previous edition.
- Finally, may I say that I don't agree with a number of the listings. Although I've checked out only a small portion of the total stores described in the book, I've found listings for stores that were closed for 5 years. Call ahead if you are driving out of your way or trusting solely this book.

There are three new American-style factory-outlet villages. The outlet malls are in the middle of nowhere, but not far from big cities.

- **Serravalle Scrivia,** a fake village atmosphere in the style most Americans adore, between Turin and Milan and usually listed in Milan shopping resources. (See p. 264.)
- Between Milan and Bologna there's **Fidenza Village;** it too is in the village format. It is somewhat difficult to get to either of these malls by public transportation.
- South of Rome, there's the brand-new **Pontina** outlets, owned by the same firm that owns Serravale Scrivia and built like an antique Roman village.

One of the older outlet malls, **FoxTown,** is technically in Switzerland—it's 5km (3 miles) from the Italian border and right near Como. Because it's in Switzerland, and Switzerland does not use the euro, you must change money to CF (Swiss francs) and the unfavorable conversion rate may not be worth it to you. Prices in Switzerland tend to be high, even on bargains.

Italy also has a system of jobbers (usually called *stochistas*) and also of free-standing outlet stores, often in the heart of a big city and easily on the tourist path. Some are as fancy as regular boutiques. Wait until you shop at the Max Mara and Etro outlets in Milan; you won't believe they are outlets until you see the price tags.

MILLS & THRILLS

Outlets can offer truly great bargains—if they are the real thing. Sometimes outlet villages are so upscale that their prices are actually between regular retail and true discount—this limbo is confusing for the shopper and provides the raison d'être for a big brand to actually go into an outlet mall in the first place—the prices are not seriously discounted and do not therefore hurt the brand's image.

Sometimes the merchandise they sell was made specifically for sale at outlets; true stock is almost always from a previous season. Others could be in the business of hustling big-city locals through warehouses in industrial suburbs that sell fakes, or are just normal businesses that market themselves as outlets. Know your stuff, know your regular retail prices, and know a few other rules of the road:

- Most outlets in factories close for lunch.
- Sales help in out-of-the-way, small communities may not speak English. It's not a bad idea to bring an Italian-English dictionary with you.
- Be sure you have a size-conversion chart, or know the sizes you want in the continental sizing system. There is a size-conversion chart inside the front cover of this book.

- Many mills are open Monday morning but close in the afternoon; others are closed the entire day. Remember the Monday rule of shopping—anything goes. Call first, especially on a Monday.
- Mills are never open on Sunday; not all are open on Saturday. Most fancy factory outlets are open on Sunday, however. In fact, in outlet malls, stores may be open 7 days a week. Welcome to the new Italy.
- Few mills will take credit cards, although Pratesi does. Outlets will take credit cards.
- If you have chosen a day trip with specific outlets and/or mills in mind, do yourself (and me) a favor—call first. Actually, have your hotel concierge call if your Italian isn't as good as his is. Get hours, credit card information, and confirmation of directions.

Chapter Three

....

MONEY MATTERS

EUROS R THEM

Italy, like most of continental Europe, adopted the euro (€) and has successfully switched from lire. Surely they did it for you, to make shopping all of Europe so much easier.

If you have old lire at the bottom of your handbag, or tucked in a safe place, you can exchange paper money for another 7 years at a bank. The rate of exchange for lire is fixed, so don't worry if the dollar is low—fluctuating rates will not affect this trade.

The good news is that the transition to euros was relatively simple. The bad news is that prices went up and people are feeling more pinched than ever. You may be shocked by prices and not find the bargains you were dreaming of.

The really bad news is that as we go to press, the euro has gained enormous strength against the U.S. dollar (the conversion rate used in this edition of *Born to Shop Italy* is 1€ = $1.10), so that the high prices I just mentioned will seem even higher to you.

As you already know, the euro is a trans-territorial currency serving the member nations; the bills are pan-European in design but the coins are created on a local basis. One side of each coin conforms with the EU master; the other side is created by individual countries. Thus, you will encounter Italian and Vatican City euro coins and sometimes euro coins minted in other member nations.

ATMS R US

The single best way to exchange money is to simply withdraw it from a wall—via an ATM. All Italian cities have banks with ATMs, so bring along your bank card. Here are two caveats:

- There are a few different types of bank machines that look similar but offer different functions—only a **bank machine/ATM** (usually marked *bancomat*) will give you a good rate. Those machines that exchange your dollars for foreign currency will cheat you, so don't be fooled.
- There is usually a fee for using an international ATM (1.40€–4.50€/$1.50–$5), just as there is at home, but you do get a good rate of exchange. However, if your bank charges a high fee, you don't want to keep going to the wall for 100€ ($110); you want to do it all at once. Ask your bank at home about its international fees. Jenny, my daughter, has a bank card that allows free international withdrawals.

Most of the ATMs operate on a 24-hour basis. Call your bank and find out if the PIN you have now will work in foreign locations, or if you need a new number. I have never had any trouble using my same old PIN with my Cirrus card.

ATMs are usually located alongside a bank so that you need not enter the building. If you need cash for a big purchase in a specific store, ask the sales clerk where the nearest ATM is located. Very often a small store will give you a sizable discount if you pay cash and are willing to forego your VAT refund. Of course, they do this because they have another set of books that Brussels knows nothing about, but what else is new?

OTHER OPTIONS

....

Check, Mates

Never travel without your checkbook. You just never know.

Send Money

You can also have money sent to you from home, in as little as 2 days. Money can be wired through Western Union (the person who's wiring you the money brings cash or a certified check and Western Union does the rest, but it may take up to a week) or through an international money order, which is cleared by telex through the bank where you cash it. Money can be wired from bank to bank, but this is a simple process only with major big-city banks that have European branches or sister banks. Banks usually charge a nice fat fee for doing you this favor. In an emergency, the American consulate may lend you money. You must repay this money. (There's no such thing as a free lunch.)

CURRENCY EXCHANGE

....

As already mentioned, currency rates and exchange rates (from dollars to euros) vary tremendously. The rate announced in the newspaper is the official bank exchange rate and does not apply to tourists. Even by trading your money at a bank, you will not get the official rate. The single best way to change dollars to euros is through an ATM. If you want a human transaction at a bank or hotel, bear the following in mind:

- While hotels give a less favorable rate of exchange than banks, they don't charge a fee to guests, are convenient, and rarely make you wait. Your time may be worth the difference.
- If you want to change money back into dollars when you leave a country, remember that you will pay a higher rate

for them. You are now "buying" dollars rather than "selling" them. Therefore, never change more money than you think you will need, unless you plan to stockpile for another trip.

TIPPING

With the arrival of the euro, tipping becomes an even more murky matter because it's a lot more expensive to be a good sport . . . and the low dollar doesn't make it the same alternative it was when the local currency was in lire. Figure 1€ ($1.10) per suitcase at a moderate hotel and 2€ ($2.20) per suitcase at a luxury hotel; 1€ ($1.10) for calling a taxi. Round up the taxi bill, but don't tip if you feel you were cheated. Sorry to say this, but with the dollar low, no one wants to be tipped in dollars.

TAXING MATTERS

Italian Tax Refunds

Let's start at the beginning so you understand the system; then I'll explain the tricky parts.

REFUNDS 101, THE EASY PART

In the U.S. when you go to pay for an item, sales tax is added at the time of purchase. In Europe, the taxes have already been added, so you pay the price on the ticket.

European Union (EU) countries have a system that allows foreign shoppers who buy goods and take them out of the country to receive a tax refund on these added taxes. In France, the tax is called TVA. In England, it's called VAT (value-added tax). In Italy, it's called IVA.

You only claim the refund when you depart the EU—this means the EU, not when you depart Italy. So if you are driving from Italy into France, you are still in the EU and can't claim the refund until you leave the EU for the U.S. If you go into Croatia, a non-EU country, you get the paperwork stamped at the border.

- When you are at the airport but before you check your luggage, go see the Customs officer.
- Mail the papers from the airport if you want a credit card refund.
- If you want an immediate refund in cash, find the cash-refund desk. Look for the desk bearing a red, white, and green logo and the sign TAX FREE FOR TOURISTS.

REFUND ME, YOU FOOL

Please note that there are several ways for you to receive a refund, and this is where it begins to get complicated.

There's the tax-free check, which you can cash or deposit at any bank; or a voucher, which can only be redeemed in currency. The voucher can be tricky because you will lose money on the conversion and have no chance to get a credit card refund. Whenever possible, have the refund applied to your credit card as you won't pay two exchange rates.

The new cash-in-town methods still mean that you have to show the goods at Customs when you depart the EU (a credit card imprint is made for the tax refund; if the store doesn't get the IVA paperwork back from Customs, you are charged the difference).

If you are leaving Italy via train or car, there are refund desks at the borders. Remember that you only do tax-free declarations at your final point of exit from the EU. Also note that by spring of 2004, the EU will further expand. This is not a Polish joke.

If you plan to hit another EU country before departing for home, you don't need to worry about Italian tax-free plans. *Ciao*, baby.

Detax Scam

Many designer shops say to you, after you inquire as to the price of a high-ticket item, "but you get a 19% discount from the tax." The implication is that the item will automatically be about 20% less, and this fact is meant to tip your judgment in favor of the sale.

There's just one problem. You don't get the full 19% back; you usually get 15% because there are various fees involved.

U.S. Customs & Duties Tips

- You are currently allowed to bring in $800 worth of duty-free merchandise per person. Each member of the family is entitled to the deduction; this includes infants.
- You pay a flat 10% duty on the next $1,000 worth of merchandise. It's worth doing—we're talking about the very small sum of $100.
- Duties thereafter are based on the type of product. They vary tremendously per item, so ask storekeepers about U.S. duties. They will know, especially in specialty stores. Note that the duty on leather goods is only 8%.
- The head of the family can make a joint declaration for all family members and should take responsibility for answering any questions that the Customs officers may ask. Have receipts ready, and make sure they match the information on the landing card. If you tell a little lie, you'll be labeled as a fibber, and they'll tear your luggage apart.
- When you make your declaration, you're supposed to include everything you obtained while abroad and are now carrying with you—this includes toothpaste (if you bring the unfinished tube back with you), items bought in duty-free shops, gifts for others, the items that other people asked you to bring home for them, and—get this—even alterations to clothing.
- For things you already owned when you left home, have the Customs registration slips in your wallet or someplace easily accessible. If you wear a Cartier watch, you should

be able to produce the registration slip. If you cannot prove that you took a foreign-made item out of the U.S. with you, you may be forced to pay duty on it when you return home!

- The unsolicited gifts you mailed from abroad do not count in the $800-per-person rate. If the value of the gift is more than $50, you pay duty when the package comes into the U.S. Remember, only one unsolicited gift per person.

- Do not attempt to bring in any illegal foodstuffs—dairy products, meats, fruits, or vegetables (coffee is okay). Generally speaking, if it's alive, it's verboten. Dried mushrooms happen to be okay.

- Antiques must be at least 100 years old to be duty-free. Provenance papers will help (so will permission actually to export the antiquity, since it could be an item of national cultural significance). Any bona fide work of art is duty-free, whether it was painted 50 years ago or just yesterday.

- Thinking of "running" one of those new Italian handbags? Forget it. New handbags shout to Customs officers.

Chapter Four

....

ITALIAN STYLE

TOGA, TOGA, TOGA

Italian style goes back, well, centuries—even before there was an Italy. It was the city-state system back then, and even up until the mid-1800s, part of what we today know as Italy was in France. What you're talking about when you think of chic is indeed half French. But not the sheets.

I sympathize with the politicos who say that modern Italy is actually two countries—North and South—and I see it in the fashions and the trends. But with a low dollar, you need not worry your pretty little head over politics—it's what's worth buying that is the real question. The answer lies within your own closet and your own lifestyle. Don't buy anything that makes sense in Italy but does not translate to your own world. At these prices, you want classics that will last 20 years.

Northern Fashion

Fashionistas in Milan are known to wear black—as they usually do in New York. To save themselves from going nuts with boredom, their black clothes have to have a style detail that makes them unique. This then is the epitome of northern Italian style—hard edged and clever details. Often the fresh approach revolves around technology and fabrics. New fabrics make the price of the garment go up.

In complete contrast to this style is another style that is worn by real people, not fashion victims—it looks like English country style and is prevalent as far south as Florence. While Italy now sells clothes from all over the world, you will find that certain brands—either Italian or global—have not ventured into the southern regions, even as far down as Florence, which is north where the south is concerned. Likewise, if you are looking to buy killer style, don't waste much time outside of Milan.

Buying Boutique Lines

If you crave the designer name but don't want to blow too much money, consider one of the lesser lines by the designer. Most of the designers have at least one, if not several, more mass-market ranges of clothing and possibly accessories. These lines are often created to be more young at heart (and price tag) so that the firm can woo the younger market and then trade them up when they are into the big euros. Newest member of the clan: T from Trussardi.

The tricky part? Big-name designers have boutique lines that may not have their names on them. You'll often find these lesser lines in department stores like Rinascente or even in the duty-free shops at the airport. In some cases, these lines end up with their own stores—such as Armani Jeans, Versus (a division of Versace), and D&G (from Dolce & Gabanna). The new T store on Via del Corso in Rome is a must.

If you see a name you don't know, ask about it. The Flexa line happens to be the young style division of Fratelli Rossetti. The Marina Rinaldi line is the large-size version of Max Mara. A. Testoni is a rather traditional line, but the Duckling line is anything but. Malizia is a lesser-priced lingerie line from La Perla, which has its own advertising so that people don't know the brands are actually competitive.

DICTIONARY OF TASTE & DESIGN

Editorial Note: Most of the brands and concepts listed below are Italian, but there are a few that are French or British or global in one way or another. If the brand is not well known in the U.S. but you have an opportunity to discover it in Italy, I have included it in this section.

Anna Molinari   The name you'll remember is not Anna's, but that of her label—Blumarine—which has been making waves for about a decade. There are now a few Blumarine boutiques. Her lesser line is called Blu Girl—very sultry and sexy.

Benetton   Benetton can only be described as a phenomenon. They hang in there and continue to reinvent, if not the wheel, then the sweater and perhaps the future. Check out some of the Benetton superstores in Italian capital cities; they even have play areas for kids.

Bottega Veneta   Tomas Maier (formerly of Hermès) came onboard 2 years ago and now everything is revitalized. There's still plenty of woven leather (in throw pillows!) and thousand-dollar handbags, but there are also more shoes and clothes and cashmeres.

Brioni   The name and brand are synonymous with men's style and elegance—James Bond (Pierce Brosnan) wears Brioni suits. There are stores—and stores that sell the brand—all over the world, but the Milan shop is the temple for service and Rome is the original flagship. The factories are in Penne.

Chocolate   Although most people don't associate Italian taste with chocolate, some of the world's most famous chocolate brands do come from Italy. See Nutella below. Perugina, the best-known mass-market brand, sells not only chocolate candy but also chocolate cooking supplies; I buy Perugina's tiny chocolate chips in the grocery store.

Coccinelle   This mass-market firm makes jazzy handbags at affordable prices and has free-standing stores in most large

---

Jenny's Turn: I Love Pocket Coffee

Sure to satisfy your caffeine addiction, pocket coffees are small, individually wrapped chocolate candies with real liquid espresso inside. Made by Ferrero, these intensely flavored confections are bought in boxes of five for about 1€ ($1.10) each and can be found in most grocery stores.

One piece of advice: Put the whole chocolate into your mouth at once, unless you want espresso squirting from your lips and dripping on your new *camiseta*.

Italian cities. Not considered a status range, but who cares? See www.coccinelle.com.

Coffee   The best-known brands make coffee for all kinds of coffee machines, not just espresso. My favorite is what I call "magic coffee"—a plastic, self-heating container with the brand name of Caldo Caldo. If you want to bring home a bag of coffee or two, try any supermarket; the best-known brands are Segafredo, Illy, and Lavazza. The grind is different for espresso. If you get hooked, fret not—Illy has a home delivery program in the U.S.; call © 877/ILLY-DIR or to go www.illyusa.com/casa.

Diego Della Valle   The man who created Tod's and Hogan (shoes) and is also responsible for the Acqua di Parma fragrance.

Diesel   Nothing to do with cars or trains but might inflame the engine of any teen or 'tween, Diesel clothing and jeans are pricey, tight, and very hot. You'll find stores in all major Italian cities, and all over the world. See their Style Lab, too.

Dolce & Gabbana   Highly influenced by their southern-Italian roots, these bad boys have reputations on the cutting edge of fashion.

Emilio Pucci   Being dead doesn't mean much when you have a name brand in Italy, or children who can carry on the business. Count Pucci's children sold to LVMH so that the Pucci brand could be revived and expanded. LVMH then did a smart thing—assigning their resident genius Christian Lacroix to also design this line. New shops and styles are popping up, and the public is Pucci-crazed all over again.

Etro   Gimmy Etro's family has been in the paisley business with some of Italy's most famous mills in the Lake Como area for centuries. The "new" Etro line is composed of fashions so chic you could swoon.

Fabriano   This firm's paper goods stand out for their excellent graphic design and format (fabulous gift items for less than 9€/$10), and its free-standing stores are opening in all major Italian cities.

Fendi   Fendi is a sisterhood of five women who run various aspects of the family business, which includes leather goods, ready-to-wear, and furs; now their children are in the business. If you just might want to gawk, check out the brand-new Palazzo Fendi in Rome, their "global store." There is also a new home-style line.

Ferragamo   Most famous for the shoes, then the silks, then the clothes, and now the hotel . . . they give away a free booklet on how to tie a silk scarf. Ask for it in one of the stores. The flagship store is in Florence, where they have expanded to take up a full city block. Sizes are in American lasts; note that large sizes are often more readily available in the U.S. than in Italy.

FNAC   Expanding into Italy, this French multimedia chain is good for books, CDs, small electronics, and supplies.

Frette   Frette has a line of Italian bed and table linens, both consumer and professional (hotel), and a somewhat new home collection that includes pajamas and robes. This brand actually began in the French Alps and then moved into Italy in the late 19th century. It has rejuvenated its look and expanded into home collections (and stores) in recent years. www.frette.com.

Gianfranco Ferré   A former architect, Ferré is known for clothing identifiable by its construction and architectural lines.

The store in Milan, which is the flagship, is gorgeous, and, of course, stunning from an architectural point of view. The clothes are divine but are crafted more for the tall woman.

Gianni Versace The line survives and thrives under Donatella's watchful eye and tender loving care. Despite Gianni's death, Versace defines shape and color, flair, drape, and humor. In most Italian cities, the men's, women's, and home-design stores are separate boutiques.

Giorgio Armani Giorgio Armani has been called one of the top five designers in the world; if you listen to *garmento* whispers, you can hear the clucking of wonder as to what will happen to his empire when he moves to the great minimalism in the sky. Meanwhile, his line and the business just keep growing. He opened headquarters in a renovated chocolate factory in Milan and then began making (and selling) chocolates.

Gucci Thanks to designer Tom Ford, Gucci is such a triumph that there's now a home collection as well as whimsical and cool must-have items, such as dog dishes. Savings are minimal (about 55€/$60 on a 545€/$600 handbag), but the cachet is high. The new Gucci means status and a whole new look—if you haven't been keeping up, you should check it out. Besides shoes and leather goods, there's clothing, scarves, and jewelry.

Jil Sander A German line sold to Italians and just rebought by Frau Sander herself. Watch this space.

Kiton This is the trade name for Ciro Paone, Neapolitan men's tailor . . . although he himself is not the tailor. In fact, there are over 200 tailors working for this men's brand.

Krizia No, Krizia isn't the designer's name—it's the name of a character from Plato. The designer behind it all is Mariuccia Mandelli, who has several licensees and creates many Krizia lines, including several fragrance lines. Imaginative, with a good sense of humor, Mandelli still manages to produce those drop-dead elegant clothes that rich women wear.

Laura Biagiotti Although she shows couture and ready-to-wear, Biagiotti is best known for her cashmere knits—and her new passion: golf. In her cut-and-sew work, Biagiotti has been known to show a sense of humor. Many of her styles are loose (they make stunning maternity dresses!) and fit nicely on women with imperfect figures. Her cashmeres are expensive but sought after. She has just announced plans to open shops in China!

Les Copains Despite the Frenchified name, this Italian sportswear company is pretty well known and pretty pricey, but not quite in the same league as Armani. The line is now designed by two young men from southern Italy—one from Sardinia and the other from Naples. It's this southern slant that makes the line hot, they claim.

Loro Piano Although most people associate this name with cashmere, the truth is its factories also make technologically advanced wools for men's suitings and produce fabrics of all kinds. Piano's cashmere is considered unique because it is Italian, not foreign. Its fascination with technology also shows up in its outerwear and Storm System products, as well as cashmere sweaters that are water repellent.

Luciano Barbera A brand so fancy that most people have never heard of it, this men's haberdashery line is carried in Bergdorf Goodman and Neiman Marcus in the U.S. Expect to pay over 909€ ($1,000) for a cashmere sweater. The reason everything costs so much is quality, created in the family mills near Biella. In Italy there is also a women's line and a golf line.

Lush A British brand but slightly re-created for the Italian market, Lush (www.lush.co.uk) makes bath and beauty products with locally made ingredients, so you get things like limoncello soap or shampoo. More than a dozen stores have popped up across Italy; the first one has just opened in the U.S., but none of the foreign branches have the Italian mode except those in Italy.

Madina This makeup line was created by the woman who is the makeup artist for La Scala opera in Milan and whose husband happens to own the chemical company that produces most of the world's designer color cosmetics. Free-standing stores are opening all over the world (visit www.madina.it).

Marni   Based in Forte di Marmi, the Palm Beach of Florence, the Marni family (actually named Castiglioni) became well known in the U.S. recently, partly because of the backing of a handful of New York specialty stores and now a shop in London. Marni does a cross between whimsy and silly, and provides clothes that people talk about—not the average bland garments, that's for sure. Lotsa flowers and bold prints.

Missoni   A family venture, the Missoni firm is famous for its use of knits and colors. They have become affiliated with architect-designer Saporitti, who has designed many of its boutiques, including the one in New York and the one in Milan. The architecture of the Milan shop is worth seeing and is an incredible example of new Italian style. Prices are high. Missoni bed linens are sold in T&J Vestor boutiques around Europe (and Italy).

MiuMiu   This childhood nickname of Mariucci Prada is also the name of the designer bridge line, with three stores in Italy: Milan, Florence, and Capri.

Moschino   The most successful ghost in Italy, Franco Moschino is actually dead, but his spirit lives on and thrives. If you have a good sense of humor and believe that fashion should be fun, you'll love the work inspired by bad boy Franco Moschino, who was what the French call a *créateur* (a big-name designer who doesn't create couture).

Nutella   The chocolate/hazelnut spread is a personal favorite of mine and one of Italy's best inventions. You can usually find it in grocery stores in the U.S.; but in Italy, you can't (and shouldn't) avoid it. I've put the stuff on just about everything. It's best on crepes, fruit, and bread, but in Italy, if you can find it, Nutella-flavored gelato is a truly legendary experience. Few gelato shops carry this amazing flavor, although many will have chocolate/hazelnut gelato; but the real Nutella flavor—now that's the good stuff. Since Italy is the home of Nutella and its makers, Ferrero, there is a certain freshness to it that you can't find anywhere else, especially in America, where it sits on grocery shelves for almost as long as Twinkies.

Patrizia Pepe   This clothing line (www.patriziapepe.com) from Prato (just north of Florence) has become so successful recently that there are now free-standing stores in the best shopping areas of all major Italian cities. This is a bridge line, somewhat hip without being totally over the top.

Pratesi   Founded in 1904 and now run by the fourth generation of the family, this small Italian bedding firm makes Italy's most luxurious sheets for Europe's crowned heads and also for the pope. It has stores in Boston, N.Y., and Beverly Hills, as well as in major Italian cities; also in Harrods in London and Lane Crawford in Hong Kong. See www.pratesi.com.

Renzo Piano   Known for his buildings all over the world, Italian architect Piano is especially talked about now because of his part in revitalizing Rome with his new music auditorium (which has a gift shop and cafe) as well as the art gallery built into the Fiat factory in Turin. Now then, this is tacky but here goes: The name of the restaurant inside the music hall in Rome is ReD, not Red like the color. It means *ristorante e design*.

Roberta di Camerino   The Venetian handbag designer who offered cult luxury product in the 1970s is now considered very "in" and also popular in vintage versions. Guiliana Camerino, the daughter, is now reissuing some old styles in various fabrics. These items are hard to find but are most easily spotted in stores in Venice.

Roberto Cavalli   A longtime legendary talent in Italy, Cavalli just made it into the global scene somewhat recently when his wild jeans were being worn by movie stars and rock artists. Then he segued into sexy chic with the lingerie look. Now he even makes lingerie. In the 1970s, his flower-power position was hip; now the clothes are featured on *Sex and the City,* and people in the street say he is the "new" Versace. He has his own restaurant in Milan.

Ruffo   Officially named Ruffo Research, this firm is famous for cutting-edge leather clothing; the star designer is actually a young Greek woman who went to school in London. (Go

Sneakers

Just like the inception of "designer" jeans, the past 2 years have seen more and more sneakers get fancy Italian makeovers. The big designer brands now make their own, with Prada leading the pack. Many of these designer shoes are incorporating leather into the sneaker for a fancy/casual look; some are still nylon and canvas.

Finding a nice pair in Italy for under 90€ ($100) is almost impossible. Even Pumas and Adidases have become status symbols and, likewise, are selling for anywhere from 82€ to 132€ ($90–$145). If you really want to find some cool sneakers without going broke, I strongly recommend going to Florence's outdoor market at Cascine on Tuesday mornings. Granted, you will find your share of the worst fake sneakers here: Adidases with four stripes, and Pumas with an upside-down logo that resembles the Nike "Swoosh" (I like to call these Pu-keys). But don't be discouraged; the bargains are here.

For me, cool sneakers are mostly about cool colors and good contrast. In Florence, I saw a very small, no-name brand called "Cric-Ups" that were well built and very cool. Best yet, they were 10€ ($11) a pair.

At the same market I found a stand with 30 boxes of Golas at 20€ ($22) per pair. Gola is a brand that was once thought of as an Adidas imposter but has really established itself in the last year as its own shoe. Before leaving New York for Italy, I was able to find Golas for 29€ ($32), a definite bargain, but since returning to the U.S., I have seen a few stores selling the new models for $72 . . . and I was gone only for a week.

figure.) The headquarters are outside Florence, although the best-known store is in Milan.

Sephora   This French chain is known for its international series of stores created in the style of a supermarket of beauty products and fragrance. Its Italian branches have a large selection

Jenny's Turn: Vintage Clothing

Wearing vintage clothes seems to be the trend that just won't end. That's fine with me; I like clothes with a history . . . just not underwear with a history. Vintage in Italy seems to be a northern thing, and Milan is the capital of the look.

The two best vintage stores on Porta Ticinese are Spazio 29 and Lo Specchio di Alice. Lo Specchio di Alice recently expanded into two adjacent stores and has a bigger selection, but I like the feel of Spazio 29 a bit better. Both have clothes from the '60s and '70s, with a few styles from the '80s.

of French and Italian brands. While there are over 100 stores in Italy alone, they are often in real-people districts and not in tourist areas. The easiest one to shop is perhaps in the Rome Centrale train station (downstairs).

Shoes   Italy has been world famous for leather shoes, gloves, and handbags for centuries. If you are looking for a fun spree without the usual tromping around stores and malls, drive the area between Padua and Venice where zillions of shoe factories dot the back roads. Most famous factory: Caovilla, where most designer shoes are made.

Valentino   The famous designer Valentino, known for his work in beige, is legally named Valentino Garavani. In some countries (for example, Japan), licensed goods are registered in his legal name. These are not necessarily the man's own designs. If you want true Valentino merchandise, you must buy it in Italy—either through Valentino couture or a shop that sells ready-to-wear.

Chapter Five

....

ROME

WELCOME TO ROME

....

I realize that Rome is known as the Eternal City and people like to think it's been this way more or less for over 2,000 years, give or take the invention of modern transportation and high-rises and a change in calendars. But the Rome you visit today is incredibly different than the Rome that existed a mere 2 years ago. There are changes everywhere and mostly in the air. *O sole mio,* this place is hot.

Rome has a new energy and excitement that were never there before (in my lifetime, anyway). While the voluptuous pleasures of the south still hang in the air, a lot of people from Milan have moved down—business is beginning to snap, crackle, and pop. *Pronto! Is that my phone ringing?*

Rome, of course, has always had a great designer upscale shopping neighborhood, but the arrival of the euro has brought new high prices. Now you shop for selection . . . or for the big brands at discount stores. Part of the glory that is Rome is that while there are heaps of designer shops, there are heaps of everything else, too. Even the magazine stands are fabulous to drool over.

Actually, truth be told, aside from the Fendi store, I'm not that knocked out with the so-called luxury Spanish Steps district. I'm not saying ignore it; I am saying that if your dollars are dear and you are not a first-timer, you may have more fun on side streets and in back alleys and away from the slick brands. My best shopping days in Rome are spent in older districts, in tiny alleys, and on back streets. I prefer to buy alternative retail, funky designs, vintage clothes, and soap. I prefer to prowl the Campo dei Fiori, to get lost in the medieval warren of streets behind the Piazza Navona.

ARRIVING IN ROME

By Plane

You can fly into Rome's airport from anyplace in the world. The airport is quite a bit out of town and a taxi will easily set you back 50€ to 73€ ($55–$80). There's also a train, but I digress.

Before arrival, please note: A private car and driver cost relatively the same thing as a taxi, by the way (a little more, but usually not much). As a result, many people book a car and driver to meet them or ask their hotel to provide this service. I've been given a source by my friend, Logan; you can call Gianni Ceglia on his mobile phone (© **0338/80-89-3970**). I now stay at the Hotel Exedra in Rome; its airport service is 50€ ($55).

If you can manage your luggage on your own, you may want to take the train from the airport right to the central train station in beautiful downtown Roma. It costs about 9€ ($10) and is a total breeze if you're not laden with heavy bags. There's also a great shopping mall in this train station, but I digress.

If you arrive in Rome from another EU country, there are no formalities. The color of your luggage tag is coded so that you don't even go through Immigration or Customs. You suddenly end up in the luggage retrieval area, watching fashion shows and car videos on large-screen TV monitors while waiting for your bags.

Luggage trolleys are free. There's both a *cambio* for changing money and a bank machine (better rates than the cambio), although the lines can be long. Still, since you have to wait for your bags to arrive, you might as well stock up on cash and be done with it.

You can connect to the train from within the arrivals terminal (it is well marked), but you must forfeit your trolley to use the escalator—so again, make sure you can handle your luggage on your own or with your travel companion. You can also get to the train station from outside, which is easier if you are a bit bulky with bags, since there are ramps for trolleys and carts.

Before you even exit the terminal, be aware that you might be assaulted by taxi drivers: These are gypsy drivers who may even have official taxis with medallions and may convince you that they are legit. Furthermore, they will quote the price in an odd manner, further confusing you. Watch out!

There is an official taxi rank, but you must find it, which I happen to have had trouble doing over a period of many years (slow learner). If you end up on the curb wondering what to do—look right and then walk right. You will find the taxi stand—I promise.

By Train

All rail tracks do indeed lead to Rome, be it intra-Italian trains or any of the fancy intra-European trains, including Eurostar (Italian Eurostar, not the Chunnel version). The Centrale train station (Termini) was spiffed up for the last Jubilee Year (2000) and is looking far better than you may remember it. The fact that it has a giant Nike shop in the front and a series of electronic kiosks for E-tickets should give you a hint that this is the New Italy.

As you emerge from the main train station, you'll see taxis everywhere; you may even be approached by some drivers who offer their services. Again, there is an official taxi stand with a very long line right in front of the train station. You wonder why you don't just hop into one of the waiting cabs, defying the queue. Why are all those people standing in line for up to 20 minutes? Because they don't want to overpay, be cheated, or come to blows with aggressive taxi drivers.

Rome wasn't built in a day, nor were the taxi scams being run out of the main train station. All those people can't be wrong. Stand in line, and you'll get a legitimate cab.

Tip: One of the reasons I now stay at the Exedra is that I can borrow a trolley from the train station and walk to the hotel.

By Ship

If by chance you are coming to Rome via ship, the port is Civitavecchia (say: *Cheat-a-veck-e-ahhhh*), along the coast north and west of Rome. It can take up to 2 hours to get into downtown Rome from here, although 1 hour is the no-traffic estimate. If you are going directly from your ship to the Rome airport, it will take 1 hour on a superhighway, and you will not actually go into Rome at all. *(Arrivederci, Roma.)*

And one final ship-to-shore report: During the summer, most stores close for the day on Saturday at 1:30pm. This isn't really a problem for you, however, because you arrive in port at 7am and make it to Rome by 9:30am, when the stores open. You have the whole morning to shop. You go to lunch at 1:30pm, when the stores close, and slowly eat a glorious Roman midday feast. Head back to the ship around 4pm and arrive in time for cocktails. Or stop off in Tarquena, a sneeze away from the port, where they have some cutie-pie retail, and yes, I thought you'd never ask, a few pottery shops.

Naturally, cruise ships offer their own shore excursions and even shopping trips. The tour offered from Civitavecchia on a recent Holland America Line cruise didn't even take you into Rome. Instead, you got "Tarquina with Shopping"—a tour that included ancient burial tombs and then a visit to the Civitavecchia Shopping Mall.

The Lay of the Land

The city of Rome is divided into 33 zones, working in circular rounds much like the *arrondisements* of Paris. The oldest part of the city is 1, Centro Storico. I have instead divided Rome into my own areas or neighborhoods; see below.

Technically speaking, Vatican City is a different city than Rome; that's why it has its own guards (who are Swiss), its own postal service, and its own euro coins, which, with Pope John Paul II's image on them, are thought to be collectable due to the Pope's advanced age and the anticipation of a new pope, whose picture will go on new euro coins.

ABOUT ADDRESSES

Addresses seem to bounce around from street to street; some alternate in a sensible way and some make no sense at all. Frequently, all the stores in a block have the same street number and are designated by letters. It's not unusual for a store to be listed according to its piazza or its street corner.

GETTING AROUND

Walk.

Okay, so it's too hot to walk that much, and the city's too spread out. So, the best time investment you can make is to organize your days so that you can do lots of walking; this keeps you out of crazy Roman traffic and on the streets so that you can count the fountains. Also, like most major Italian cities, Rome has new laws about motor traffic, and only certain cars with certain permits are allowed in certain areas.

Taxi   Taxi drivers in Rome are known to be difficult, especially to tourists, especially to Americans who can't speak Italian, and most especially to women traveling without men. Be prepared to occasionally have to argue with the driver if you take cabs; be aware of when you should pay a supplement (for extra baggage and for rides after 9pm and on Sun and holidays). I continue to have unpleasant situations with taxi drivers, enough so that I think the difference between Italy and France can be summed up in the way you are treated by taxis. But enough about me.

Rome & Its Shopping Neighborhoods

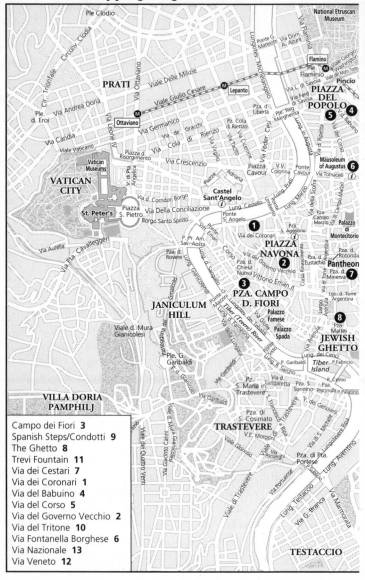

Campo dei Fiori 3
Spanish Steps/Condotti 9
The Ghetto 8
Trevi Fountain 11
Via dei Cestari 7
Via dei Coronari 1
Via del Babuino 4
Via del Corso 5
Via del Governo Vecchio 2
Via del Tritone 10
Via Fontanella Borghese 6
Via Nazionale 13
Via Veneto 12

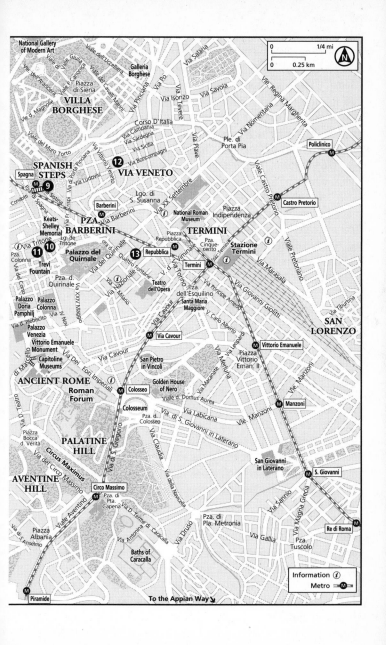

Legitimate taxis carry a shield with a number. Cars for hire are black with a shield. Taking any other car can be dangerous.

Metro   There is a metro, the Metropolitana. It's nice and gets you to most of the touristy attractions, but it does not blanket the city. You may find the walk from your hotel to the nearest stop (look for the big red M sign) worthy of a taxi in itself. One of the reasons I switched hotels to the Exedra is that it is 50m (164 ft.) from the Repubblica metro stop. These days, these things count.

To ride the metro, have change to put into the ticket machine, or look around for a machine that produces change. You must get your ticket from one of the machines; there is no booth selling tickets. (The newsstand will not give you change without a purchase.) Because the metro is not too involved, it is easy to ride, and safe. A Metrobus card, which costs about 2.75€ ($3) per day, allows you unlimited use of the metro and buses. It's sold in train stations and at *tabac* stands.

Bus   I love to take the bus in Rome, although many people will tell you that buses are slow and not dependable, especially in the rain. But the bus gives you a nice view of this gorgeous city and gets you easily to the main attractions. To find out which bus to take, you can buy a bus map at a newsstand, you can ask your concierge, or you can read the sign at the bus stop that lists all the stops. Also check inside the telephone book in your hotel room, which may have a bus and metro map.

I once took the right bus in the wrong direction—a typical mistake for those who don't speak the language or know their way around the city very well—but I had a great time and saw a lot of sights.

Rome has many bus islands that act as little stations where buses congregate. There's one such island in front of the Vittorio Emanuele monument in the old city, and another called San Silvestro, which is in the heart of the shopping district at the base of the Via Veneto and halfway to the Spanish Steps.

The bus system in Rome is similar to those in other Italian cities: You must purchase your ticket at a tobacco stand or newsstand ahead of time (they do not sell tickets on the bus or take money); you enter from the rear and cancel your own ticket in the box; and you exit from the center of the bus. Instructions in English and Italian are inside the bus.

SLEEPING IN ROME

....

American Chains

The American hotel chains have made a comfortable dent in the Roman scene; they often offer deals (in dollars, no less) that are too good to be true. While there are several chains (see below), note that with the addition of a spa, the Hilton has reached icon status. While it has a slightly screwy location, it has become a major, major player. See below for more on the Hilton.

Hilton Originally, I thought this hotel would be inconvenient for a shopper, but years ago I decided to give it a whirl. After all, the hotel has a shuttle bus to the shopping districts as well as special promotional rates. Furthermore, it has its own swimming pool and a resort ambience—perfect for summer in Rome, which is always a scorching situation. We all know to trust the Hilton brand, but few of us know that this is one of the most famous, and different, Hilton hotels in the system.

The hotel has a fabulous, and famous, rooftop restaurant, La Pergola. But it gets better: Always famous for its swimming pool and parklike grounds, this Hilton now has a spa. Not just any old spa, as is the rage among all hotels, but a spa of such grand proportions that it was possibly created to make Cleopatra roll over in her grave. This spa has become so important in the local landscape that now zillions of celebs stay here. The buzz on the hotel has changed from that of insider's secret to bastion of hip.

Holiday Inn/Crowne Plaza The Holiday Inn in Rome is the Minerva. It, too, is a five-star hotel, so in some ways it competes with the bigger names listed here. Children up to age 19 stay free in their parents' room in all Holiday Inn properties, so this is something to consider. When I called Holiday Inn, they explained that prices change on a daily basis, depending on availability, but rates booked in U.S. dollars are guaranteed at that rate. Furthermore, I was offered an additional discount for being an AAA member, which brought my room rate for a fall booking to $309.25. Not bad, considering that the regular rate on these rooms is often over $380.

InterContinental   The Hotel de la Ville InterContinental Roma has the best location of any of the U.S. chains for shopping, as well as some rather good deals. Last time I looked, the Hotel de la Ville was booking at $250 per night, guaranteed in U.S. dollars. Note that you get breakfast with this rate, as well as 500 frequent-flier miles. Also note that the Hotel de la Ville is next door to the Hassler, one of the most famous hotels in Rome, known for its excellent location at the top of the Spanish Steps.

Marriott   Rome Hotel Grand Flora is now open on the famous shopping street Via Veneto. Marriott is in business with the Bulgari family.

Sheraton   Sheraton/Starwood has long had an interesting position in Rome. They have a modern hotel in the middle of nowhere, halfway between Rome and the airport; it's frequently booked by cruise companies for turning around passengers. **Westin** has taken most of the Ciga properties that Sheraton was holding onto, including the Hotel Excelsior, well located on the Via Veneto and also often booked for cruise passengers. It is a gloriously old-fashioned grande-dame hotel worthy of royalty. Please note that special rates almost always have to be booked before you arrive.

Westin   In Rome it's the Excelsior—grande-dame hotel right on the Via Veneto just up the block from the American Embassy. There are also Sheraton hotels—they are mostly on the outskirts of large cities or attached to business parks.

Addresses and phones are below.

CAVALIERI HILTON
Via Cadiolo 101
U.S.: ✆ 800/HILTONS

CROWNE PLAZA MINERVA
Piazza della Minerva 49
U.S.: © 800/465-4329

EXCELSIOR HOTEL (WESTIN)
Via Veneto 125
U.S. and Canada: © 800/325-3589

HOTEL DE LA VILLE INTERCONTINENTAL ROMA
Via Sistina 69
U.S.: © 800/327-0200

MARRIOTT GRAND FLORA
Via Veneto 191
U.S.: © 888/236-2427

SHERATON ROMA
Vialle del Pattinaggio
© 06/545-31; or 800/325-3535 in the U.S.

Dream Hotels

EXEDRA
Piazza della Repubblica 47 (metro: Repubblica).

This hotel changed my life and my vision of Rome. It's new inside, old outside, and built over ruins, which can be seen through glass floors on the lower level. Just head down to the Business Center.

The restaurant is designed by my hero Adam Tihany. The hotel location right above a metro station makes transportation a breeze. Furthermore, you can walk to the main train station. (The taxi line was so long when I arrived in Rome that I popped my bags on a trolley and arrived at the hotel pushing the trolley and pulling my dog.) The staff is dressed in very chic black on black; everyone is friendly and helpful; and because the hotel is so new, you have the feeling of having made a great discovery.

There's a cooking school, sumptuous rooms, and, get this, a McDonald's next door. Any luxury hotel with a McDonald's is my kind of place, although I hear they are trying to ease out the fast food. There's also a movie theatre (with some selections in English), a rooftop pool and spa, and more chic than the average person can begin to absorb.

But wait, I'm not finished. I brought my dog with me, and when we arrived in the room, there was a large VIP basket for her, filled with dog food, biscuits, a toy, etc. Now that's catering to a client's special needs. Rooms begin at 296€ ($325). For reservations, call © 800/337-4685 in the U.S. Local phone 06/489-381. exedra.boscolohotels.com. Do not confuse this hotel with the trendy Es Hotel.

ALEPH HOTEL
Via di San Basilio 15 (metro: Barberini).

Considering my heartthrob Adam Tihany designed this hotel, it's a pity I had to stare at it without sleeping in it. Indeed this is the small, cozy, artsy boutique hotel for those who want luxury on the sly. There's a spa, a Moroccan-style restaurant, and a location nestled not too far from the Spanish Steps and Via Veneto. For reservations, call © 800/337-4685 in the U.S. Local phone 06/422-901. aleph.boscolohotels.com.

HOTEL DE RUSSIE
Via del Babuino 9 (metro: Spagna).

While I am not a big fan of modern hotels, I admit to falling head over heels in love with this one, a recent entry from Sir Rocco Forte and as delicious and decadent as the Delano in Miami Beach. On top of all that: a fabulous shopping location at the Piazza del Popolo. Sir Rocco Forte also re-created the Savoy in Florence (see chapter 6). For reservations, call © 800/323-7500 in the U.S. Local phone 06/32-88-81.

Four-Star Finds

HOTEL CARRIAGE
Via delle Carrozze 36 (metro: Spagna).

This is just one of those "finds" that I discovered while shopping in the Spanish Steps district. I stumbled on it, so I did not stay here but did do an inspection. This is indeed a find—a great shopping location and a nice little four-star for those who would rather put their extra euros into their shopping sprees. The hotel has the tiny, clubby, modest feel of home.

Singles start at 136€ ($150); a suite is about 227€ ($250). Local phone ✆ **06/69-91-24.** Fax 06/678-82-79. hotel.carriage@fanet.it.

JOLLY HOTEL VITTORIO VENETO
Corso Italia 1 (metro: Barberini).

One of those newfangled, post–World War II, high-style modern Italian buildings, the Jolly gives you the best of both worlds. Your room overlooks the park, and you are situated at the top of the Via Veneto, so you can just roll out of bed and into the stores. It's rare to find the American crowd here; the hotel is often frequented by businesspeople. Rates, which include a big breakfast buffet, start at around 182€ ($200)—a great price for Rome. There are also various promotional deals, including a package called Mitica Roma (available for all four Jolly hotels in Rome), which puts a room at less than 182€ ($200) per night, and weekend nights, when added on, are about 109€ ($120) per night for two. For reservations, call ✆ **800/221-2626** in the U.S. Local phone 167/01-77-03 (toll-free) or 06/84-951. www.jollyhotels.it.

SOFITEL ROMA
Via Lombardia 47 (metro: Spagna).

One of Sofitel's new and grand hotels, a renovated mansion near the Borghese Gardens. This is the former Hotel Boston, in case you or your taxi driver is confused. Don't miss the fifth-floor terrace. Prices are not low and can be over 364€ ($400) per room if you don't get a promotional deal. For reservations, call ✆ **800/SOFITEL** in the U.S. Local phone 06/47-80-29-58. www.sofitel.com.

Snack & Shop

LA CARBONARA
Piazza Campo dei Fiori 23 (no nearby metro).

This is one of the few places in Rome where it is as pleasant to eat inside as outside, where your experience is as special in winter as in spring. Located right on the Campo dei Fiori, this seems to be the nicest of the surrounding cafes. The interior is done in a rustic country style, with some tables overlooking the piazza. The daily fruit and flower market adds to the charm of the location and makes this restaurant a must. This is one of the few restaurants in the area that is open on Sunday, but the flower market is closed on Sunday. For reservations, call © 06/686-47-83. Closed Tuesday.

MCDONALD'S
Piazza di Spagna, near the Spanish Steps (metro: Spagna).

Stop laughing. I love this McDonald's, and not just because my son does. The architecture (it's in a fake villa) is astounding, the location is sublime, and the food is inexpensive for Rome, if not by U.S. standards. You can get the usual burgers and McNuggets, or load up at the salad bar, where you can get tomatoes and mozzarella. You have to see this place. The crowd it gets is amazing. It's a good place to rest between stores. Logan says to sit downstairs where it's less noisy, and where ice cream and Baci (the chocolates) are sold.

NINO
Via Borgognona 11 (metro: Spagna).

My favorite restaurant in Rome, Nino is a small bistro with dark wood walls, and it's located right in the heart of the Spanish Steps shopping area. It attracts a nice, fashionable crowd without being chi-chi.

Prices are moderate by Rome standards, which to me is incredibly inexpensive, especially for this location and style. I just got my Visa bill: My last lunch at Nino, an admittedly simple affair consisting of bottled water, one Coca-Cola, spaghetti, and a coffee, was all of 13€ ($14). Tip included. The waiters are friendly; I often eat here solo and feel comfortable doing so. If you get here early (by local standards) for lunch, you don't need a reservation. Or you can plan ahead and call © **06/679-56-76.** Closed Sunday.

But wait! I just got a letter from a reader who loves Nino and bemoaned the Sunday closure to the waiter Lorenzo. Lorenzo sent them to **Ristorante 34,** which they adored. By mentioning that Lorenzo sent them, they got VIP treatment.

RISTORANTE GIRARROSTO TOSCANO
Via Campania 29 (no nearby metro).

This country-style place is at the top of the Via Veneto (across the street from the Jolly, around the corner from the Excelsior). Sit down and feast on the antipasti, for which there is a flat charge per person, no matter how much you eat. After you've eaten more than you knew possible, they bring dinner. The cooking style is Florentine; the wine is Chianti (although there are plenty of others); the atmosphere is adorable (covered in tiles and charm); the crowd is well heeled, although there are some tourists. And prices are moderate. Book a reservation (© **06/ 482-18-99),** especially for after 8pm, as the place does fill up. Closed Wednesday.

THE SHOPPING SCENE

Shopping is something you do in Rome while you are doing Rome . . . or in between meals. Aside from making a frontal attack on Via Condotti and the fancy stores in that area, you will find shopping ops as you explore Rome, and not vice versa.

Roman style is still a little bit old couture, but mostly Roman fashion reflects Rome's geographic location: This is philosophically—and fashion wise—the south of Italy. As such, Rome is rather like the Beverly Hills of Italy, and the clothes for sale here have a glitz and gleam to them that you won't find up north. Even the Milanese who have moved on down here don't wear black. Colors are hot in Rome. Women are not flat-chested in Rome. Skirts are shorter in Rome. Nailheads, studs, bugle beads, and sequins with, yes, truly, little bits of fur—faux and/or real—can be found sewn to clothing and, hmm, even shoes.

The globalization of money and designer franchises means that Italian designers sell their lines all over their own country, most certainly in Rome, and in just about every other country as well. The line may be most fully shown in stores in Milan, but you can find an excellent selection of these designer clothes in Rome. In a few cases, the Rome store is better than the Milan store.

Best Buys

Rome doesn't have any cheap best buys, unless you are ready to spring for Italian designer fashions, in which case everything is a best buy. Oops, I lied.

Designer Fashions   You won't find too many designer bargains unless you hit a sale, but then things can really go your way. If you are bargain conscious, the best deals in Rome are at a few outlet shops (see below) or in the airport, which has a gigantic duty-free shopping area. If you are status conscious, these are best buys because the selection of styles in any given designer brand goes beyond what you'd find in other cities in the world.

Please note that items imported to Italy for sale at the duty-free shops at the airport (English sweaters, for example) are 19% cheaper than they are in a regular Italian store, but they are still outrageously expensive. Buy Italian when in Italy; forget everything else. Also note that not every store in the Rome Airport is a duty-free shop, even though it may look like one.

Ties   I got caught up in how many status ties are for sale in various shops in Rome. Prices are less expensive than in the U.S. and the U.K. In fact, prices can be so low you may giggle. The average price of a power tie in New York, without

New York State sales tax, is $95 to $135. The same ties in Rome cost 59€ to 100€ ($65–$110). You can even buy a power tie in Rome for 32€ ($35). I kid you knot.

Home Style   From Tad to Lisa Corti, the sexy colors and the mix of imported looks with Italian chic have arrived. This is mondo home style, from Asia, from sub-continent, and from all over shaken up with the Italian touch. Lisa Corti is sold at Saks Fifth Avenue, but the Italian prices—even in euros—are better than the U.S. prices. If you can't stand the colors, back into beige or monotones in the bed line, from Frette or Pratesi.

Shopping Hours

Hours in Rome are the same as in all of Italy, but Sunday is really loosening up. In fact, the department store La Rinascente is open on Sunday from noon to 5pm. Wonders never cease.

For normal retail days (Tues–Fri), shops open at 9:30am and close at 1 or 1:30pm for lunch. They reopen at 3:30pm in winter and at 4pm in summer. In the summer, stores stay open until 8pm. Because Romans (as do all Europeans) dine late, many people are out shopping until midnight. Do not let any hotel concierge or signpost lead you to believe that stores in Rome open at 9am—even if it says so on the door. This is Rome, remember?

If you don't like to give up shopping for lunch, the department stores and mass merchandisers stay open during these hours, and a growing number of high-end merchants are following suit. Fendi is open through lunch, as are many other stores on Via Borgognona and in the Spanish Steps area.

Now then, the odd days are Monday, Saturday, and Sunday. Some stores are closed Monday morning; in summer, they are often also closed Saturday afternoon. But that's not a rule. On my last Monday in Rome, I found that mass-market stores and chains are open by 10am on Monday. Designer shops open at 3:30pm on Monday. For Sunday shopping, stores that are open may close for lunch and then be open again from 4 to 7pm.

Closed Out

Watch out for those August closures—some stores call it curtains, totally. Only madmen go to Rome in August. The sales are in July.

Personal Needs

You will find neither grocery stores nor real-people department stores in the middle of the usual tourist shopping haunts, although there's a branch of **La Rinascente** and of **Upim** just near San Silvestro, close to the main tourist areas such as the Trevi Fountain and the Spanish Steps. But you have to know how to find them . . . or to even look for them.

Ask your concierge for the nearest pharmacy or grocery.

Note: The Centrale train station has a fabulous mall underneath it and can meet most needs. Rome has several dozen all-night pharmacies, including one at the airport. The pharmacy at the main train station is open until 11:30pm daily.

There are three branches of **Standa**—the Kmart-like department store locals rely on—in Rome; the one in Trastevere (Viale Trastevere 60) also has a supermarket. Upim stores are closing like mad.

Rome is more spread out than some of the other cities you'll visit; you may need to take a walk around your hotel to learn the whereabouts of your own minimart for buying water, snacks, and all those things that cost too much from your minibar.

Special-Event Retailing

If you happen to be in Rome between December 15 and January 6, get yourself (and your kids) over to the Piazza Navona, where there is an annual Christmas fair. Stalls surround the large square and offer food, candies, and crafts. You can buy tree ornaments and crèches. *Warning:* Much of the Hong Kong–made merchandise is less expensive in the U.S. Stick to locally crafted items at the fair, and you won't get ripped off.

Because Easter in Rome is also a big deal, there are more vendors in Vatican City at this time.

Shopping Neighborhoods

Spanish Steps/Condotti   No matter what season of the year, the Spanish Steps are so gorgeous that you can't help but be drawn to them. They are particularly magical because they lead to all the best big-name stores. Don't forget that there's an **American Express** office at the Steps, so when you run out of money on a shopping spree, you can get more without missing a beat, and then get right back to spending it.

The **Via Condotti** is the leading shopping street of the high-rent Spanish Steps neighborhood—but it is not the only game in town, or even on the block. The area between the Spanish Steps and the Via del Corso is a grid system of streets, all packed with designer shops.

Via Condotti has the most famous big names and is the equivalent of Rodeo Drive, but you'd be missing a lot of great stuff (and the American designer stores) if you didn't get to the side streets, all of which combine to make up the area I hereby name Spanish Steps/Condotti.

Note: There is one street that leads away from the Spanish Steps, the Via del Babuino (yes, it's the baboon street), which appears to be an equal spoke from the Steps but actually has a very different neighborhood feel to it, so I have separated it from the rest (see below).

If you have only a few hours to shop in Rome and you are seriously interested in designer fashion, your assignment, should you accept it or not, is to shop the Spanish Steps/Condotti area and to get to some of—or all of—the Via del Babuino and a block or two of the Via del Corso down at the Condotti end. By all means, make it into the recently refurbished Fendi, which is like an art gallery of creativity. If you can't stand all these fancy stores and have no need to be toting the next or newest Gucci bamboo handle, then head over to Via Vittoria, one of the tiny side streets in the area where many young and hip shops are having their day. My fave is **Il Baco da Seta** (no. 75).

Via Veneto   I know that every American in Rome has heard of the Via Veneto, if only from the movies. While I invariably stay at a hotel in this area, note that the shopping here is nothing to write home about or to go out of your way to visit. The large bookstalls on the street corners are handy for a vast selection of magazines (all languages) and supplies, from post-cards to videos (yes, even dirty movies) to paperback bestsellers in English. There are some shoe shops and several glitzy cafes. It's a pleasant street to wander, but not exceptional. If you are staying in the area, you will probably enjoy the side streets more.

Via Nazionale   This is a very long street, but its best parts—between Repubblica and Termini—have a slew of fashion shops for young women and a few big names. More and more big names are opening here, but you can now find Max Mara, Frette, and a few others. The Upim here has closed to make room for more fancy fare. Stay tuned.

Trevi   From the Spanish Steps, you can walk to the Trevi Fountain and segue into several "real-people" Rome neighborhoods. First hit **Via del Tritone;** both sides of the street have good offerings. See the listing below.

Via dei Coronari   You say you like to stroll down medieval streets and look at antiques shops? Hmm. Well, guys, have I got a street for you. This particular street takes you back to a previous century, and has the best antiques stores in Rome. Located right around the corner from the Piazza Navona, the Via dei Coronari is very small; study your map first.

Walk down one side of the street and back up the other, an area of maybe 2 or 3 blocks. Some of the shops are extremely fancy salons with priceless pieces; others are a little funkier. Almost all of the dealers take credit cards. Those who don't speak English may speak French if your Italian isn't too good. The shop numbers will go to the middle 200s before you've seen it all; there are possibly 100 dealers here.

The dealers are very community minded and have their own block association that has various parties and promotions for the public. They've organized a few nights in May when the

Via dei Coronari

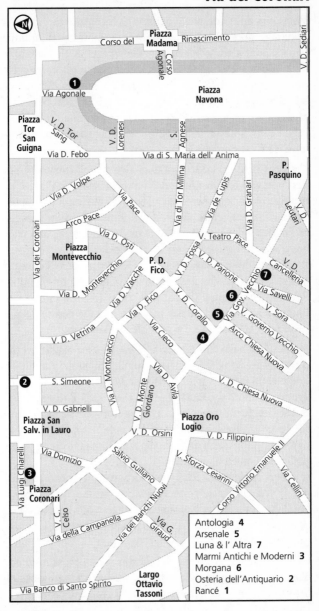

Antologia **4**
Arsenale **5**
Luna & l' Altra **7**
Marmi Antichi e Moderni **3**
Morgana **6**
Osteria dell'Antiquario **2**
Rancé **1**

stores stay open late, and a party in October, also for late-night strolling and shopping (officially called the local **Antiques Fair**). Candles and torches light the way.

If you are looking for someplace super to eat in the midst of the antiques stores, try **Osteria dell'Antiquario,** Piazzetta di San Simeone (© **06/68-79-694**). You can eat outdoors or in at this simple but elegant place that's also quite "in." Lunch for two costs about 73€ ($80). Don't let the address throw you; it's right on the Via dei Coronari.

Via del Corso Via del Corso is a very long street; the part that you will be most interested in begins where Via del Tritone intersects it and extends all the way to Piazza del Popolo. Both sides of the street are lined with stores; many are branches of famous names, such as Frette or even Benetton, and many are stores that I just like for local color.

The really hot part of Via del Corso is right below the Spanish Steps in the area from Via Condotti to Piazza del Popolo, where you'll find all the fancy designer shops, a zillion teen shops (rock music blaring), and the new version of neon rock fashions for 14-year-olds—like **Onyx.**

Via del Tritone This is a big real-people shopping street that connects the Via del Corso and Spanish Steps area to the Via Veneto and Piazza Barberini area; it is also an extension of the Trevi neighborhood. At the top is the **Piazza Barberini,** with the Bernini Bristol Hotel and a metro stop. As you move down the street until it dead-ends into Via del Corso, you have a lot of regular shops with more moderate prices than the big-name designer shops 3 blocks away.

There is a large **La Rinascente** department store on the corner. If you walk a few blocks away from the Spanish Steps, you'll be at the Trevi Fountain, so to get your bearings, look at a map, and see that Via del Tritone is between Trevi and the Spanish Steps.

Campo dei Fiori Campo dei Fiori is one of those neighborhoods that is beginning to attract tourists and will certainly be ruined in no time at all; right now it is a genuine daily fruit and flower market that packs up by about 1pm. Get there mid-morning, browse the stalls and photograph the fruits, and then plop down at any of the dozen or so cafes nearby. There are also pizza places, if you don't want a 55€ ($60) lunch.

Aside from the market, you are in the midst of an old Roman neighborhood, where rents are lower and fun shops are opening up. There are a number of food and cookware stores surrounding the Campo dei Fiori. Just a few blocks away is the Piazza Navona, where you can visit the **Rancé** soap shop and stroll around the piazza, of course. *Note:* There is no market at Campo dei Fiori on Sunday.

Via del Governo Vecchio   This is sort of a hidden street, between the Piazza Navona and the Campo dei Fiori. Before you attempt to find it on foot, first try to locate it on a map. The street is dark, narrow, medieval, and blessed with a few vintage clothing shops. Some are the Army-Navy type; others sell serious vintage—I had my 45€ ($50) Pucci triumph on this street, although the actual store where I got lucky is now gone.

Aside from the vintage stores, there are some cutting-edge fashion boutiques. I like **Morgana** (no. 27) and **Arsenale;** both are hot and happening. This neighborhood is easy to reach, is fun to shop, and gives you a less touristy perspective on Rome. Also be sure to take in **Antologia** (no. 49), for women's clothing, and **Luna & l'Altra** (no. 105). Luna sells Dries and Kenzo and style, for those who know what it means.

Via Fontanella Borghese   Right now, this is still coming into its own as an extension of the Via Condotti on the other side of the Via del Corso. This street is quiet, unvisited by tourists, and home to several new branches of big-name designer shops, such as **Fendi** (no. 57). In this same quiet area is the new **Lisa Corti** store, Via di Pallacorda 14.

Via del Babuino   Remember when I told you that Spanish Steps/Condotti had another part to it that was the same but different? Well, this is it. This is one of the antiques neighborhoods of Rome, and boasts some snazzy designer shops, too. It's a fun neighborhood, especially if you're just looking for furniture, paintings, or the hottest items in Europe these days: Art Deco tabletop accessories. I take it back—this is more than a fun neighborhood. This is a must-do.

Via del Babuino stretches from the Spanish Steps to Piazza del Popolo, and is filled with interior-design experts, antiques shops, and fabric and lighting showrooms, as well as a few leather-goods hot shots and designer somebodies. **Emporio Armani** (no. 13) begins the parade—although it is almost directly across the street from **Etro** (no. 102) at the beginning of the shopping windfall. Then comes **Chanel**, etc. Further along you'll get to **AJ** (no. 70A), which is Armani Jeans, the Italian version of AX, although not identical.

Don't forget that right off this street, where you least expect it, is one of the better designer discount stores of Rome, **Il Discount dell'Alta Moda** (Via di Gesù e Maria 16 and 14, the new men's shop). If you stay on Baboon Street, it dead-ends at the Piazza del Popolo and the **Hotel Russie,** which you must wander through. But before you can rest and relax at the hotel, be sure to hit **Tad** (no. 155a). For that matter, Tad also has a cafe.

The Ghetto   This is a far cry from the Grand Hotel, but for those of you who want to stay in a fabulous hotel but then travel to the grittier parts of the city, you are off on a crazy adventure. Take a bus from the train station to the Vittorio Emanuele monument and walk, or just taxi, right to the oldest part of Rome, where the ghetto was.

Take the **Via delle Botteghe Oscure** for 2 short blocks, note all the fabric jobbers (wholesalers), then turn left at the **Piazza Paganica.** You'll now enter a small neighborhood that seems very residential. Wander the weaving streets looking for the shops that interest you. This is the kind of adventure that is welcomed by a true *garmento,* someone who likes to see bolts of fabric piled up in store windows and doesn't care about fancy architecture or salespeople in matching uniforms. The area is charming, very old, crumbling, and undiscovered by tourists. All of these stores are jobbers; you'll find jeans and underwear and sweats and even a few jewelry stores. *Don't miss:* Leone

Limentani, Via Portico d'Ottavia 47, a discounter with mounds of dishes and china—even Richard Ginori patterns.

Via dei Cestari If you're looking for a unique shopping experience, a unique gift, or just something special and different, after you visit the Pantheon (bad gift stalls), check out the Via dei Cestari, which is filled with ecclesiastical shops selling ribbons, robes, socks, and all sorts of fascinating supplies. Start at **De Ritis** (no. 48) and check out all the surrounding stores. Many also sell chalices and religious souvenirs.

Five Best Stores of Rome

IL BACO DA SETA
Via Vittoria 75 (metro: Spagna).

Droopy and divine fashions in easy-to-wear silk in dreamy colors; also some accessories. Fair prices in the 136€ to 181€ ($150–$200) range.

LUNA & L'ALTRA
Via del Governo Vecchio 105; no nearby metro.

This store isn't much bigger than a walk-in closet, but it carries an international cadre of funky-chic names such as Issey Miyake and Dries Van Noten, and puts it all together in a look that is comfortable and fabulous.

MARMI ANTICHI E MODERNI
Via dei Coronari 113–114 (no nearby metro).

Maybe this store is only great to me—it is a matter of taste. While the store may at first seem like a tourist trap (TT) or at best a place that sells marble stuff you may or may not be interested in, stay a few seconds and find the fruit. It's very expensive (about 18€/$20 per piece), but it is so chic you could pass out.

TAD
Via Babuino 155a (metro: Spagna).

Home style by the mile, even though it's not that hard-line Italian look. Ask them for the address of the stock shop, which was around the corner when I visited, but may have moved. There is a cafe, too.

TERMINI ROMA MALL
Rome Main Train Station (metro: Termini).

Perhaps you can never take the love of a mall out of the American heart. This is truly an American-style mall located underneath the main train station, but it has French and Italian stores and places to eat—and it is great fun. There's one shop devoted just to merchandise for race-car drivers and wannabes. There's a Sephora, the beauty supermarket. There is a real supermarket. There's everything. I love it here. Aboveground, on the main level, there's a tease of what's below—a Nike shop, a Benetton, a bookstore, etc.

ALSO-RAN

LISA CORTI HOME TEXTILE EMPORIUM
Via di Pallacorda 14 (metro: Spagna).

This store opened a month after I left Rome, but because I am such a Lisa Corti fan and because I have seen color pictures of this venue, I send you here with delight. It's right near the Piazza Fontanella Borghese, not too far from the Spanish Steps. Look for the look in any Saks Fifth Avenue catalog and compare prices.

ROME RESOURCES FROM A TO Z

Antiques

While I can't go so far as to suggest you actually buy antiques in Rome, this is the Italian center of fancy antiques shops. There are several streets where stores abound, including **Via del Babuino** and **Via dei Coronari** (see above). If you're shopping for serious antiques and looking for a dealer to trust, look for the gold seal representing the Associazione Romana Antiquari. Note that each fall, for 1 week, there's an antiques market at Pala Parioli, and the shops on Via dei Coronari are usually open at night.

Beauty

AVEDA
Rampa Mignanelli 9 (metro: Spagna).

Although this address sounds screwy, actually "rampa" very well describes the fact that the shop is on a ramp to the Spanish Steps. This is an American brand, and prices are slightly higher in Rome than in the U.S., but it's a high-quality brand and good for travel sizes if you need products.

BEAUTY PLANET
Grand Hotel Palace, Via Veneto 66–70 (metro: Repubblica).

Full-service spa and beauty center. Closed Sunday.

SERGIO VALENTE
Via Condotti 11 (metro: Spagna).

Logan says this is the must-do salon if you need your hair done. It has been the "in" fashion hairstylist salon for 3 decades. Closed Monday. *Note:* Cash only.

Books

The large news kiosks on the Via Veneto sell paperback books in many languages, including English.

FELTRINELLI
Via VE Orlando 79–87 (metro: Repubblica).

This is a famous chain with stores here and there in busy shopping districts. This one is divided into a few stores in a row, the **International** shop—with books in English—is at no. 87. There's also a ton of guidebooks and a wide selection of videos and DVDs of famous Italian movies. Yes, they even have *Flesh Gordon* [sic]. They are open on Sundays, 10am to 1:30pm and 4 to 7pm.

LION BOOKSHOP & CAFÉ
Via dei Greci 33 (metro: Spagna).

Located in the Spanish Steps shopping district, this store specializes in English-language books; they also have great stuff for kids. Closed Sunday and Monday.

RIZZOLI ROMA
Largo Chigi 15;
Via Tomacelli 156 (metro: Spagna).

Tomacelli is the larger of the two shops; both are open on Sunday at 10:30am until 1:30pm, and then 4 to 8pm. During the week, hours are nonstop. Italy's best bookstore with books in all languages.

Cashmere

AMINA RUBINACCI
Via Bocca di Leone 51 (metro: Spagna).

Visitors to Capri will know the name of this famed Neapolitan source that has recently opened a small shop in Rome specializing in cashmeres, but there are also cottons and cashmere blends. To die for.

MALO
Via Bocca di Leone 79 (metro: Spagna).

Flagship of the famed brand, which has home style, gift items, accessories, and more cashmere than you can dream of. They do have an outlet store (p. 158) located outside of Florence.

SOLO CASHMERE
Via del Babuino 55a (metro: Spagna).

This is a small shop selling garments made of 100% Italian cashmere, which is of very high quality with very high price tags. Still, check out the sales and the selection of styles, which are both sublime.

Cooking Classes

DIANE SEED
Via del Plebiscito 112.

Call © **06/679-7103.**

FROM MARKET TO TABLE
Via dei Due Macelli 106.

Jon Eldan (a baker) and Carla Lionello (a cook) offer assorted tours and cooking classes and workshops for food lovers, including a market-day workshop that runs from 9am to 2pm and costs 159€ ($175) for two people, with lunch included. You can e-mail this young team for more information at j.eldan@agora.stm.it or call © **06/69-92-04-35** for information and reservations. While I haven't done their class, I did a similar one in France and loved it. I'd consider this a must-do for any foodie. Yes, of course, it's all done in English.

Costume Jewelry

CASTELLI
Via Condotti 22 and 6 (metro: Spagna);
Via Frattina 18 and 54 (metro: Spagna).

This small, wood-paneled shop is crammed with perfume, beauty supplies, and a wonderful collection of costume jewelry. Don't miss the variety of evening bags. I saw this fabulous hair contraption in chenille (sort of a chignon catcher), but it cost 91€ ($100)—and that was when the value of the dollar was strong. The store at Via Condotti 22 is open nonstop (through lunch, that is).

CONSUELO BOZART
Via Bocca di Leone 4 (metro: Spagna).

You can leave here with a collection of fake Art Deco and other costume jewelry. The styles and selection are great; this place is definitely worth the stop if you didn't get what you wanted in Florence. It's famous in designer circles.

Department Stores

Italy doesn't have great department stores, and I don't suggest you go out of your way to shop in one. There are two that are somewhat convenient to mainstream tourist shopping: a branch of **La Rinascente** at Via del Corso 189; and a branch of **Coin** at Piazzale Appio, which is across the street from the Via Sannio market and may possibly be on your itinerary (if you are spending a week in Rome and can't stand to look at another fountain).

Upim, the dime-store version of an Italian department store (which may be a contradiction in terms), has stores at Via del Tritone 172 and Via Nazionale 211. The **Standa** at Viale Trastevere 60 has a supermarket downstairs.

Designer Boutiques

CONTINENTAL BIG NAMES

CARTIER
Via Condotti 83 (metro: Spagna).

CÈLINE
Via Condotti 20 (metro: Spagna).

CHANEL
Via del Babuino 98–100 (metro: Spagna).

ESCADA
Salita San Sebasstianello 8 (metro: Spagna).

FOGAL
Via Condotti 55 (metro: Spagna).

HERMÈS
Via Condotti 60 (metro: Spagna).

KENZO
Via del Babuino 124 (metro: Spagna).

KOOKAI
Via Bocca di Leone 5 (metro: Spagna).

LOUIS VUITTON
Via Condotti 15 (metro: Spagna).

SWATCH
Via Condotti 33 (metro: Spagna).

UNGARO
Via Bocca di Leone 24 (metro: Spagna).

YVES SAINT LAURENT RIVE GAUCHE
Via Bocca di Leone 35 (metro: Spagna).

ITALIAN BIG NAMES

BENETTON
Piazza di Spagna 94 (metro: Spagna).

BOTTEGA VENETA
Piazza San Lorenzo 9 (metro: Spagna).

BRIONI
Via Condotti 21a (metro: Spagna).

BYBLOS
Via Borgognona 7 (metro: Spagna).

DOLCE & GABBANA
Piazza di Spagna 82–83 (metro: Spagna);
Via Borgognona 7d (metro: Spagna).

EMPORIO ARMANI
Via del Babuino 140 (metro: Spagna).

ETRO
Via del Babuino 102 (metro: Spagna).

FENDI
Via Borgognona 36–49 (metro: Spagna);
Via Fontanella di Borghese 57 (metro: Spagna).

FERRAGAMO
Via Condotti 73 (metro: Spagna).

GIANFRANCO FERRÉ
Via Borgognona 42 (metro: Spagna).

GIANNI VERSACE (MEN)
Via Borgognona 24 (metro: Spagna).

GIANNI VERSACE (WOMEN)
Via Bocca di Leone 26 (metro: Spagna).

GIORGIO ARMANI
Via Condotti 77 (metro: Spagna).

GUCCI
Via Condotti 8 (metro: Spagna).

LA PERLA
Via Condotti 79 (metro: Spagna).

LAURA BIAGIOTTI
Via Borgognona 43 (metro: Spagna).

LES COPAINS
Piazza di Spagna 32–35 (metro: Spagna).

MAX & CO.
Via Condotti 46 (metro: Spagna).

MAX MARA
Via Condotti 17–19 (metro: Spagna);
Via Frattina 28 (metro: Spagna).

MISSONI
Piazza di Spagna 78 (metro: Spagna).

PRADA
Via Condotti 92–95 (metro: Spagna).

TRUSSARDI
Via Condotti 49 (metro: Spagna).

VALENTINO
Via Condotti 13 (metro: Spagna).

ZEGNA
Via Borgognona 7 (metro: Spagna).

Discounters

DISCOUNT SYSTEM
Via Viminale 35 (metro: Repubblica).

This store is possibly owned by the same people who own Il Discount Dell Alta Moda, or else it is just patterned after it. They have a very similar brochure and the same price system—that means to get the accurate price, you must deduct 50% from the marked price on the tag. So don't let the price tags throw you.

In terms of selection, Discount System is a larger store and has a much, much, much greater selection. I spent an hour here touching everything and trying to buy something but left empty-handed. But Barbara Lessona has bought tons of Prada. There's menswear, womenswear, shoes, handbags, luggage, belts, ties, dressy dresses, and every big-name Italian designer in some form or another. The clothes are at least a year old.

The location is convenient enough to make this a thought-provoking choice for bargain shoppers. It's around the corner from the Grand Hotel and down the street from the main train station; you can take the metro to Repubblica and walk. The same metro will also take you to Piazza di Spagna and the Spanish Steps.

I once began my morning here (the store does not open promptly at 9:30am, so take your time) then walked the few blocks to the metro and went on to Piazza di Spagna, where I shopped the Baboon Street and ended up at Via di Gesù e Maria for the other discount store. Seeing both discount stores in 1 day made it a brilliant experience.

Il Discount dell'Alta Moda
Via di Gesù e Maria 16 and 14 (men's store; metro: Spagna).

Both designer clothes and accessories are at discounted prices—the problem is lack of range, lack of sizes, and sometimes high prices (even at a discount, some of these prices will make you wince). *Important note:* The price is one-half of the price marked on the ticket. So if you are going to wince, do so accurately. The help may not speak English, and you may not feel comfortable with the system until you figure out how to read the price tags properly.

Now for the good news: There are plenty of big names and the store is easy to shop because it is arranged by color group. The handbags are probably the best deal.

The best news is the new men's store, two doors down, at no. 14. This huge store is well stocked and has many things that will fit women. While Armani jeans at 107€ ($118) weren't my idea of a bargain, I wanted everything. There were men's suits in the far rear. The style and colors and sophistication are beyond compare.

Shock Stock
Via della Farnesina 99–101 (no nearby metro).

This is one of Barbara Lessona's finds. It's not far from Campo dei Fiori and carries brand-name clothes and cashmeres. It is open in August but closed Saturday afternoon during that month.

Gifts

Fabriano
Via del Babuino 173 (metro: Spagna).

Another find from Milan, this store sells pens, writing goods, bound notebooks, and papers. There are some great gifts with tons of style for not much money.

Gloves

MEROLA
Via del Corso 143 (metro: Spagna).

This is the oldest glove shop in Rome and a far cry from much of the rest of the fare on Via del Corso, which nowadays seems to cater to teens. Yes, Audrey Hepburn's gloves in *Roman Holiday* came from here.

Home Style

C.U.C.I.N.A.
Via Mario de Fiori, 68 (metro: Spagna).

This store is actually similar to Pottery Barn or Crate & Barrel in the U.S. or even Conran's in London, but this is the Italian version. It's a must for foodies and those seeking gifts for cooks and gourmands; lots of little doodads. For those who have visited the store before, yes, this is a new address.

FRETTE
Piazza di Spagna 11 (metro: Spagna).

This is a branch of the famous Italian linen house that sells both luxury linen and a hotel line, which is high quality but less expensive.

TAD
Via del Babuino 155a (metro: Spagna).

TAD'S STOCK
Ask at regular store to verify it's still nearby (metro: Spagna).

I first discovered Tad in Milan, and yes, this is a branch of the same store. However, the Rome store is better—more color, more whimsy—and the stock shop is tons of fun and located about a block away from the regular store. Much of the merchandise comes from Viet Nam and/or has an ethnic hint to it, but it's also very Mediterranean looking. Prices are fair; they are downright cheap at the Stock shop.

Malls

CINECITTA'DUE SHOPPING CENTER
Via Togliatti 2 (metro: Subaugusta-Cinecitta).

My God, what is Rome coming to? It's an American-style shopping mall with more than 100 stores; open "nonstop." This mall is for locals; I cannot imagine why a tourist would visit, but there you go.

FORUM TERMINI
Rome Termini Train Station (metro: Termini).

Most of the mall is downstairs, but there are plenty of stores on the ground level, including a **Nike** and a **Benetton.** There's a branch of the makeup supermarket **Sephora** on the lower level, as well as a real supermarket that sells everything. There's a store that sells race-car-driving souvenirs and the usual stores for clothing, telephones, CDs, books, etc. If you haven't seen the brand **Bottega Verde,** this is a place to check it out—sort of the local version of The Body Shop.

ROMA DOWNTOWN
Via di Propaganda 7a (metro: Spagna).

This is a store with the concept of a mall—major brands and goodies all located under one roof. At least it's conveniently located near the Spanish Steps. It's for tourists and it is open on Sunday. Hours are unusual, so please note: Monday, Tuesday, and Thursday to Sunday 10am to 8pm; Wednesday 3 to 8pm. Popular with Japanese visitors.

Markets

Although Rome's main flea market at Porta Portese is famous, I've never found it that good—except when I needed to buy extra luggage because I'd gone wild at Fendi. The biggie is held on

Sunday from 6am to 2pm. You can get there at 8am and do fine; this is not like the Bermondsey Market in London, where you must be there in the dark with a flashlight in your hand. (In fact, in Rome, please go to flea markets only in daylight.) Officially called the **Mercato Di Porta Portese;** it stretches for about a mile along the Tiber River, where about 1,000 vendors are selling everything imaginable—a lot of which is fake or hot (or both). Enter the market about halfway down Viale Traste-vere, where the old clothes are. This way you avoid miles of auto accessories. You can give it a miss as far as I am concerned.

The big news in Rome, though, is that "private" flea markets are popping up—real people just rent a table and sell off last year's fashions or whatever turns up in grandma's palazzo. Often the sellers are aristos or celebs. Check the Friday edition of the local newspaper *La Repubblica* for the weekend market schedule, listed under a heading called *Mercatini* (Markets) on the weekend's "what's happening" page.

Typically these events are held on Sunday, may cost 1.80€ to 7.30€ ($2–$8) to attend, and have a few hundred vendors. They do not open super early but struggle to open around 10am and are hottest from noon to 1pm; most are in areas off the beaten track and may require a bit of a taxi ride.

The newest flea is held monthly, beginning on Saturday after-noon (3–7pm) and running all day on Sunday, starting at 9am on the banks of the Tiber between Ponte Milvio and Ponte Duca d'Aosta. Most people call it the **Ponte Milvio Market.**

Via Sannio is a busy "real people" market area with all kinds of fabulous junk. Everything is cheap in price and quality. The goods are all new, no antiques. Many of the vendors who sell on Sunday at Porta Portese end up here during the week, so if you miss Sunday in Rome, don't fret. Just c'mon over here. The crime problem (pickpockets) seems to be less during the week, also. There's a **Coin** department store on the corner. You can get here by bus or metro; because it's in a corner of central Rome, the taxi fare can be steep.

Piazza Fontanella Borghese, not far from the Spanish Steps, has 24 stalls selling prints, maps, books, coins, and some antiques. Good fun; a class act. Open Monday to Saturday 9am to 6pm, possibly later on summer evenings.

Outlets

MacArthur Glen Outlets
Pontina, opening Oct 2003.

Timberland Factory Outlet
Centro Commerciale Arcom, Via Orvietto 36 (no nearby metro).

To drive, head south to Exit 27 (Torvaianica-Pomezia, Castelli Romani). ☎ 06/91-60-22-37.

Pharmacies & Soap Sellers

Farmaceutica di Santa Maria Novella
Corso Rinascimento 47 (no nearby metro).

Hmm, this isn't a traditional pharmacy, even though it calls itself a pharmacy. Yes, this is a branch of the famous Florentine address. They have expanded enormously in the past few years with stores in many European capital cities. This one, small and new, is a block from Piazza Navona. The salespeople do not speak English, but if you give it some time and some mime, you'll sample everything and figure it all out. The Weekend soap, for 9€ ($10), is one of my favorite gifts.

Rancé
Piazza Navona 53 (no nearby metro).

This firm was from the south of France, where its ingredients originate, but it has since become Italian. Although most famous for its soap, it now has a full line of bath and beauty products as well as scents. The brand is sold mostly through catalogs in the U.S. but costs half the U.S. price when bought in the new shop in Rome. You'll have a wonderful time with the assortment and with making up gift baskets and packs. There is a booklet in English that explains the French origins of the goodies as well as all the properties of the line.

Plus Sizes

Elena Miro/Sorriso
Via Frattina 11 (metro: Spagna).

Designed by Spanish maven Elena Miro, this line begins at size 46 (about a U.S. size 14). The store is a chain with stores popping up all over Europe selling chic and stylish work and play fashions for less money than Marina Rinaldi. Sort of in the Ann Taylor look and price league.

Marina Rinaldi
Largo Goldoni 43 (metro: Spagna).

A division of the design firm Max Mara, Marina Rinaldi is now a global brand with chic fashions for the large-size woman. The brand's sizing system is strange, so please try on before you buy. Even if you use the chart that compares Marina Rinaldi's sizes to American sizes, you may be in for a surprise. I wear a size 16 in American sizes, but according to the chart, I wear a 12 in American sizes, which in Marina Rinaldi's system is a size 21.

Shoes & Handbags

There are scads of little shops selling leather goods all over Rome, and all over every other major Italian city, for that matter.

Bottega Veneta
Piazza San Lorenzo 9 (metro: Spagna).

This gorgeous Bottega shop is new. It's across the way from the newer Louis Vuitton that has newly become luxe headquarters off of the Spanish Steps shopping district; it is hard to find unless you know where to look. Is the store worth finding? Well, yes. Prices are less than in the U.S., but there are no

Papal Shopping

If you are on a quest for religious items (nonantique variety), a dozen shops surrounding St. Peter's Square offer everything you've been looking for. Most of the shops will send out your purchase to be blessed by the pope. Allow 24 hours for this service. Some of the stores will then deliver the items to your hotel; others ask you to return for them. If you are having items blessed, make sure you understand how you will be getting your merchandise back.

Merchandise ranges from the serious to the kitsch. Papal shopping falls into three categories: There are a number of gift stands and shops scattered throughout the Vatican; there is a string of stores in Vatican City; and there are vendors who sell from card tables on the sidewalks as you walk from the entrance/exit of the Vatican Museum (this way to the Sistine Chapel) to the front of St. Peter's.

Buy everything from the sublime to the ridiculous: Bart-Simpson-meets-the-pope T-shirts, rosaries, medals, glow-in-the-dark 3-D postcards—all tastes, all price ranges.

If you are a postcard freak, remember that Vatican City is an independent state; it has its own post office and its own stamps.

---

bargains here. That won't shock anyone, as Bottega has never had inexpensive merchandise, anyway. The store has two levels and many collections, and is to drool for.

FRAGIACOMO
Via Condotti 35 (metro: Spagna).

This store has goods for him and her, and high-quality goods at that, with prices closer to 90€ ($100) than 180€ ($200), which is more the average for this kind of quality. Many of the looks are adaptations of the current faves—a Chanel-style pump, etc. There are many low-heeled, fashionable styles as well as ballet flats for 90€ ($100), which isn't the lowest price in Rome but is pretty good. This is one of those bread-and-butter resources.

FRATELLI ROSSETTI
Via Borgognona 69 (metro: Spagna).

The Rossetti brothers are at it again—shoes, shoes, shoes, and now at somewhat affordable prices. There are men's and women's shoes as well as belts and even some clothes.

TOD'S/HOGAN
Via Borgognona 45 (metro: Spagna).

Tod's is significantly less expensive in Italy than in the U.S. Although the scene started with the driving shoe, the cult is so well established that now there's the Hogan line of sports shoes, high heels in the Tod's line, and very fancy (and expensive) leather handbags. Shoes begin at around 182€ ($200). Note that this brand used to be called jpTod's but has now streamlined to simply Tod's.

Teens

DIESEL
Via del Corso 184 (metro: Spagna).

This Italian firm sells jeans and other casual clothing items, a must-do for the local scene and the perfect gift for any blue-jeans snob. The Style Lab is upstairs.

ONYX
Via del Corso (metro: Spagna).

There's another Onyx on the Via Frattina and stores all over the world; this Roman flagship is a block deep and lined with video screens, blue neon lights, teenage girls, and copies of the latest looks re-created into inexpensive clothing and trends. Even if you buy nothing and know no teens, come by just to wander around and marvel at what has happened to civilization.

ROME ON A SCHEDULE

Knowing your way around Rome is great; browsing all the stores between the Exedra Hotel and the Piazza Navona is fun. But let's get small.

The best designer shopping in Rome is in the Spanish Steps area, and what you really need is a good understanding of how to tackle that vicinity. Essentially, what you should do is walk up and down every street from the Via Frattina to the Via Vittoria, between the Via del Corso and the Piazza di Spagna, including the fabulous Via del Babuino, which shoots off beside the Piazza di Spagna heading to the Piazza del Popolo. Should you be a little sick of the big names, concentrate on the Via Vittoria and the Via del Babuino.

If you are thorough and really enjoy each of the shops, you can probably do this in a week. If you are swift, you'll do it in a day. If you are desperate, you can manage in a half day. Obviously, you'll just go into those stores that beckon you.

Once you reach Piazza del Popolo, make sure you walk back toward the Spanish Steps on the Via del Corso. That's after you have peeked at the **Hotel de Russie,** of course.

Via del Corso   Forgive me for raving, but I think this is tons of fun. It's a "real people" shopping street with normal stores, lots of locals, and a lot of teenage shops. You may even find the Via del Corso refreshing, after you've seen the high prices in the tony shops along the Via Condotti.

Via dei Due Macelli   This one runs parallel to the Via del Corso, but at the top of the shopping trapezoid, so it bumps into the Spanish Steps. This is a more upscale street than the Via del Corso. It is considered a fine address, harking back to the immediate post–World War II years. **Pineider** has a shop here (no. 68), one of their nicest shops in all of Italy for paper goods, office items, and stationery chic. The Via dei Due Macelli runs right into the **Piazza di Spagna,** so it's a good path to walk if you are coming from the Via del Tritone. If you're hungry for home, don't miss **McDonald's** (no. 46), which is hard to find because it does not have a big sign and is hidden in a pseudo-villa.

Via Frattina   This is the first serious shopping street, as you approach from the Via del Tritone area. It is very different from the rest of the Spanish Steps streets, because it still has reasonably priced stores on it and is by no means as hoity-toity as the rest of the neighborhood. Among the finds are two identical Castelli shops—perfumeries that sell lots of hair clips, earrings, costume jewelry, and fun doodads.

Via Borgognona   This is now the best of the Spanish Steps streets, although shopkeepers on the Via Condotti may argue otherwise. I like it best because it's low-key but luxe; it's also home to restaurant **Nino.** Whether you shop Fendi or not, you must see this store; consider it an art gallery and cultural experience.

Via Condotti   This is the best-known shopping street of Rome with the most famous names on it. It is an old-fashioned area and still has many of the big-time shops, where you should at least check the windows. Over the years Max Mara has bought up most of the storefronts, so the space goes on forever. But then there's Gucci, Prada, etc.

Via Vittoria   This is the funkiest of the streets; I think the best in providing a sense of discovery. **Il Baco da Seta** (no. 75)— the kiss of silk—is here for droopy clothes in mid-range prices with tons-o-style (see "Five Best Stores of Rome," p. 85).

TOUR 2: BACK-STREETS SHOPPING TOUR

This tour assumes you have already done Tour 1 and shopped your heart out in the nirvana of Italian big-name retail around the Spanish Steps area. If you didn't finish that tour, you can piggyback it onto this tour as the first part.

1. Walk along the Via del Corso from where it begins at the Piazza del Popolo. Within a block you'll be surrounded by shops that specialize in the Italian version of the American look. If you

have teens with you, be prepared to spend. If you haven't had a shot at the Italian version of Loehmann's yet, then make a quick detour on Via di Gesù e Maria and pop into the discount designer shop at no. 16, and then into its other part, No. 14. Then hop right back onto Via del Corso and continue walking. Don't miss **T-store** (no. 203), which is the young-people store from Trussardi.

2. When you get to the Piazza San Lorenzo, which is right near the Plaza Hotel, hang a right. You'll see a cinema, but since you are on a shopping tour, instead head for **Deco** (Piazza San Lorenzo in Lucina 2), a knickknack designer store where even if you don't smoke you'll have to marvel at the ashtrays and other objects.

3. At the end of this piazza, tuck into the left on Via Campo Marzio and enjoy the tiny shops and workshops that make Italy what it is.

4. Curve around the little streets, shopping wherever you please until you hit the Piazza Navona. Should you get lost in this area of old-fashioned cobblestones, just ask for the Piazza Navona. If you do not mind paying 12€ ($13) for an ice cream (ouch!), you can sit down at one of the cafes on the piazza for a break. You can shop the tourist stalls, have your caricature painted, or keep on moving right through to the end of the piazza to cross the Corso Vittorio Emanuele II.

5. Once across the street, you are walking straight, but the street is now named Via Baullari; it leads you directly to the Campo dei Fiori. Ready for lunch? *Si!*

Chapter Six

....

FLORENCE

WELCOME TO FLORENCE

....

I am suffering from a love-hate relationship with Florence. I love the city and its treasures (which includes stores, of course) but I hate the tourist crowds, I hate the prices, and I hate the atmosphere in which local shopkeepers know that you will buy or eat or favor their firms and so they provide little as they laugh all the way to the *bancomat*.

Florence has changed enormously . . . even Siena has changed. I sometimes think that today Siena offers what we all used to go to Florence to find. But wait, I'm not bad-mouthing Florence—I'm just warning you. And asking you to note that I am reporting in these pages on several different faces of Florence, as I search for hidden values and hidden finds. There is much in Florence to enjoy, so step this way.

In terms of shopping, Florence does not offer as much of the classic, big-name, big-ticket Italian designer shopping as Rome or Milan, although Florence does have a street of dream shops and a side street of fashionable big names. Every shoe maven knows the address of the flagship Ferragamo store, located in the heart of the best shopping and expanding to eat up much of the fancy shopping street.

Yet Florence is in many ways the unofficial beginning of the south of Italy—many fashion stores don't dare even open here, for various marketing reasons relating to the southern Italian style. You won't find a branch of Chanel, or even Missoni. You won't find the mass-market stores Zara (a Spanish brand) or H&M (Swedish), both of which are strong in Milan and internationally. Few people here wear black; there is no hard-edged fashion. In fact, you are more likely to find English-influenced country styles on the locals with money and pedigree.

This is not a case of keeping Italy for Italians or keeping out northern, big-city style. It's cultural. Strangely enough, you will find many French chains have invaded not only the tourist shopping areas, but the real-world parts of town. There are also Blockbuster Video stores in residential areas, an American contribution, and a Lush bath-and-beauty store from London in the heart of tourist land. I love that limoncello soap. Even French super-chef Alain Ducasse has opened a restaurant in Tuscany as the area becomes more international and less related to Milan.

Florentine Choices

Florence does indeed offer a charming, country-elegant shopping paradise that combines every element of retail: boutiques representing many of the hottest designers in the world, trendy local shops offering the best of finely crafted gift items, several flea markets, and a fabulous old bridge jammed with jewelry shops. It also has two competing department stores a block from each other, so you have more shopping ops right there; some nice flea markets, a truly great Tuesday real-people market . . . and best of all, Florence serves as the gateway to some superlative factory outlets and the wonders of everything else under the Tuscan sun.

Because the city offers so many faces and opportunities, you will have to make choices in terms of what kinds of sights you want to see and stores you want to shop. And with the prices so high, you may want to change your orientation a bit.

- Choose a hotel on the edge of town if you want to get away and onto the road or into real-people parts. If you want to be in the thick of it all, choose a hotel well located in the city center. Make a list of your priorities in terms of having a real experience, not just mingling with the tours behind the red umbrella.

- Book a day with Faith Heller Willinger, the famous American food maven living in Florence, or one of the other people who offer cooking classes (p. 130).

- Think of foodstuffs in terms of shopping and gifts to bring home, and tastings in terms of sightseeing. Get back to the land.

- Shop at outlets. Window-shop in Florence if you want, but get a car or a car and driver, and take a day trip to the nearby outlets for serious savings.

- Look beneath the surface; head to the fringes of the tourist districts. You might want to book a day with Maria Teresa Berdondini of Tuscany by Tuscans (© and fax **0572/70-467;** tuscany@italway.it), who does a Hidden Florence tour that will touch your soul, show you artisans and craftspeople behind closed doors, and turn shopping into a religious experience.

ARRIVING IN FLORENCE

....

By Train

If you are coming to town by train, do pay attention: There are several train stations in Florence, and while you probably won't get off at the wrong one, you may have a few very nervous moments. You want the **Santa Maria Novella** (often written as S.M.N.) rail station. If you're arriving by plane from Pisa, you can take the train directly from the Pisa airport to Florence. There is no train from the Florence airport.

The Florence train station is smaller than the one in Milan and less intimidating. To get a taxi, follow signs to the left side of the station (left if you are arriving and walking toward the front of the station). There are a few stores in the arrivals area (and a McDonald's); there's a small mall beneath the station.

The train ride from Rome takes about 2 hours; from Milan, about 3 hours. Note that there are Eurostar trains and IC (Inter-City) trains; the IC takes a half-hour longer to Rome but may be less expensive or included without a supplement in your travel pass. Ask.

By Plane

Before small intra-European airlines were fashionable, you had to fly into Pisa to fly to Florence. While you still have that option and the Pisa airport is larger, you can now fly directly into Florence.

Please note that the airport is lovely (good shopping for such a small airport), but there are often weather problems, and you can't count on a timely arrival or departure. But then, this is Italy after all.

Most people still use the Rome airport because you get your long-haul flights there and can easily connect to Florence by train from Rome, although there is no longer a train from the Rome airport straight to Florence. Still, you can connect through the Centrale station quite easily.

Getting Around

It's a good thing you can walk just about everywhere in central Florence, because more and more bans are being put on vehicular traffic. This is true not only in Florence, but also in Siena and other nearby towns. To enter the historical parts of town, a car must have a specific sticker in the windshield. Rental cars do not come with these stickers.

TAXIS

You can get a taxi at the train station; taxis have stickers. There are no free-roaming taxis driving around town—you don't just hail a taxi. You must call ahead. If you need a taxi to pick you up somewhere, call © 055/43-90 or 055/42-42. Your hotel probably has a button or direct hot line that summons taxis in a matter of minutes.

Florence

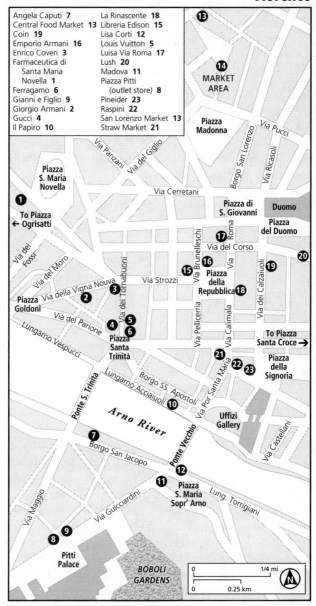

Angela Caputi **7**
Central Food Market **13**
Coin **19**
Emporio Armani **16**
Enrico Coveri **3**
Farmaceutica di
  Santa Maria
  Novella **1**
Ferragamo **6**
Gianni e Figlio **9**
Giorgio Armani **2**
Gucci **4**
Il Papiro **10**

La Rinascente **18**
Libreria Edison **15**
Lisa Corti **12**
Louis Vuitton **5**
Luisa Via Roma **17**
Lush **20**
Madova **11**
Piazza Pitti
  (outlet store) **8**
Pineider **23**
Raspini **22**
San Lorenzo Market **13**
Straw Market **21**

MARKET
AREA

Piazza
Madonna

Via Pucci

Piazza
S. Maria
Novella

Via Panzani

Via del Giglio

Borgo San Lorenzo

Via Ricasoli

Via Cerretani

Piazza di
S. Giovanni

Duomo

To Piazza
← Ogrisatti

Piazza
del Duomo

Via dei Fossi

Via del Moro

Via della Vigna Nouva

Via de' Tornabuoni

Via Strozzi

Via Brunelleschi

Via Roma

Via del Corso

Via de' Calzaiuoli

Piazza
Goldoni

Via del Parione

Piazza
della
Repubblica

Piazza
Santa
Trinità

Via Pellicceria

Via Calimala

To Piazza
Santa Croce →

Lungarno Vespucci

Piazza
della
Signoria

Ponte S. Trinità

Lungarno Acciaiuoli

Borgo SS. Apostoli

Via Por Santa Maria

Arno River

Uffizi
Gallery

Via Castellani

Borgo San Jacopo

Ponte Vecchio

Piazza
S. Maria
Sopr' Arno

Lung. Torrigiani

Via Maggio

Via Guicciardini

Pitti
Palace

BOBOLI
GARDENS

0   1/4 mi

0   0.25 km

N

Bus

For your day trip to Siena (see below), you'll want to take the **SITA bus.** The SITA station (© 055/214-721) is across the street from the Santa Maria Novella train station, and it's an easy walk from most hotels.

For your day trip to **Forte dei Marmi,** you'll need the **LAZZI line** (© 055/215-154), also located near the Santa Maria Novella station. Note that if you are going on to the new Ducasse restaurant nearby, you will want a car or a taxi to connect you from Forte dei Marmi.

Car Service

Most hotels will offer you car service, but it's rather pricey. I prefer to book through Maria Teresa Berdondini of Tuscany by Tuscans (© and fax **0572/70-467;** tuscany@italway.it) because she has better rates and most drivers speak English. A legit car service has the proper license to enter city streets forbidden to regular traffic.

SLEEPING IN FLORENCE

GRAND HOTEL VILLA MEDICI
Via il Prato 42.

I have been hanging out at this hotel for years, and while the location at first seems slightly off, it's actually great—you are within walking distance of the train station, the bus station, and city center, and, importantly, not far from the *autostrada.* This is the hotel you pick if you want to visit outside of Florence, if you are headed to the outlets, or if you're going to Siena or the countryside. It's also near the Tuesday open-air market and a 10-minute taxi ride from the airport. Traffic problems in Florence cannot be underestimated, and location becomes one of this hotel's major selling points.

Meanwhile, the charm of the hotel is the property itself—it has a garden, and you can see mountains out your window.

The furnishings fall into the shabby-chic mode, which means that while the hotel is a palace, it's a comfortable palace and the kind of palace you would want to have for your own; it's not stiff and formal or forbidding.

On my last visit I had what they call an apartment, which is sort of a suite, but it has two bathrooms, and the living room has a sofa bed; this is great for those traveling with kids.

The hotel has numerous rates and promotions based on the season; doubles are about 273€ ($300) without a promotion.

Since the hotel is a member of Leading Hotels of the World, you can book a room by calling ✆ **800/233-6800** in the U.S. Local phone 055/238-13-31. www.villa.medici@fi.flashnet.it.

Note: Do not confuse this hotel with the Grand Hotel.

HOTEL BERNINI PALACE
Piazza San Firenze 29.

If only I knew a hotel like this in every city. This is the hotel of my dreams—newly renovated but still a little funky and local and charming and intimate. Not too big, not too small. If you want a hotel in the historical center of town, you cannot find one with a better location.

Just refurbished, the hotel has great bathrooms, but a comfort zone of interior design that isn't too hard-edged or chic. It's more like home than a magazine spread. Breakfast is served in the room where the Italian parliament met in the 1860s.

Rates vary between 182€ and 273€ ($200–$300) per night depending on the season; there are various promotional offers and online deals. *Note: Born to Shop* readers may write ahead or show their book at check-in for an upgrade, based on availability. No toll-free U.S. phone number. Local phone ✆ **055/28-86-21.** www.baglionihotels.com.

JOLLY HOTEL FIRENZE
Piazza Vittorio Veneto 4a.

Jolly is a chain that I frequent; this hotel on the edge of Florence is modern and ugly from outside, but great inside and very well priced. Being on the edge of town is a blessing due to some of the traffic problems—you can walk or bus into the historical center but you can also get out of town quickly. The hotel is also directly across the street from the Tuesday open-air market I love so much. Prices vary with season and promotion, but a double can still be yours for under 182€ ($200). To make a reservation, call © **800/247-1277** in the U.S. Local phone 055/27-70. www.jollyhotels.it.

SAVOY HOTEL
Piazza della Repubblica 7.

If I hadn't seen it, I wouldn't have believed it. This dumpy old grande dame was bought by Sir Rocco Forte and totally redone. It's now similar to the Hotel Russie in Rome and a must-do in terms of gawking. Pop in for a drink or to sit in the library of the lobby if you don't want to spend the night.

The style is neoclassical Miami Beach super chic and oh-so-moderne, elegant, and plush. It's in the center of the city and a fabulous shopping location, as well. Doubles begin around 364€ ($400). Book through Leading Hotels in the U.S., © **800/233-6800.** Local phone 055/273-51. www.rfhotels.com.

THE SHOPPING SCENE

If you're in Florence for the first time, you may be overwhelmed . . . or just plain faint. If you are combining art, culture, and shopping on a short time schedule, you will most certainly be dizzy. If this is a repeat trip and you have a discerning eye, you may want to take shortcuts. Certainly the shopping scene is changing quickly, and sophisticated travelers may not be pleased. Fret not and follow me. But remember, we don't buy junk anymore—those days are gone.

Here are some tips:

- Do your serious fashion shopping in other cities (Rome and Milan have more designer stores) and save Florence for specialty shopping, unique items, and shopping experiences you simply can't get elsewhere.

- Florence and the surrounding area are good destinations for buying $5 to $10 gifts that don't look junky; see "The Best Buys in Florence," below.
- Museums all have gift shops, most of which offer unique gift items at reasonable prices. Crowds may be thinner there, too.
- The Straw and San Lorenzo markets are both wonderful fun, but they have very, very similar merchandise, and, let's face it, it's mostly junky and touristy. If time is truly limited, choose one. It won't hurt you to miss them both. (Foodies should pick San Lorenzo.)

The Best Buys in Florence

Junk   I love junk; I love 5€ to 23€ ($5–$25) gift items. But we don't want it to look cheap or tacky or end up at someone's yard sale next summer. So buy carefully.

Smalls   This is what I am calling small stylish items with low prices that could be called tasteful junk. The markets are a good source only if you have a discerning eye. Grocery stores are filled with choices. Even Lush, the British store for bath and beauty, has Italian-influenced products. Florence provides better-quality, easier-to-get-to smalls than any other major Italian city.

Olive Oil   Olive oil is much like wine, with olives very much like grapes. Often, vineyards that make wine also make olive oil and have wine shops *(entoca)* that sell it. The airport in Florence has an excellent selection; otherwise, you can try a wine shop, a grocery store, or even some of the specialty sources directly. There are many tours and tastings that help educate your palate. Remember, the good stuff isn't cheap; it usually comes in a glass bottle and is heavy and fragile. Expect to pay 18€ ($20) per bottle. The selection at **Baroni** at the **Central Market** (near San Lorenzo) is excellent; check them out online at www.baronialimentari.it.

Ceramics & Faience If you get into the hill towns and pottery towns, you will save off Florence prices. If you don't have the opportunity to get out of town, you'll find plenty to choose from in Florence—from the huge jardinières to the little rooster jugs. I am horrified at how expensive these items have become—I can't fall in love with a plate to hang on the wall for 45€ ($50) and up. But, you can get a salad serving set for 4.55€ to 7.30€ ($5–$8). Some items are sold in the two town markets; better-quality items are sold in specialty shops around town. Remember: Prices for ceramics are lower in Siena, just an hour away. They are even better in Deruta, 2 hours away.

Paper If you didn't get your fill of Italian-style paper goods in Venice, you can buy more in Florence. The assorted merchandise is so classy looking that it makes a marvelous gift; pencils cost less than .90€ ($1) each. There are about half a dozen stores in central Florence that specialize in Florentine paper works; items of less quality are sold at souvenir stands and in the markets. *Note:* I am seeing less marble paper here and more engineered prints.

Cheap Handbags I am only slightly ashamed to tell you this: The triumph of one trip to Florence was a faux reptile-printed plastic Birkin-style handbag for 27€ ($30) that is so stunning you could faint. Because it is textured, it's harder to detect that it's plastic, and it's absolutely fabulous with gray flannel. It's also great for travel because it's not too fragile. Despite the plethora of cheap bags, I've never seen one this great since.

Designer Brands at Nearby Outlets It takes some time and trouble to get to, but it's worth it.

Secret Dealings

To compensate for lack of sales in off periods, many store owners, especially those outside the deluxe brands, will make deals. I saved about 91€ ($100) on a handbag once because I was able to go down the street to the cash machine and pay in cash and was equally willing to waive the tax refund paperwork.

Hidden Finds in Florence

If you are offended by all the tourist junk in Florence, fear not. There are a handful of hidden places that are yummy and worth the slight trouble it takes to find them.

ALESSANDRO DARI
Via San Niccolo 115R.

I don't know how to say this except with honesty, and if you think I am weird, so be it. I found my visit to this shop to be a religious experience . . . or, at least, a very spiritual one. I don't mean because there is religious merchandise, but I felt myself surrounded by the work of a master, perhaps the Michelangelo of our time. I felt as if Dari's work was straight from the angels or even God.

This is both a workshop and jewelry shop, so you can commission a piece or buy from the display cases. Prices start at 409€ ($450), but for less than 909€ ($1,000) you can have some serious work. There are rings that are buildings, rings that do tricks, and pieces with hidden mechanisms and secrets.

The shop is a short walk from the Ponte Vecchio. If you want to make an appointment, call © **055/244-747**; browsers are welcome.

ANTICO SETIFICIO FIORENTINO
Via Bartolini 4.

Within easy walking distance of the center of downtown, this factory is truly hidden in an industrial neighborhood, behind a high fence. Once through the gate, you will step back in time to the 18th century. The compound includes a private house, a factory (hear the hum of the shuttles?), and a showroom laden with fabric and ribbons. The showroom is organized by price and by type of silk and cotton: Prices are not low. To visit this factory is an almost religious experience. If you don't intend to buy $100-a-yard (or more) goods, don't worry. You can afford a small bag of potpourri. You may want your concierge to phone ahead, as you need an appointment (© 055/21-38-61) and may be asked to pay for the right to visit.

CHIANTI CASHMERE COMPANY
Call or e-mail for directions.

American Nora Kravis breeds cashmere goats in the Tuscan hills midway between Florence and Siena, just outside of Radda in Chianti. She uses the milk from these goats to make soap and skin-care products. Check them out online at www. chianticashmere.com. For directions, call © 0577/738-080 or send an e-mail to info@chianticashmere.com.

FARMACEUTICA DI SANTA MARIA NOVELLA
Via della Scala 16r.

This is by no means a new source or much of a secret, but it is a little hard to find and fits with the mood of most of the other shops on this list—it is a step back in time as you enter a former convent that looks like a museum. The usual soaps and skin creams are sold in the front rooms; in the rear, a newly opened room sells herbal cures.

LORENZO VILLORESI
Via dei Bardi 14.

This place is as hidden and private as they get, and you must telephone for an appointment at least a day in advance (© 055/234-11-87). Mr. Villoresi is a nose who has created some big-time scents for some big-time firms, but he will grant you a private workshop with him. It costs 250€ ($275) and takes as long as it takes, because the two of you will create your own fragrance from scratch. Heaven scent.

Shoppers Beware

Be careful when buying . . .

Leather Goods   I know Italy, especially Florence, is famous for its leather goods; I know, I know. I'm not telling you to refrain from a leather purchase. I merely ask that you purchase slowly and carefully. There are so many fake leather factories in Florence and so many handbags for sale in markets and on the street that you will lose your mind in short order. More important, leather goods in Italy are well made but expensive. If it's not expensive, it might not have been made in Italy.

For real value in leather goods, you'll do far better spending a little more money and buying from a big-name leather-goods house with a reputation to back up the goods. And forget about those so-called outlets.

Do note that there is a huge no-man's-land: no-name, no-brand handbags and leather goods that are not inexpensive (227€/$250 and up) but offer great value if bought properly. Buying and bargaining for them is tricky.

Gold   There are plenty of jewelers on the Ponte Vecchio, but I can't give you one good reason why you should buy from them unless you have romance in mind and are willing to pay for it. Despite the hype, this is not the place where you must buy. If you are looking for a Nomination bracelet—gold or silver—try jewelers on the side streets.

Silk   I have to steer you away from the silk scarves and the silk ties in Florence; to me, the patterns are all cheap copies of famous works and they simply miss. Years ago you could buy marvelous fake scarves in the San Lorenzo market; no more. Most of the market stock comes from the Orient. Check edges to see if they are hand-stitched; make sure it's silk and not polyester—unless you want polyester, which is less expensive. Silks for home style are expensive but sumptuous.

Shopping Hours

Like all Italy, Florence is celebrating a new world in shopping hours. The two big department stores are open on Sunday, and there's a lot going on that didn't used to be happening. Many stores still close at lunchtime during the week, but Florence doesn't close tight for lunch. You can find some life if you look for it.

Shops are basically closed Sunday and Monday, or at least on Monday until 3:30pm. In summer, they also close on Saturday afternoon at 1pm. Remember, though, Sunday (even Sun morning) is surprising in Florence, so don't stay in your room making false assumptions—get out there and shop. Sunday hours for those stores that are open are 10am to 4pm or 11am to 5pm.

Also note that the last Sunday of the month is a special day in retail, so more stores are open then (there's also a cute flea market that day) than on the first Sunday of the month. The suburban American-style shopping mall is also open on Sunday. So are most of the big factory outlets, but check before you make the trek.

Markets always close for holidays but do not necessarily close for lunch. The San Lorenzo market is closed on Sunday and Monday, but is open during lunch on other days. The Straw Market is open but not in full bloom on Monday; it is open during lunch every day—except Sunday.

Food stores are open Monday morning. In winter, food stores are also open on Saturday afternoon but are closed on Wednesday afternoon. In June, the pattern switches, and the food stores close on Saturday afternoon and stay open on Wednesday afternoon.

Speaking of summer hours, except for the major tourist traps, everything is closed from mid-August through the rest of the month.

Sunday Shopping

While Sunday isn't a big shopping day in most of Italy, if the weather is nice, or if the tourists are in season, you'd be surprised at just how much business goes on. The Straw Market has sellers who open up their carts. It's not as hot and happening as Venice, but Sunday is beginning to catch on. On the last Sunday of each month, stores do open. Every Sunday, there's a big bookstore open (see "Florence Resources from A to Z," later in this chapter).

There is action on the **Ponte Vecchio.** The usual shops are indeed shuttered, but on the walkway over the bridge, standing shoulder to shoulder on both sides of the walk, is an incredible array of vendors—from boys with imitation Louis Vuitton tote bags, to hippies with poorly made jewelry, to real artisans with well-crafted pieces. Much of what you will see here is delightful junk—the exact kind of thing you want to see on a Sunday. But there are a few buys.

There's also a vast amount of Sunday shopping available in the so-called in-town factory outlets and tourist traps (TTs) that stretch from the Duomo to Santa Croce. I think the single best store for Sunday shopping (if you have to pick one) is **Ducci** (Lungarno Corsini 24r), a dressed-up version of a TT that's more like an art gallery.

But the real factory outlets—outside of town—are also open afternoons only. Some open at 2pm, others at 3pm—so check before you drive or hire car service. Don't be surprised if there are lines out front before the outlets open. At Prada, you take a number—and the cafe is open before the shop.

If you like upscale, tony shopping rather than touristy stuff, there's magnificent shopping in **Forte dei Marmi** on Sunday. It's just an hour from Florence. Alternatively, you can go to **Montecatini,** a town famous for its spa, where stores are also open.

About Addresses

Florence is stricter than many other Italian cities about its numbering system; stores (to differentiate them from residences) are zoned red, or *rosa,* and therefore usually have an "r" after their street numbers. The same number in black (to depict a residence) is somewhere else entirely on the street. Go figure.

Sending It Home

If you don't feel like schlepping your purchases with you, there's a giant post office in the heart of town—right near the Straw Market—that offers what's called **Express Mail.** Italian mail makes me nervous; you can use Federal Express if you prefer, or if cost is no object.

There is also a branch of **Mail Boxes Etc.** (Via della Scala 13r; © 055/268-173), which does shipping, packing, money-grams, etc. Store hours are Monday through Friday from 9am to 1pm and from 3:30 to 6:30pm. Mail Boxes Etc. franchises are turning into UPS stations over time, so don't freak.

Scams & Rip-offs

While Florence is not a high-crime city by any means, it is a very sophisticated city where many people come to shop and trade goods. As a result, expect the usual international deals and scams:

- Pickpockets abound (especially in San Lorenzo market).
- Be wary of Etruscan art that's too good to be true—it is the most highly imitated art form sold in Italy.
- If a store says it has a factory on the premises, don't assume the store is a factory outlet and therefore cheaper; many of those factories are just for show. If you are taken to a factory or a resource by your tour director, expect that he or she is getting a kickback. Ask for free time to do your own exploring. On the other hand, maybe the tour director is taking you to a great place.
- Prices on similar goods are the same all over town, but the quality may be better at certain vendors; not all cheap sweaters were created equal.

Scams & Rip-offs: The Revenge

This is a terrifying piece of news, but I got it from the *International Herald Tribune* and many journalists as well, so I am taking it as true. The word is that all those fake Prada handbags sold on the streets in Italy and all over the world are actually real and come directly from Prada! Prada makes them and supplies them to the street dealers. In short, business is business in Florence as elsewhere. Life is pretty hard when you can't tell the good guys from the bad guys. Buy with care and maybe a giggle.

Snack & Shop

FRESCOBALDI WINE BAR
Via de' Magazzini 2–4r.

This is around the corner from my beloved Bernini Palace Hotel and so hidden that it takes a local to point it out. Here you can get a meal or simply have wine by the glass. Inside it's all medieval, with sponged walls and vaulted ceilings, but it has a sleek bar with a very hip local crowd. ✆ 055/284-724.

LA CANTINETTA
Via Borgo San Lorenzo 14r.

Yeah, I know this is a tourist trap kind of place—but I am in love with the concept of a spaghetti bar and I also appreciate being able to eat a meal for a total of less than 9€ ($10). It's cafeteria style and you can choose various kinds of pasta or salads, wine, or soft drinks. Great if you have kids or want a fast meal; close to the Duomo and on the way to San Lorenzo market. No reservations; ✆ 055/213-525.

SHOPPING NEIGHBORHOODS

In Town

Tornabuoni The Via dei Tornabuoni is the main whoop-de-do, big-time street for the mainline tourist shopping of the gold coast kind. This is where most of the big-name designers have their shops, and where the cute little specialty stores and leather-goods makers cluster. This is where you'll find everyone from **Gucci** (Via dei Tornabuoni 73r) to **Ferragamo** (Via dei Tornabuoni 16r), but, alas, no Chanel. Who needs Chanel with the Ferragamo museum to keep you busy? If you have only an hour for seeing the best shopping in Florence, perhaps you just want to stroll this street. Although most of the hotsy-totsy names are on Tornabuoni, some of them are on nearby side streets, especially on **Via della Vigna Nuova,** which you will recognize because it has the **Enrico Coveri** shop on the corner (Via della Vigna Nuova 27–29r).

The Tornabuoni area begins (or ends) at the Piazza di San Trinita, which is a small *piazza* (plaza) with a very tall, skinny obelisk. The Via dei Tornabuoni itself leads easily into Via della Vigna Nuova, but don't think it ends there. Stay with the street as the numbers climb because **Profumeria Inglese** (no. 97r) is well past the thick of things, but it's a great place for perfumes and beauty supplies (assuming you are not going to France).

Also check out **Via degli Strozzi,** the connector between Tornabuoni and the Piazza della Repubblica. **Emporio Armani** (Piazza Strozzi) is here.

Excelsior/Grand   The Westin Excelsior/Grand neighborhood backs up to Tornabuoni, where the famed hotels are located. Many good stores are actually on **Piazza Ognissanti;** the rest line **Borgo Ognissanti** until it hits Piazza Goldini and becomes Via della Vigna Nuova. If all this sounds confusing, don't panic.

The neighborhoods are close to each other and could even be considered one neighborhood, which is why staying at either of these hotels makes good sense if you love shopping, want to walk, and need a luxury property.

The shops in the Excelsior/Grand area are less touristy and more mom-and-pop than the big names in Tornabuoni, but the area does include a big name or two, such as **Bottega Veneta** (Piazza Ognissanti 3).

Grand/Medici   You can walk from the luxury hotels at Borgo Ognissanti all the way to the Grand Hotel Villa Medici, another luxury hotel only 2 blocks away. In doing so, you will pass several local resources and a discount shop as well as two major American car-rental agencies, Avis and Europcar (National). If you want a discount shop, check out **One Price** (Borgo Ognissanti 74r), where the sweaters come in dreamy colors (all lamb's wool) and sell for about 23€ ($25). Then there's **Porta**

del Tartufo (Borgo Ognissanti 133r), a gourmet food shop that specializes in truffles but has other food products as well.

Excelsior/Grand Antiques   There are two main antiques areas in Florence, one near the Pitti Palace and the other right beside the Excelsior/Grand area at **Piazza Ognissanti.** If you face the Excelsior Hotel (with the Grand Hotel to your rear, the Arno River to your right, and a church to your left) and start walking, you'll pass a small street called Via del Porcellana. From there, look across Borgo Ognissanti to **Fioretto Giampaolo** (no. 43r). Stop in, and then walk a block toward Tornabuoni until you get to the Piazza Goldini.

At the Piazza Goldini, you'll discover **Via dei Fossi,** which is crammed with antiques dealers. In fact, the area between the two streets and including the **Via del Moro,** which runs next to Via dei Fossi, is host to almost two dozen dealers. Most of these stores sell larger pieces of furniture and medium-to-important antiques; there's not too much junk. There are some businesses that are geared to the design trade without being in the antiques business—like **Riccardo Barthel** (Via dei Forri 11r), which does tiles. One Sunday each fall (ask your concierge for the exact date because it varies from year to year), all the dealers in the area have open houses.

Arno Alley   The Arno is a river, not a neighborhood; the main street along each bank of the river changes its name every few blocks. On the Duomo side of the river, the portion of street named **Lungarno Amerigo Vespucci,** which becomes **Lungarno Corsini,** is crammed with shops, hotels, and even the famous Harry's Bar.

Some of these shops sell antiques; several of them sell statues and reproductions of major works; some sell shoes, clothes, and/or handbags; and one or two are just fancy TTs.

Note: Several of these shops are open on Sunday.

Duomo Center   As in Milan, there is excellent shopping around the Duomo. Naturally, this is an older, more traditional area. Most of these stores are in older buildings. Locals as well as tourists shop here. This area has gotten so built up and is filled with an overwhelming number of stores. There are stores around all four sides of the church. There's even shopping in the church, in the little museum store downstairs, and in the little side streets stretching from the church as well. This is where **Pegna** is located.

The main shopping street of this part of town is called **Via dei Calzaiuoli,** and it's directly behind the Duomo and runs right smack into the Uffizi. It is closed to street traffic, so pedestrians can wander freely from the Duomo to the Piazza della Signoria, another large piazza filled with pigeons, postcards, incredible fountains and statues, tourists and locals, charm and glamour, and everything you think Florence should have. You can't rave about an area too much more than that, can you?

A second main shopping street, **Via Roma,** connects the Duomo and the Ponte Vecchio and runs past Piazza della Repubblica, where many traditional stores are located. This street runs parallel to Via dei Calzaiuoli, and you could mistake it for the main shopping street of town unless you knew better. The Savoy Hotel is on Via Roma.

Just before it reaches the Ponte Vecchio, Via Roma becomes Via por Santa Maria. Don't miss **Luisa Via Roma** (Via Roma 21r), which is sort of the local version of Barney's.

Streets that run from the Duomo in the direction of Santa Croce in the city center are chockablock with cute stores. The best ones are **Via del Corso** (which becomes Borgo Albizi) and **Via Tavolini,** which will change its name each block and runs exactly parallel to the Via del Corso. Be sure to take some time to look at the old houses here and to smell the coffee. You'll find the local branch of **Lush** in this part of town; many of the branches of French stores are here, as are a few discounters.

Ponte Vecchio   If you keep walking a few hundred meters from Piazza della Signoria right to the banks of the Arno River, you will see the Ponte Vecchio. You'll zig to the right a few yards, and then walk left to get across the bridge. Or you can connect by continuing straight along Via Roma, which will change its name each block and become the Ponte Vecchio 3 blocks after you pass the Duomo.

By my definition, the Ponte Vecchio neighborhood includes the bridge and the retailers on the Duomo side of the bridge.

Once you cross over the bridge, you are in another neighborhood: Pitti.

I consider Ponte Vecchio a distinct area, however, because the entire bridge is populated by jewelry shops. Prices are very high, but looking in windows is free. *Note:* Once you are on the Pitti side, if you make a sharp left and then turn to face the river, you'll find the very well hidden **Lisa Corti** shop.

Over the Bridge (Pitti & Santo Spirito)   Once you cross over the Ponte Vecchio, you reach a different retailing climate. You are now on the Pitti side of the bridge. The stores are smaller but no less touristy; you get the feeling that real people also shop here. You can wander, discovering your own personal finds; you can stop and get the makings of a picnic or grab a piece of pizza. The shopping goes in two directions: toward the Pitti Palace or uptown along the Arno. (If your back is to the Duomo, turn left along the Arno to head uptown.) See both areas, looking at shops on **Borgo San Jacopo** and on **Via Guicciardini.**

If you are headed for the once-a-month flea market or looking for antiques shops and crafts vendors, the Santo Spirito neighborhood—actually part of Pitti—is where you want to be. Santo Spirito may not be on the tiny freebie maps handed out all over town, but it is truly convenient and easy to find: If you are standing in front of the Pitti with the Pitti behind you, walk straight 1 block.

If you are looking for **Lisa Corti,** it's on the Via Bardi, which is the street to your left, if your back is to the bridge. The store is hidden, so dart into the bridge area from the side to find it.

Santa Croce & Bernini Back Alley   A sneeze behind the Piazza Signoria is the Bernini Palace Hotel and the Borgo dei Greci, which leads to Santa Croce. Shoppers know this area mostly because of the famous Leather School located inside the Santa Croce church. It's nice to wander around this area because it *feels* like it's a little off the beaten track and seems more natural than the parts of town where tourists swarm (yet this is a major tourist area with many, many TTs). Face it, it's all tourist shops. There are also some cafes and pizza eats, more so-called leather factory outlets than you ever care to see in your lifetime, one or two fun antiques-cum-junk stores (the best kind), and a good bit of Sunday retail. If you are lucky enough to catch the Sunday flea market, it's even deeper into this area. If you want a grocery store, there's a **Standa** not too far away— take the Via Verdi to the post office, and *volare.*

FLORENCE RESOURCES FROM A TO Z

Antiques

As an antiques center, Florence gets pieces from the entire Tuscan area. The problem of fakes, which is severe in Rome, is not as great here. Anyone can get taken, that's well known, but the chances are less in Florence than in Rome.

- Antiques are available at a flea market at the **Piazza dei Ciompi,** but this is really grandmother's attic, fun stuff. We're talking tag-sale quality here, but you may uncover a find every now and then (or absolutely nothing). Note that there are two parts to this market, the regulars who are open every day in the center aisles in little huts, and the people who set up on tables in the open air on the last Sunday of each month.
- For more serious stuff, check out any of the following streets: Via Guicciardini, Via Maggio, Via dei Tornabuoni, Via della Vigna Nuova, Via del Porcellana, Borgo Santi Apostoli, Via dei Fossi, Via del Moro, Via di Santo Spirito, or Via della Spada. There's a string of fun shops for everything from old postcards to 1950s jewelry on the Borgo San Jacopo right over the bridge. I happen to like Via dei Fossi for medium-range antiques—possibly affordable.
- Affordable antiques are best bought at flea markets that are regular events, most often held once a month.
- Many locals like to go to **Viterbo,** a city about 45 minutes away, because it has a fairly decent Sunday flea market for antiques. Viterbo also gets a less touristy crowd.
- The best flea market in Florence proper is the monthly event held at **Santo Spirito** every second Sunday.

- There's an antiques fair in **Pistoia,** a half-hour away, on the second Saturday and Sunday of each month; the market is covered and houses about 150 stalls. There is no market in July and August. Head for the **Via Ciglliegiale.**

- There's a market in **Pisa** on the second Sunday of each month and the Saturday that precedes it. Located on **Via XX Settembre,** this market, which also has about 150 dealers, is known for its furniture, which can be bought at a low price and then restored. The market is not held in July and August.

- The town of **Siena** has a flea market on the third Sunday of each month. Located at the **Piazza del Mercato,** the market has only about 60 dealers, but it does get a lot of "smalls" (the trade term for small objets d'art) and locals selling off estate pieces, so buyers can hope to get lucky here. There's no market in August.

- The biggest (and best) antiques fair in Italy is held in **Arezzo,** about an hour south of Florence by train. It's held the first Sunday of each month and the Saturday that precedes it. There are over 600 dealers at this event, and it does not close in the summer months. Head to the **Piazza Vasari** and work the area to the **Piazza San Francesco.**

Please note that the laws defining what is and is not an antique are different in Italy than in many other countries, so that items made from old wood or from older items may be classified as antiques even if they were made yesterday! The craftspeople in the area are gifted at making repros that are so good you can't tell how old they are.

Bath Balms & Erbolistas

BIZARRE
Via della Condotta 32r.

This is the secret source of spices and essences for Logan Bentley (my Italian correspondent). Some people in town claim it's a hangout for local witches.

CHIANTI CASHMERE COMPANY
Just outside the village of Radda.

Soap made from cashmere goats on a Tuscan farm (for more information, go to www.chianticashmere.com).

DEHERBORE
Via del Proconsolo, 43r.

Another source for great looking (and smelling) gift items and cures. This is on the way to Santa Croce, just past the Hotel Bernini Palace.

ERBORISTERIA PALAZZO VECCHIO
Via Vacchereccia 9r.

This is an herbalist, not a pharmacist—puh-lease! Buy hair tonic, bosom tonics, and much more. It's right in the thick of the shopping in central downtown, the packaging is good, and the opportunity for fun gifts is strong.

LUSH
Via del Corso 23r.

This British bath firm has stores all over Italy and makes a great effort to create Italian products with local ingredients, so they are different from offerings in other Lush shops. I am addicted to the limoncello soap and shampoo.

Books

ART STORE
Piazza del Duomo 50r.

This appears to be a museum shop but has an entrance separate from that of the museum next door, and offers mostly books. There are art books as well as guides, children's books, the usual souvenirs, and gifts with an artistic bent.

BM Book Shop
Borgo Ognissanti 4r.

This English-language bookshop, right smack in the heart of everything, specializes in American and British books; it's a great place to hang out and ask questions or touch base with the owners.

Libreria Edison
Piazza della Repubblica 27r.

This is sort of the local Barnes & Noble. Although most of the books are in Italian, there are also foreign-language books, which means you will pay 10€ ($11) for a paperback. The store is large, continues on the lower and upper levels, and sells everything in book- and communications-related media, from postcards to CDs. The shop is open on Sunday from 10am to 1:30pm and from 3:30 until 8pm. Other days of the week (including Mon), it's open nonstop from 9am to 8pm.

Boutiques

Luisa Via Roma
Via Roma 19–21r.

One of the best stores in town—maybe the world—when it comes to fashion, style, whimsy, and the look we crave but usually can't achieve or afford.

Raspini
Via por Santa Maria 72r.

This firm once owned a ton of boutiques carrying designer brands; now they have cut back but still have some of the world's best-known labels. Most are Italian, but there are some international makers also. This is near the Straw Market.

Cooking Classes

CUCINA TOSCANA (FAITH HELLER WILLINGER)
Near Pitti Palace (get the address when you book a class).

Every Wednesday Faith Willinger, famous for her books and articles and importance in the world of Italian food and wine, gives a private cooking lesson in her home in the heart of town near the Pitti Palace. I have not included the address because, after all, this is Faith's home and the woman does deserve a little privacy.

Technicalities first: The class costs $450 for the day but will be discounted to $400 per day if you mention *Born to Shop* when you book. Yes, you get more than $450 worth of fun, and an excellent goody bag to take away with you.

The class begins with a lesson in making the perfect espresso, and then you're off to the market to pick out lunch. The class makes lunch together, gets a few life lessons from Faith, and then eats the lunch ensemble. Sometimes there is a guest chef at lunch.

I'm sure I don't need to tell you that Faith is warm, funny, fabulous, and lives in a dream apartment (very funky). To book a class, go to her website: www.faithwillinger.com.

GIULIANO BUGIALLI
(See website.)

These English-speaking classes specialize in homemade pasta. In the U.S., call © **212/813-9552;** www.bugialli.com.

LA CUCHINA FIORENTINA
(Location varies.)

These are group classes (in English) for up to eight participants—you get a trip to market and then kitchen and cooking time, for about 182€ ($200) per person. The exact site of the class varies according to the group; when you reserve, you'll find out where to go. This is organized through a private eating club and is booked through Tuscany by Tuscans (www.tuscanyby tuscans.it; tuscany@italway.it).

Costume Jewelry

ANGELA CAPUTI
Borgo San Jacopo 82.

This place serves up dynamite creative costume jewelry with bright-colored plastics and lots of inventive twists and turns. Prices range from 9€ to 91€ ($10–$100). Caputi is well known in designer circles as a hot talent and now has young, modern clothes to go with her jewelry. She should stick to jewelry. This is on the Pitti side of the Ponte Vecchio.

MARCELLA INNOCENTI
Loggo del Mercato Nuovo 3r.

This small shop, right across from the Straw Market, seems so fancy you might think the jewels in the window are real. But they are faux, and the prices are so low you will giggle. I got a pair of gold earrings with "diamonds" for 18€ ($20). If you don't see what you are looking for, ask and the trays will come out.

Department Stores

COIN
Via dei Calzaiuoli 56r.

A small department store concentrating on ready-to-wear. It features quasi-modern architecture in a multilevel space that exhibits a little of everything for men, women, and children. It's a good place to sniff out next season's fashion direction. Prices aren't at the bargain level, but they are moderate for Italy. *Remember:* When the elevator says T, you are at street level; S stands for second floor. The biggest news here is that they have totally eliminated makeup and perfume and have only a MAC boutique on the ground floor right at the front door.

La Rinascente
Piazza Repubblica.

La Rinascente is right in the heart of town, obviously put there to compete with the lovely Coin. The store is moderately priced, light, modern, fun to shop, and open on Sunday. It is not a great store, so don't be too hurt.

Designer Boutiques
Continental Big Names

Cartier
Via dei Tornabuoni 40r.

Escada
Via Strozzi 30 and 36.

Hermès
Piazza degli Antinori 6r.

Lacoste
Via della Vigna Nuova 33r.

Laurel
Via della Vigna Nuova 67–69r.

Louis Vuitton
Via dei Tornabuoni 2.

Wolford
Via della Vigna Nuova 93–95r.

Italian Big Names

Accessories of Benetton
Via Degli Speziali 6–8r.

Benetton
Via por Santa Maria 68r, Bottega Veneta.

Brioni
Via Calimala 22r.

EMPORIO ARMANI
Piazza Strozzi.

ENRICO COVERI
Via della Vigna Nuova 27–29r.

ERMENEGILDO ZEGNA
Piazza dei Rucellai 4–7r.

FERRAGAMO
Via dei Tornabuoni 16.

FRETTE
Via Cavour 2.

GENNY
Via dei Tornabuoni 35.

GIANFRANCO FERRÉ
Via dei Tosinghi 52r.

GIORGIO ARMANI
Via della Vigna Nuova 51r.

GUCCI
Via dei Tornabuoni 73r;
Via Roma 32r.

LORO PIANO
Via della Vigna Nuova 37r.

MARINA RINALDI
Via Panzani 1.

MAX & CO.
Via de Calzaiuoli 89r.

MAX MARA
Via dei Pecori 23r.

PRATESI
Lungarno Corsini 32–34r;
Lungarno Corsini 36–38r.

PUCCI
Via della Vigna Nuova 97–99r.

TRUSSARDI
Via dei Tornabuoni 34–36r.

VERSACE
Via dei Tornabuoni 13r.

VERSUS
Via della Vigna Nuova 36–38r.

ZEGNA SPORT
Via della Vigne Nuovo 62r.

Foodstuffs

BARONI
Mercato Centrale, via Galluzzo.

The entire indoor Mercato Centrale is a fabulous source for foods, souvenirs, and memories. Of the many stalls, this is one of the more famous for 30-year-old cheeses that are not exported, designer olive oils, and much, much more. The staff speaks English.

PEGNA
Via dello Studio 8.

Oh boy, have I got a store for you. Despite the fact that this is a few feet from the Duomo, I needed a local friend to find it for me—it is hidden in plain sight and could be the most exciting stop in town, if you are a foodie, anyway. This is an old-fashioned grocery store that sells everything, including English brands of cleaning products. There are foods to take home, foods for picnics, and even gift items in soaps or foodstuffs. Don't miss it.

Home Style

DITTA LUCA DELLA ROBBIA
Via del Proconsolo 19r.

Carrying plates, tiles, religious souvenirs, and more, this place is a little bit off the beaten path (but not enough to count) and is one of the best pottery shops in town. I dare you not to buy. Shipping is available—although it may double the price of your goods. The shop is located between Piazza della Signoria and Santa Croce.

GALLERIA MACHIAVELLI
Via por Santa Maria 39.

Despite the stupid name for a shop, this is one of the best resources in town for country wares and ceramics. It's located right in the center of downtown, so you can easily pop in. Shipping is available.

LISA CORTI
Via del Bardi 58.

I am perhaps Lisa Corti's biggest fan—and yet I am forced to tell you that the Florence store does not do her work justice and you may think I am nuts when you get here. So, some background. Lisa Corti is from Milan and sells in the U.S. through Saks Fifth Avenue. Her shop in Milan is off the beaten path but wonderful; she is also sold in Positano at La Sirenuese, which is where I discovered this brand.

Corti designs fabrics in bright swirls of color with a southern Italian flair and feel. Her stuff is mostly home style, although there are some clothes and even pieces of pottery. Because the goods are printed in India, some locals tend to dismiss this brand, which is silly. Very silly.

The shop in Florence is hard to find, and it takes real patience to fully explore the merchandise, which is mostly put away. If you don't know this stuff is great, you won't be impressed by the shop. Best buys are table linens, which begin around 68€ ($75).

PASSAMANERIA TOSCANA
Piazza San Lorenzo 12r, at the corner of Via della Vigna Nuova and Via dei Federighi.

Maybe you don't plan your travels around your ability to find trim or tassels, but when you luck into a source that makes the best in the world and is affordable, it's time to celebrate.

This firm actually has two shops—both in neighborhoods that you will be visiting anyway. I've been buying my cotton multicolor tassels in Paris for about 4.50€ ($5) each (at the flea market, no less)—in Florence, they are 5.45€ ($6) each! You'll also find pillowcases, embroideries, brocades, assorted trims, and fabrics. The San Lorenzo shop is larger. Chic, but expensive.

PASSAMANERIA VALMAR
Via Porta Rossa 53r.

This shop is right in the heart of town; just look at your map for easy access to one of the best sources in town for tassels, tiebacks, trims, cushions, and more.

RICHARD GINORI
Via Rondinelli 17.

RICHARD GINORI OUTLET STORE
Sesto Fiorentino.

Richard Ginori is one of the most famous international names in bone china; Ginori's fruit pattern (and the price per plate) has been known to make brides faint. While the firm is in fine shape, it has lost its luster as a retail resource—the Via Condotti (Rome) store has closed, and the shop in Florence is less than memorable and carries other brands besides Ginori.

Your best bet, if you believe in the tooth fairy or have the time and the adventuresome spirit of a true shopper, is to stop by the factory outlet shop (© 055/421-04-72) in Sesto, a small village about 20 minutes outside Florence. Give it a try if you have a car, don't mind splurging on a taxi (have your driver wait), or hire a car and driver. The factory shop is open Monday to Friday 9am to 1pm and 3:30 to 7pm. It does not take credit cards. *Note:* The outlet is on the way to the Pratesi outlet, off the A11.

Linens & Lace

PRATESI
Lungarno Corsini 32–34r and 36–38r.

This is a new shop, although old-timers who remember the old store will know this store is nearby. Business has been so great that it expanded into the space next door, hence the two street numbers. Once you waltz inside, you'll know why business is so good and swoon from wanting to touch or snuggle up into the gorgeous linens. There's nothing old-fashioned here; the store not only has the full line of Pratesi merchandise but will also custom make whatever you need.

And for the tacky people who want to know the same things I do—yes, many (most of) prints here were not at the outlet. While the quality is the same, the selection in the store is larger and broader, and they will make anything you need in any size in any print or fabric you select. There's also a beach line, a baby line, and a cashmere collection. Oh Athos, you did good, my friend.

BRUNNETO PRATESI
Via Montalbano 41, Pistoia.

See "Day Trip 1: Pistoia," later in this chapter, for how to visit this factory store, which is just a half-hour outside of Florence in the town of Pistoia. Brunneto Pratesi founded the firm named after him; his grandson was my friend Athos Pratesi, who passed away a few years before my husband. Now the company is run by Athos's son Frederico. This is one of the last merchant-prince manufacturing Italian families.

LORETTA CAPONI
Piazza Antinori 4r.

If you've ever dreamed of being either a Lady Who Lunches or a Lady Who Sleeps Late, this lingerie store is for you. Here you'll find the dreamiest silks in underwear, linen, negligees, and more, as well as some cottons and table linens. This is what having money is all about.

Makeup & Perfume

If you can help it, don't buy makeup in Florence—it's expensive, and the choices are pretty average. If you're desperate, go to department stores such as **Coin** or **La Rinascente.**

The **Profumeria Inglese** (Via dei Tornabuoni 97r) is a temple to good taste, fine goods, and every imaginable brand, right in the heart of the shopping district. There are no bargains here. For beauty cures and treatments, check the pharmacy listings below or the local *erbolistas*—listed in "Bath Balms & Erbolistas," earlier in this section.

Markets

MERCATO DELLE CASCINE
Piazzale Vittorio Veneto.

Held once a week (Tues only), this market is famous with locals because it serves them in the same way a department store might. The various vendors are regulars, so everyone gets to know everyone, and some of the vendors even have famous reputations. I found the market fabulous from an academic standpoint, but not actually the kind of place with much to buy.

Granted, a lot of that depends on luck and taste, but I just didn't need new pots, pans, dishes, tires, or baby clothes. I was wildly interested in the heap of designer handbags that Faith and I have decided must have been fake; there are handbags beginning at 5.45€ ($6). I like the local fabrics, tablecloths, and dish towels; I love the few food vendors. I did work my way through mounds of used clothes and linens in hopes of finding something I had to have.

The market opens at 7am; I got there at 8am, and vendors were still setting up. Another time I arrived at 11am and it was just fine.

To get there, take a bus to the Jolly Hotel or walk along the Arno—it's a bit of a walk from the center of town, considering that once you get to the market you are going to walk even more, but you can do it.

MERCATO DELLE PULCI
Piazza dei Ciompi.

This is the local flea market that sells everything from furniture to pictures, coins, and jewelry; it's great fun, especially if the weather is fair. Held the last Sunday of each month. Meanwhile, every week, Tuesday through Saturday (not at all the same as the once-a-month affair), the regular dealers in a small strip of stalls are open. Possibly not worth the trip.

The Sunday market is an all-day job beginning around 9am; the daily market closes for lunch and follows more traditional business hours. To get there, walk out the back end of the Duomo onto Via dell Oriuolo, pass the Piazza Salvemini, and hit Via Popolo, which in 1 block takes you to the flea market. It's an easy walk. On Sunday, the nearby **Standa** is open.

SAN LORENZO
Piazza del Mercato Centrale.

I'm sad to report that San Lorenzo does not offer the thrills of years gone by. Either I can't stand a bad fake anymore, or the fakes are going downhill. But wait, all is not lost—the gorgeous sweater for 14€ ($15) brightened me right up. I'm also pleased with the dealer who sells pottery and faience; I found shawls and a few pieces of ready-to-wear I just couldn't live without. And the food market, hidden beyond all the junky stalls, is heaven on earth.

You name it, and San Lorenzo has it. Specifically, San Lorenzo is good for cheapie ties and scarves and gifts galore, cheap clothing for kids or teens, T-shirts, and souvenirs. The selection of leather jackets doesn't cut the mustard with me—I think you can do better in the U.S. I didn't see any handbags that even looked kosher to me.

The market has a few pushcart dealers, and then several rows of stalls that lead around a bend. The stalls are very well organized; this is a legal fair, and stallholders pay tax to the city. Many of the stalls give you shopping bags with their numbers printed on them. Now, that's class.

With the recent crackdown on phony big-name merchandise, few of the pushcarts have imitations. *A word of caution:* Do not get so excited with the bargains that you don't cast an eagle eye over the goods or, in your haste, think that these are real designer goods. Look for defects; look for details. I have yet to find a faux designer scarf here that really looks good enough to pass as the evil twin sister.

Most stall owners take plastic. The market is open Tuesday to Saturday from 9am to 7pm. Closed Sunday and Monday.

SANTA MARIA NOVELLA TRAIN STATION
Santa Maria Novella.

Technically speaking, the main train station is a train station and not a market. But it functions as a marketplace. There's a McDonald's, stores, and plenty of people and action. There is a mall underneath.

STRAW MARKET
Via por Santa Maria.

The best thing about the Straw Market is that it doesn't close during lunchtime. It's also within walking distance of the Ponte Vecchio, the Duomo, and all the other parts of Florence you want to see, so you can make your day's itinerary and get it all in. Locals call this market *Porcellino,* in honor of the boar statue that stands here.

This market sells far more junk and much more in the way of souvenirs than the other markets. It also gets more crowded than other markets. Still, it's a marvelous TT and worth a visit, if only to fill a lunch void. The merchandise varies with the season, as it should. It takes a good eye and a steady hand.

The market is open daily, from 9am to 5pm in winter, and from 9am to 7pm in summer. Closed tight on Sunday.

Outlets & Stock Shops

See "Beyond Florence," p. 151, for factory outlets.

Il Gaurdaroba
Via Verdi 28r.

You will walk by here anyway, so why not pop in for discounted designer clothes for men and women?

Piazza Pitti
Piazza Pitti 32r.

Good news, bad news. This large outlet store is right across from the Pitti Palace, so you have no excuse not to stop in. Once there, you have to get lucky in terms of sizes and brands—but this is an off-pricer that gets current clothes from the major brands. I even spotted some Missoni.

Paper Goods

Florentine paper is one of Florence's greatest contributions to bookbinding and gift giving. There are two styles, marbleized and block printed. The marbleized style is readily found in Venice; neither style is handily found in Milan or Rome.

In Florence, there are scads of stores selling papered gift items; such items are even sold from souvenir stands, in markets, and at the train station. Prices are generally modest, although they can get up there with larger items.

BOTTEGA ARTIGIANA DEL LIBRO
Lungarno Corsini 38–40r.

This is a small shop, next to the Arno, that has beautiful things and can solve many a gift quandary. Small address books are around 7.30€ ($8); pencils are stunning and inexpensive; picture frames range from 4.50€ to 14€ ($5–$15), depending on the size. These frames have plastic fronts, not glass. There are photo albums, bound blank books, and all sorts of other items. Note the business cards printed on the back of marbleized paper swatches.

CARTOLERIA PARIONE
Via Parione 10r.

I got a letter from a reader a few years ago, a professional photographer, who was looking for marbleized photo albums that she could use to show her work. She said she could find them in the U.S., but they cost about $100 and could I find some in Italy for less. Well, it took me a year, but yes, Virginia, here you go—this store, which sells many of the usual paper goods, also has the photo albums. They come in various sizes, and prices begin at 27€ ($30)! They will ship (fax your order to 055/21-56-84). The shop is located right in the heart of the Tornabuoni shopping district.

GIANNINI E FIGLIO
Piazza Pitti 37r.

Historically well known for the marbleized type of Florentine paper, this shop has been in business for centuries. They also make bookplates, calling cards, and items for all other paper needs. I think several paper-wrapped pencils tied with a bow make a great gift; the price obviously depends on how many pencils you buy, but you can put together a beautiful 9€ ($10) package. There are many good paper shops in Florence, but this is the single most famous.

Il Papiro
Lungarno Acciaioli 112r.

This is the most commercially successful of the marbleized-paper stores, with branches all over Italy and in the U.S.

Pineider
Piazza della Signoria 13r.

Do you love to mail handwritten notes? How about thick formal note cards that smell of old money and inseparable style? At this shop you'll find very conservative, old-time stationery as well as some gift items and the new designs by Rebecca Moses. Prices are steep. This is a serious international status symbol.

Pharmacies

Not the kind of pharmacy you go to when you need an *aspirina,* these pharmacies seem to be a specialty of Florence—they are old-fashioned, fancy-dancy places where you can buy creams and goos and local brews and various homeopathic treatments, as well as European brands or local homemade potions for all sorts of things. There are tons of these places in Florence. One or two will be all you need for great gifts and, possibly, dinner-table conversation.

Farmaceutica di Santa Maria Novella
Via della Scala 16r.

Yep. This is the one—the one you've read about in every American and English fashion and beauty magazine, the one where you buy the almond cream. At least, that's what I buy here. Go nuts. (Almonds are nuts, so go nuts.) Fabulous gift items, fabulous fun. It's located near the train station and downtown—go out of your way to find it. I had to ask three times just to find it; I was even stumped when I was standing outside the front door. Never mind—walk in! It looks unusual because it's a convent, not a storefront. All the more yummy.

FARMACIA MOLTENI
Via Calzaiuoli 7r.

Remember this one because it's open every day of the week, 24 hours a day. It's centrally located, and it's where you go in case of a medical emergency of the pharmaceutical kind. It's also gorgeous.

Shoes & Handbags

BAJOLA
Via Rondinelli 25r.

If only old-world style will do for you, but you find Louis Vuitton too obvious, you probably want luggage from Bajola, which was founded in 1896. This is a very local kind of resource, one that the "in" society knows about, but the American tourist does not. It's not far from the Richard Ginori regular retail store, on your way to (or from) the main train station.

DESMO
Piazza del Rucellai 10r.

Desmo is one of my best Italian secrets for reasons of pride and pocketbook—excuse the double entendre. They make a top-of-the-line, high-quality, equal-to-the-best-of-them handbag at a less-than-top-of-the-line price. Years ago they made their name as a maker of leather clothing, shoes, and accessories, copying Bottega Veneta creations; now they have their own style and plenty of winners. Colors are always fashionable and up-to-date; the prices are pretty good—few items in the house top 182€ ($200), and you can get much for considerably less.

Now then, don't let the address throw you; Piazza del Rucellai is a little dip in the Via della Vigna Nuova—you can't miss the shop when you are in the thick of the designer stores. See "Logan's Outlets" at the end of this chapter for information on Desmo's factory outlet.

GHERARDINI
Via della Vigna Nuova 57r;
Via degli Strozzi 25r.

One of the biggest leather-goods names in Italy and Asia but little known otherwise, Gherardini offers a specific look in luggage, shoes for men and women, belts, and accessories. I find their conservative designs drop-dead elegant with old-money style. They also have some tote bags and a printed canvas/vinyl line that is status-y as well as practical. There are two stores in Florence, both in the heart of the central downtown shopping district.

HERMINE'S
Via Pietrapiana 72r.

One of the reasons I like this store is that it doesn't claim to be making Hermès goods—it goes out of the way to show you the differences. Which aren't obvious. Nonetheless, the prices are high . . . as is the quality. The store is near the Standa grocery store and off the tourist path, but not far from city center and Santa Croce.

IL PONTE VECCHIO
Piazza del Mercato Nuovo 18r.

This is a very unusual store, in that the goods are magnificent, but they are very expensive; and when you ask why the prices are so high, you may well be told that these are Hermès goods without the Hermès price tags, made in the same factories. I don't know if I have a bridge to sell you or not, but the goods here are worth drooling over. Every color imaginable and every Hermès style. But 182€ ($200) for a wallet? Not me; not these days.

LEATHER SCHOOL
Monastery of Santa Croce, Piazza Santa Croce.

If you insist on shopping in one of the many leather factories in Florence, you may as well go to the best—it's actually inside the Santa Croce church and is a leather school with a factory on the premises. The school is open Monday through Saturday year-round, and on Sunday from April 15 to November 15. You enter through the church, except on Sunday, when you enter through the garden.

MADOVA
Via Guicciardini 1.

Gloves are back in style, so stock up. I'll take the yellow, cashmere-lined, butter-soft leather ones . . . or should I think pink? Maybe both? Unlined gloves are about 27€ ($30) and come in about a million colors. There's everything here, from the kind of white kid gloves we used to wear in the 1960s to men's driving gloves to very ornately designed, superbly made, high-button gloves.

MANTELASSI
Piazza della Repubblica 25r.

If made-to-measure shoes are what you have in mind, step this way with your instep. Men and women can design their own, bring a shoe to be copied, or choose from the many styles displayed.

SALVATORE FERRAGAMO
Via dei Tornabuoni 16r.

Yes, there are Ferragamo shops all over Italy and all over the world. But none of them comes near the parent shop in Florence, which is in a building erected in 1215, complete with vaulted ceilings, stained-glass windows, and enough ambience to bring out your camera. The shop has several connecting antechambers with an incredible selection of shoes, boots, and ready-to-wear . . . as well as a library and a kiddie playroom. Shoes are in American sizes; however, there is a limited selection in big sizes.

Upstairs is the museum, which is *fab-u-lous*. It is not open to the public all day, or open every day, so call to ask for the hours (© **055/29-21-23**) and to make an appointment—they are strict on the appointment stuff. There is also a research library for designers and a small museum gift shop with great merchandise but very high prices. The postcards cost three times what they should. Save up for shoes, instead.

Each January and July there's a clear-it-all-out sale, but I confess that I left brokenhearted last January. Clothing provided better deals than the shoes. Prices were not as good as the sale at Saks. The sale is held in the basement, which has an entrance at the side door; there are guards and usually lines to get in.

Sergio Rossi
Via Roma 15r.

Even though this brand is part of one of the French luxury conglomerates, it's true Italian style in high heels and luxe leathers.

Tanino Crisci
Via dei Tornabuoni 43–45.

Tanino Crisci is a big name in Italian shoes and leather goods with an international reputation, but there are not many stores in the U.S., so Americans may not be familiar with the brand. This is a chain of moderate-to-expensive shoes in sort of sporty, conservative styles. There's something a bit chunky about a lot of the styles, but the look wears forever and looks better every year. Very preppy. The quality is well known; prices range from 127€ ($140) to over 182€ ($200). This is a very specific look that is either your style or not.

They make men's and women's shoes, dress and sports models; and also have belts and small leather goods.

FLORENCE ON A SCHEDULE

TOUR 1: FULL-DAY FLORENTINE DRAMA

1. Begin the tour at **Ferragamo,** at the Piazza di San Trinita, at 9:30am. Hopefully you also have an appointment at 10am to tour the shoe museum upstairs. Then, walk down **Via dei Tornabuoni** to see the designer boutiques.

2. The fancy shopping ends in time for you to turn right onto the Via degli Strozzi and be at the Strozzi Palace, where **Emporio** is housed. Then walk another block to Piazza della Repubblica and head left on Via Roma, toward the Duomo. You are now passing some of the older, established shops, as well as places like **Luisa Via Roma** for young looks, impor- tant designer clothes, and local pizzazz. When finished here, you can have a coffee in the rear of the store or go across the street to the **Hotel Savoy** to have a coffee in the library. Once back on the street, note that at the corner, Via Roma becomes a much smaller street called Borgo San Lorenzo. Follow it for 1 long block. You are still walking straight, but the sub- text of the street has changed. At the end of the block you will arrive at the back end of the **San Lorenzo market,** which you will know by the stalls in the street. If there are no stalls in the street, it must be Monday.

3. Explore the market area until you're exhausted or ready for lunch. You may want to return to your hotel to dump your packages. Most shops in Florence will close from 1 or 1:30 to 3:30pm, so if you want, this is your chance for lunch and a foot soak.

4. Or stroll back the way you came, pass the Duomo, and head toward the **Straw Market** on the Via por Santa Maria. The Straw Market is open during lunchtime. There are also two pizza joints right around here, so you can grab a quick bite to eat. My regular one is called Piccadilly. We're not talking charm or big-time taste, just a snack. You are near the **Diesel** jeans

shop, so avoid anything too fattening. Then walk back to Ponte Vecchio so you are on the bridge when the shops open after lunch at around 3:30pm.

5. Walk across the bridge on the right side of the street, visiting any of the tiny jewelry shops that meet your fancy. ***Tip:*** The stores are more expensive on the near side of the bridge, and many of them sell the same merchandise. When you get to the other side of the Arno, turn right onto the Via San Jacopo; don't miss the **Angela Caputi** shop and a look at Ferragamo's new family hotel, the Continental.

6. At the end of that block, turn around and do the other side of San Jacopo. When you get back to via Guicciardini, hang a right and walk toward the Pitti Palace, shopping as you go. Too bad, no time for the art. (What a Pitti!) After the paper-goods store **Giannini E Figlio,** there is an outlet store where you could get lucky—then turn right around and head back toward the Arno, now walking the other side of Via Guicciardini.

7. Before you hit the bridge, turn right on the Via Bardi and cross the street so you are almost in the river. Find the tiny **Lisa Corti** shop and explore and dream of colors and dinner parties to be. Look out the window at the Arno before you leave.

8. Then walk back across the Arno on the right side of the bridge, which will be the side opposite the one you crossed on.

9. Once over the Arno, turn right immediately on Lungarno Generale Diaz. Please note that the main drag running along the Arno changes its name at every bridge, so while you've probably been on the street before and will be again later in the day, its name will change and you may get confused. Walk to the **Uffizi,** only a few yards away. Take in the beautiful view of the river, the excellent postcard dealer, and then the museum.

10. After your tour of the Uffizi, turn left into the courtyard and walk across to the Piazza della Signoria, which has a fabulous fountain, some cute little horse-and-buggies, a zillion

tourists, and an even better postcard dealer. Cross the piazza to Via dei Calzaiuoli, a famous shopping street. Walk toward the Duomo, making certain not to miss the **Coin** department store. Then round the corner to the main shopping street and **La Rinascente,** an even better Italian department store.

11. Lesser shoppers would call it a day, but you are just ready for tea and a short pit stop. From the Duomo, head into the warren of back streets where old mansions have been turned into hip and hot shops; take Via del Corso; and just wander, shop, and dream that someday you will live here. Tired? Stop for a coffee at the swank **Savoy Hotel,** gather strength, and decide if you want to push on.

12. Of course you're going on! Now you can return to the flea market at **San Lorenzo** and buy whatever you wanted but didn't buy earlier in the morning. By now you know the lay of the land and have seen a tremendous amount of retail goods.

TOUR 2: QUICKIE FLORENCE HALF-DAY TOWN TOUR

1. Begin at the **Ponte Vecchio,** window-shop along the bridge; if it's Sunday, the bridge will be lined with vendors.

2. Turn right after you cross the bridge and stick to the right-hand side of the street as you walk along the **Borgo San Jacopo,** darting in and out of the antiques stores and window-shopping the rest. You'll find a few restaurants and a deli or two along here, if you need a snack. After a block or 2, cross back and walk along the other side of the street: You are now headed back to the Ponte Vecchio.

3. Do not turn left and cross the bridge, but stay to your right, headed for the **Pitti Palace.** Window-shop (and more) and then take in the Pitti. As you walk, you'll note a few more cafes and pizza places if you are hungry. You can even buy a slice of pizza and take it with you as you stroll. But please, no pizza in the Pitti. Then, shop your way back into town as time permits.

BEYOND FLORENCE

If head-for-the-hills is your choice of neighborhood, you've picked a great part of Italy to explore. Yes, you can rent a car and drive; but, if you want someone else to drive you, then you need only contact my friend Maria Teresa Berdondini of Tuscany by Tuscans (© and fax **0572/70-467;** tuscany@ italway.it), who has a private tour service and will arrange anything you want, from olive-oil tastings to private tours to trips to the outlets.

Prices are based on whether or not you have an English-speaking escort with you and how far you go. Prices include departure and return to any hotel in Florence:

1. Half-day shopping tour (5 hr.) with car and driver—Gucci and Prada outlets: 200€ ($220).
2. Full-day tour with car and driver (6 hr.)—Gucci, Prada, and Malo outlets: 250€ ($275).
3. Full day with car and driver (7 hr.)—Gucci, Prada, Malo, Pratesi, and Ralph Lauren: 300€ ($330).
4. Full day (6 hr.) as above in no. 2, plus English-speaking guide and a visit to olive oil mill and castle: 450€ ($495).
5. Full day as above in no. 3, with escort and visit to a local winery or to Montecatini: 500€ ($550).

Day Trip 1: Pistoia

Okay, okay, so you weren't planning on a side trip to Pistoia. In fact, you've never even heard of it and perhaps think you can survive without it. Wrong. Pistoia may not be the garden spot of Italy, but it is the home of the **Brunetto Pratesi** factory. At the Pratesi factory there is a little shop that sells—you guessed it—seconds. If you show your copy of this book, or say you are a friend of the family, you will be allowed to shop there.

Pratesi, as you probably know, is a family business that makes sheets for the royalty of Europe and the movie stars of Hollywood. They are sticklers for perfection: A computer counts

Aaron's Turn: Nearer My Outlet to Thee

Prada   The line outside of the Prada outlet, prior to its opening, was what you might expect to see at a Strokes concert in Milan. It was packed with hipsters and Eurotrash that were so tragically hip that they probably got sad when they had to take their clothes off each night. Yet their worship was understandable: Inside there were bargains to be found. Most clothes were 30% off and some had markings for additional discounts on top of that. You could try the clothes on; the sales help spoke English. I flipped for a Prada suit at 182€ ($200). Didn't fit.

Giorgio Armani, Armani Express, Armani Jeans   The Armania of this store is a bit overwhelming. It really is one store divided into three by well-placed curtains. The prices were pretty far from discount, with some short-sleeve shirts at 82€ ($90). The selection was good except for the Armani Jeans division. I mean, for designer jeans, some of the pairs at this store really made me want to hurl (and from the looks of the color combinations, it looked like somebody beat me to it). There were faded jeans that weren't so much faded with a yellow or gray undertone, but more of a tie-dye. So, for people who are touring with the new incarnation of the Grateful Dead, and want to spend 60 bucks on a pair of "discount" jeans, I strongly recommend the Armani Outlets. For anyone else, don't bother.

Dolce & Gabbana   Bad prices and reject clothes. There's not much else to say; this place wasn't worth it on the day we visited. Some of the 45€ to 55€ ($50–$60) T-shirts they had made me feel sorry that humanity could have created them. And what kind of person wears this kind of shirt? By far, this is the worst of all of the outlet stores in the Florence area.

Pratesi   We went to Pratesi on a different day, since it was a different direction and we wanted to have plenty of time and not be too wiped, or whipped, by Outlet Exhaustion. My mom first met Athos Pratesi when she was pregnant with me and got her first Pratesi sheets as a baby gift when I was born, so we all go way back with this family, and of course I had to listen to all kinds of stories about when I was a baby, which is always embarrassing and especially so when you just want to see the prices and hope to afford something good. I know these sheets last forever because my mom's are almost 25 years old and still going strong.

Jenny and I were also excited to visit the outlet as we have been buying sheets and home goods at Target and Kmart. Because my mom has always bought the Pratesi sheets with little flowers on them, I didn't know they made anything different, so it was pretty cool to see solids and monochromes, jacquard stripes, and things that weren't too girly. Jenny really flipped out for the beach line and got shoes (20€/$22!) and a tote and all sorts of things at really great prices.

the number of stitches in each quilt. If there are five stitches too many, the quilt is a reject! What do they do with this poor, unfortunate, deformed quilt? It will never see the light of day in Beverly Hills, Manhattan, Palm Beach, or even Rome. No, because it has all of five stitches too many, it will be considered a reject, a defect, a second. It will be sold, at a fraction of its *wholesale* price, in the company shop. It's your lucky day.

The store is in the factory, a low-lying modern building, set off the street on your left as you come off the highway, and distinguished only by the discreet signs that say BRUNETTO PRATESI. Not to worry—because it's the most famous factory in the area, everyone knows where it is. Show the printed address (below) to anyone at a nearby gas station or inn, and you will get directions. Don't be intimidated; it's not that hard.

If all this truly makes you nervous, ask your concierge to call ahead and get very specific directions for you: He or she can even arrange a person for you to call in case you get lost.

The factory is located at Via Montalbano 41r (© 0573/ 52-68-68). Store hours are Monday 2 to 7pm; Tuesday to Friday 9am to noon and 2 to 7pm; Saturday 9am to 1pm.

Like all factory outlets, the store sells what it has; you may be lucky or you may not. Last time I was there, the showroom was filled with quilts, nightgowns, and gift items, but low on matched sets. There were blanket covers in various sizes, but you could not put together a whole queen-size bed set. The one total set I priced was no bargain. Price on an item varies depending on the defect; some items are visibly damaged, some are not. Prices are essentially half of what you would pay at regular retail—a blanket cover that retails for 818€ ($900) costs 364€ ($400) here. If you were expecting giveaway prices, think twice. Then look at the beach totes for 18€ ($20) and faint from their chic and your need to own everything in the line.

Pratesi is one of the leading linen makers in the world, and their goods compete with Porthault as the most sought-after by the rich and famous. Considering the quality, these are bargain prices. Do note, however, that Pratesi has sales once a year (in Jan) in their stores in Italy, and twice a year in some other cities around the world. In January in Italy, the prices are marked down 30% off retail, and you have the whole store to choose from.

The scenery on the way to Pistoia is not gorgeous, but you drive on a freeway (A11), so you don't need to worry about getting lost on winding country roads. The town of Pistoia itself has a good bit of medieval charm, and there's a wonderful country inn–type family restaurant that I adore. So, all in all, you'll have a wonderful time. You can also go by train—get the train at Santa Maria Novella (S.M.N.) in Florence for Pistoia; you can catch a taxi at the station in Pistoia.

Day Trip 2: Siena

Siena is not very far from Florence, but it takes some thinking about should you decide to go, unless you have your trusty rent-a-car and are totally free and independent. It's a very pleasant day trip, especially nice for a Monday morning when most of the stores in Florence are closed or a Wednesday morning when market is in full thrall. (Beware, it's mobbed.)

There are prepackaged day trips just to Siena or to Siena and medieval San Gimignano, which is not a shopping town but rather one of those incredible hilltop villages. Do note that if you buy a tour you will pay about 45€ ($50) per person for the day trip, whereas if you do it all yourself, it will cost less than 18€ ($20).

The train ride, which is free if you have a railroad pass, is very long (over 2 hr.) and often involves changing trains. It's a better use of your time to pay an additional 14€ ($15; round-trip) and buy a bus ticket via SITA; you want the *corse rapide* to Siena, which is direct. The bus takes 1 hour and 20 minutes. It drops you on the edge of town, next to the market and within walking distance of everything.

There is basically a bus every hour, although peak travel times have several buses. Best bet is to travel via SITA, on Via Santa Caterina da Siena 15. It's about a block from the S.M.N. train station. Round-trip tickets are discounted slightly.

The SITA station has a sign outdoors directing you where to buy tickets (the *biglietteria*) and an information booth outside of the ticket area. After you buy your tickets, you then must find out which lane your bus will be loading from; there is a large sign high up on the wall near the ticket office.

If you take the bus, it may make local stops as you approach Siena. Don't panic. Your stop is the end of the line, San Domenico Church. When you get off the bus, note the public bathrooms (very clean, pay toilets) and the tourist information office where they'll sell you a map to the city. If you are standing with your back to the church facing the tourist information office, you'll see that there are two streets to your right. One bears off slightly, and the other turns more dramatically and goes down.

If you are doing this on a Monday morning, most of the stores in downtown Siena will be closed. However, if you take the low road, you'll see many touristy stores that are open, even on Monday. While some open at 9am, many more will open at 11am. In fact, the best time to be in Siena is on a Monday morning between 9 and 11am because you'll have it almost to yourself and you'll still get to go shopping.

The main shopping street is Via Banchi di Sopra, which leads right to the Campo and then goes up the hill as the Via di Citta. Take this to the Duomo (well marked) and then follow the signs back down and up the Via della Sapienza, which will bring you back to the bus stop at San Domenico.

Via della Sapienza has a good number of wine (this is Chianti country) and tourist shops, especially close to the bus stop, that remain open during lunchtime, too.

As you approach the Campo, you'll notice various alleys that lead into the square. Some have steps; others are ramps for horses. Each entryway seems to be named for a saint. Many of the alleyways that lead from the shopping street to the Campo are filled with booths or touristy stands. There are more free-standing booths on the Campo itself.

The Campo is surrounded by shops, many of which specialize in pottery, hand-painted in dusty shades and following centuries-old patterns. Some of them are even branches of other stores you will find up the hill, closer to the Duomo. The best shops are clustered up the Via di Citta, close to the Duomo—you will automatically pass them as you walk around and up.

Day Trip 3: Outlet Stores Near Florence

For the younger generation's take on this shopping experience, see Aaron's report, "Nearer My Outlet to Thee," above. For information on the Pratesi factory store, see Day Trip 1.

The Mall
Via Aretina 63 Regello, Localita Lecci, Montevarchi.

This outlet mall is very chic and modern, stark and well designed, up to the standards of any Gucci store. Ignore the busloads of tourists who are pushing about you. If you are driving, call

© 055/865-77-75 for exact directions. There are many shops, variously connected parts to The Mall. They do accept credit cards, and they have sales during which everything is half off the lowest price. All the stores offer VAT-refund materials.

I Pellettieri d'Italia
Localita Levanella, Montevarchi.

I have listed the official name of this factory, although everyone just calls this "The Prada Outlet." Yes dear, you heard right. Montevarchi is an industrial area outside of Arezzo. How far is Arezzo, you are asking now? Well, about an hour or so by train from Rome and Florence—it's mid-distance between the two, actually, and right on the main train line. It's about a half-hour drive from The Mall.

This situation is a little more formal, and you may feel like you are going to prison. You go behind wire and are given an ID number. The store is large and beautifully arranged and organized. There are other brands here besides Prada and MiuMiu (I found Helmut Lang), and there are shoes as well as sunglasses, clothes, handbags, totes, etc.

It's hit or miss, but worth the adventure if you are nearby. The store (© 055/919-95-95 or 055/978-94-81) now accepts credit cards. On weekdays, it's open from 9am to 12:30pm and 3 to 7pm; it's also open all day Saturday and on Sunday afternoon beginning at 2pm.

Modulo
Via Pian dell'Isola 66, Punto Vendita.

This is the outlet center for Celine and Loewe. Both are owned by LVMH, if you are wondering what they have in common. Loewe is a Spanish leather goods firm, sort of equal to Hermès but not as well known. Both outlets sell leather goods as well as clothing for men and women. Prices are not to swoon for but are better than regular retail.

Logan's Outlets

BIG BERTHA CASHMERE
Via dell'Industria 19, Perugia.

Only Logan could come up with a resource with a name like this—it's a catalog company for cashmeres, and better yet, it does *not* close at lunchtime. There's a large selection of sizes and colors. Local phone © 075/599-75-72.

DESMO
Via Matteotti 22b Donato, Fronzano, Reggello, outside Florence.

Call © 055/865-23-11 for specific directions; you will need to hit the *autostrada* going toward Reggello. No credit cards, but savings of about 30% on Desmo brand handbags.

ELLESSE
Via Filippo Turati 22, Ellera Umbria Ponte San Giovanni.

I always thought this was a French line, but it appears to be made locally. Tons of tennis togs and other sportswear. The exit from the autostrada is Corciano; the factory is 500m (1,500 ft.) from the highway and is clearly marked. Local phone © 075/503-91.

MALO (MAC)
Via di Limite 164, Campi Bosenzio.

As soon as I gave away all my cashmeres because they gave me hot flashes, I discovered the Malo outlet where I almost wept with contempt for the insults of middle age. I was forced to buy cashmeres for others, but did get some suede shoes for myself.

Be still my heart—you could faint from the glory of all the colors, let alone the stunningly low prices. Two-ply cashmere sweaters were in the 91€ ($100) price range; four-ply were 136€ ($150). I don't know if I was there for a sale, or if this is the regular drill, but you take half off the price on the tag. Ask!

Note: This outlet is the closest to Florence, but has moved to this address rather recently, so there may be a conflict with other guidebooks. The sign outside not only says MAC, but uses the same typeface as MAC cosmetics, so it's confusing. Cope. If you are driving and want precise directions, call ℂ 055/894-53-06.

Many Americans are not familiar with the Malo brand because there are only a few Malo stores in the U.S. This is one of the top Italian brands of cashmere, and for a small pittance, you can buy sweaters that would retail from 273€ to 545€ ($300–$600). I could barely breathe, I was having so much fun.

By the way, Malo does make a few other things besides sweaters. Years ago my late husband bought the world's most chic bathing suit at a Malo store. They had hats and handbags when I was there, fabulous little suede slip-on shoes, and some fashions a la Donna Karan in cotton and silk. I was there in winter, so I would guess seasonal stuff turns up toward summer.

Chapter Seven

······················

VENICE

WELCOME TO VENICE

··

In season, Venice is people, people everywhere; you have to be a little bit clever to actually enjoy shopping, or even to want to set foot in a crowded shop. Not to worry: Buy yourself a straw boater—yes, from that tourist trap (TT) right over there—buy a bag of pigeon food, and hit the back alleys where you have to get lost to get found. Or follow a few of my tricks—last time I went to Venice, I stayed at the new Sofitel hotel on a private island across the lagoon from San Marco. You could take a private boat to San Marco, do your shopping thing, and then escape.

Venice and shopping are made for each other; you're going to have the time of your life—even in that crowded high season. In winter, the city can be a little bit chilly or damp, but the town is yours, and you will more than fill your senses . . . and your shopping bags. I went for New Year's Eve last year. The stores were open until almost the last moment, the weather was fair, the crowds were thin (although all the hotels were sold out), and the shopping was as much fun as ever.

- You can buy what they sell at Bergdorf Goodman for a fraction of the U.S. price.

- You can walk into an ordinary shop in Murano and pay 41€ ($45) for what would cost 10 times that in an ordinary shop in New York.
- You can load up on tourist junk, take it away from Venice, and turn it into great gifts for your loved ones—it won't even look like tourist junk.
- You can buy your dog a gondolier's hat and take pictures—I did it.
- You can wander around and never find where you are going and still manage to buy velvet espadrilles (fall season) on the Rialto bridge, pasta in the shape of sombreros (you stuff them), and magnifying glasses with Murano-glass handles . . . for a mere 27€ ($30).

Venetian Shopping History

Venice was founded in the 5th century by survivors fleeing from Lombard invaders after the fall of the Roman Empire. She provided a cultural and political link between Eastern and Western civilizations for many centuries; by the 13th century, the city was a leading (and very wealthy) port of trade. People have been shopping here ever since.

The absence of cars allows leisurely browsing of the shops, churches, piazzas, and palaces. Every area contains boutiques stocked with the lace, fine glass, paper goods, and leather items for which Venice has become famous. The best thing about shopping in Venice is that you are forced to walk just about everywhere—even if you are just a museum person, you still pass by the shops and can look in the windows.

Conversely, even the most dedicated shopper is going to get an extra surge of excitement just from walking by the churches and museums. In Venice, culture and clutter, of the retailing sort, are all tied into one very attractive bundle.

Most shopkeepers speak English and are quite accustomed to tourists. All shops are anxious for business. Adjustments in price will reflect just how anxious for business shopkeepers are—in season (Carnevale–Oct), when tourists are plentiful, prices are higher, and bargaining is unheard of. In winter, things are sweeter—and cheaper.

ARRIVING IN VENICE

By Plane

Although the Venice airport is a tad inconvenient, it makes European flight connections a breeze and is worth using if you can afford water-taxi connections. Note that if you take a water taxi to/from Marco Polo International Airport and Venice proper, it will cost about 73€ ($80).

By Train

To ride the regular express trains, I usually purchase an **Italian Rail Pass** (see chapter 2) or a **Eurailpass** . . . or simply buy a ticket from Milan and hop onboard the fast train to Venice. There are about 20 trains a day between Venice and Milan. Some go faster than others; the fastest train is 2 hours 40 minutes.

Sometimes I do second class, but if I'm worried about getting a seat at what might be a peak travel time, I buy a first-class seat and a seat reservation so that I have a specific seat assigned to me. My most recent trip in a first-class seat cost 27€ ($30) one-way and took a mere 3 hours. The concierge at the Hotel Principe de Savoia got me the ticket, so it couldn't have been easier. Also note that many of the main hotels in Milan are 5 minutes from the Centrale train station.

Learn how to read an Italian rail schedule, and allow yourself plenty of time for the asking of many, many questions. I once found an intercity train (fast train) on my timetable that appeared perfect—it was outbound from Venice and was stopping in Milan but was marked for Geneva. Had I merely read the board in the station, there was no way I could have known

about that train. If I'd taken the train marked Milano, I would have wasted 2 hours.

By Bus

If you are staying in Mestre or Treviso or in the 'burbs, you can take the bus into town—or the train.

By Ship

I don't need to tell you that Venice has been a favored cruise destination for, uh, centuries. Some of the most famous shipyards in the world are outside Venice, and many of today's modern ocean liners are built right there. The number of passengers in recent cruise history who have come to Venice by ship has increased enormously in the past 10 years: Some 1 million people a year are expected just as cruisers.

Ships disembark at VTP (Venezia Terminal Passeggeri), which is being renovated to handle the mob scene. The terminal has access for both ferries and cruise ships, and each area is color coordinated so that passengers can easily find the right check-in zones. For details, you can always call © 041/533-48-60.

Getting to Your Hotel

You certainly don't want to drive to Venice, but if you do, and have a rental car, you will have to leave it in one of the major parking lots (where you'll pay by the 24-hr. period) on the mainland in Mestre and come back later. So you'll probably be arriving by bus, train, or plane. No matter how you arrive, you will eventually need to arrange some sort of water transport (see below) to take you—and your luggage—to your hotel.

The key to smooth sailing, in all senses of the word, is to pack light and know that you can check baggage at the stations—even overnight or over many nights. In these days of international terrorism, it's not easy to find a place to leave unaccompanied baggage.

Some hotels will arrange to meet you and will handle luggage for you; many hotels have their own boats to take you back and forth from the airport. Put your Vuitton right here, madame. Fax or e-mail your hotel in advance of your trip to arrange to be met. You'll pay for the service, but it may make your trip a lot more pleasant.

There used to be porters who met the water bus *(vaporetto)* at the train station and then again at San Marco and would help you get to your hotel, but sometimes these guys are nowhere to be seen. This, then, is another reason to travel in winter; there were tons of them on my last December trip.

The more reasonable approach to local transportation is the vaporetto (plural: *vaporetti*). These water buses go around town in two different directions: one via the Grand Canal, the other via the Adriatic to San Marco. There are additional routes to various islands and specialty destinations. If you get on (or off) the water bus at the train station, you are at Ferrovia; the

Jenny Does Mestre: To Stay or Not To Stay

Just a hop, skip, and confusing bus ride away from beautiful Venice is not-as-beautiful Mestre.

Mestre is the equivalent of a suburb that surrounds a cool city; it strives to be cool too, but it's just not quite there. Originally, the town was a haven for tourists who didn't want to pay overinflated Venice prices for food and lodging, and perhaps it still is during the high season, but that's not what we found. Aaron and I were there in shoulder season and during a war, so prices in Venice were more flexible. But we didn't know that.

We decided to test Mestre because we thought Venice would be full and, since we had no hotel reservations, did not want to schlep around trying to figure out what to do. Getting off the train in Mestre, we wandered into the Hotel Information room at the train station to see what the town had to offer.

The "helpful" woman at the desk asked how much we wanted to spend in her delightful city. After hearing "about 50€ a night," she laughed, almost offensively, and said she didn't think she could find a place that low.

She told us about a "charming" little bed-and-breakfast, *La Residenza,* for 70€ ($77) per night. One catch, she warned: This charming little bed-and-breakfast provided a bed but no breakfast. Still, we bit. We were tired.

In order to get to our "bed," we had to go to another hotel, in the Piazza Ferretto, Hotel Vivit. The train station woman called and told them we were on our way and told us everything was square, after taking a small deposit.

Then the real fun began. After our 10€ ($11) cab ride for only a short distance and then a short walk through the piazza, we found the hotel. The innkeeper informed us that the B&B we had agreed to stay in was full. We would have to stay in the hotel that night (for the same price) and move to the B&B the next morning. We were too weary from traveling to argue. The room was cute. Small, but not uncomfortable. No frills, but no cockroaches, either.

The next morning we packed up our bags and marched them downstairs to the lobby, so we could get our key to our new accommodations. We told the concierge about our situation, to which he replied, "No, no, you rest here tonight." So, a little confused and apprehensive, we schlepped our bags back upstairs. Considering that we only had 1 day to be in Venice, the waste of all this time ticked away in our minds.

On checkout day, we went again down to the lobby, a little worried about what would occur as we paid the bill. We were expecting perhaps a different rate, a cheaper rate, as we had not gotten to stay in the "charming" B&B we were hoping for. We thought wrong. Not only did we not get the room for cheaper, even though the man told us, "is cheaper here, you pay same price," but he then informed us they will not accept credit cards, and there is a cash machine just outside.

Aaron rushed off to get cash when I noticed something out of the corner of my eye: MasterCard, Visa, and American Express stickers posted on the hotel desk. They did take credit cards. We inquired about it and they quickly told us that yes, they do in fact take credit cards, they just couldn't with us because we were getting "a special price." In other words, we were getting screwed.

I think that Mestre has a big business preying on tourists, students, and young people who come to town to save money but then waste time and don't get the best deals. While we were in Venice, we went into a randomly chosen three-star hotel near San Marco. We asked about price, haggled a bit, and were offered a nice room for 50€ ($55), far less than that in Mestre.

The moral of this story? If you are going to Venice, go to Venice. Not Mestre.

bus station is Piazzale Roma. The lines (and routes) are clearly marked; some lines offer express service with fewer stops. You can get a schedule at the Centro Informazioni ACTV at Piazzale Roma.

Buy a ticket before you board, if possible; it costs slightly more if purchased onboard. You can also buy tickets at any

Central Venice

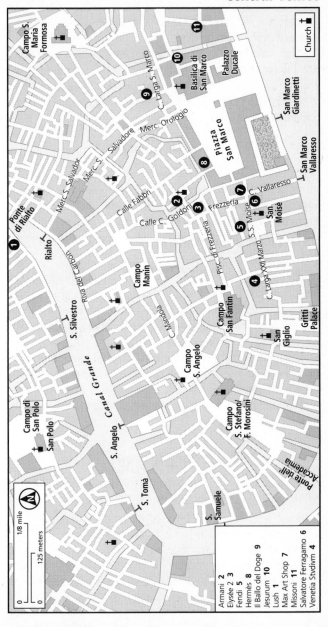

Church ✚

Campo S. Maria Formosa

Ponte di Rialto

C. Larga S. Marco

Basilica di San Marco

Palazzo Ducale

Merc. Orologio

San Marco Giardinetti

Merc. S. Salvador

Merc. S. Salvadore

Piazza San Marco

San Marco Vallaresso

Calle Fabbri

Frezzeria

C. Vallaresso

Calle C. Goldoni

San Moisè

Pisc. di Frezzeria

S.S. Moisè

Rialto

Riva del Carbon

Campo Manin

C. Larga XXII Marzo

Gritti Palade

Campo San Fantin

C. Mariola

San Giglio

Canal Grande

Campo di San Polo

San Polo

S. Silvestro

Campo S. Angelo

Campo S. Stefano/ F. Morosini

S. Angelo

Ponte dell' Accademia

S. Tomà

S. Samuele

0   1/8 mile
0   125 meters

Armani **2**
Elysée 2 **3**
Fendi **5**
Hermès **8**
Il Ballo del Doge **9**
Jesurum **10**
Lush **1**
Max Art Shop **7**
Missoni **11**
Salvatore Ferragamo **6**
Venetia Stvdivm **4**

shop displaying a sign that says ACTV. Prices have more than doubled in the past 2 years.

The water bus may be a little confusing at first, since there are different little floating stations for the different lines. Read the destinations listed, buy your ticket accordingly, and give it to the ticket taker when he comes around to ask for it. Sometimes he doesn't ask.

Getting Around

Walk. Get lost. Enjoy it. Take the vaporetto. And yes, take a ride in a gondola at least once in your life. Do not buy a multitrip vaporetto taxi until you have vaguely costed it out in your head. I lost money on my last one because I did so much walking and didn't really use the pass often enough for it to be worth its cost.

About Addresses

No city in Italy has a more screwy system for writing addresses; they are virtually impossible to read or to use because there is one address for mail and another for the actual building. My advice? Forget addresses. Walk; enjoy.

If you must get to a specific resource and haven't found it in your general lost-and-found, search-and-shop technique, ask your hotel's concierge to mark it for you on a map. Also take business cards that have maps on them so that you can get back to a specific source.

SLEEPING IN VENICE

My best money-saving trick? Don't sleep in Venice. Come in for a day trip. Padua is only 40km (25 miles) from Venice, an easy commute. Venice is just a 3-hour train ride from Milan. For something like Carnevale, where you want to be part of the action and then get out as fast as you can before you have a screaming breakdown (some 250,000 people jam San Marco each day on the Carnevale weekends!), this is an ideal ploy.

But since you've probably come to stay for a night or 2 or 3, then just about any hotel will do. Some happen to be a little more magical than others. In Venice, you really pay for location. Since I tend to be there for only a short period of time and every moment is precious to me, I splurge on the hotel. As a repeat customer, I also know my way around from only a handful of hotels; not getting lost is money in the bank of time.

Super Shopping Hotels

BAGLIONI LUNA
San Marco 1243, Bocca di Paizza (ACTV: San Marco).

This is one of my best finds lately because of the combination of location, luxury, and price. Right off San Marco, this is an ideal shopping location that also has strong promotions. It's not inexpensive, and it is a member of Leading Hotels of the World. There is no toll-free reservations phone number. Local phone © 041/52-89-840. www.baglionihotels.com.

HOTEL BAUER
Campo San Moisè, San Marco 1459 (ACTV: San Marco or San Moisè).

Few moments in my life will I cherish with as much passion as when my private water taxi pulls up to the side of the hotel and I enter through the "water door." The Bauer is my palace, and I am the princess when my boat comes in. I especially like the approach from the water because the front door on the street is very 1950s, but the rear is very 1450s.

Rooms have recently been renovated in this hotel—my last room had 6m (20-ft.) ceilings, a gilt wooden bed, and white embroidered damask hung on the walls and bed. Naturally, there was a view of the Grand Canal. Add to that the fabulous bathroom amenities, the best shopping location in town (across the walkway from Versace, next door to the new Ferragamo, and two steps from American Express—how convenient), and Leading Hotels of the World charm, and, well, you can't beat it. As an added plus, I had breakfast on the seventh floor with all of Venice spread around me.

For reservations from the U.S., call © **800/223-6800**. Local phone 041/52-07-022. Fax 041/52-75-57. www.lhw.com/bauer.

HOTEL DANIELI
Riva degli Schiavoni, Castello 4196 (ACTV: San Zaccaria).

The Danieli also has a good shopping location; it's on the other side of San Marco from the Bauer. It, too, is a renovated palace, done more in the Byzantine fashion. Located on the far edge of San Marco, it even has its own gondola stop: San Zaccaria. Best yet, there is a rooftop restaurant and terrace with a view that cannot adequately be described. Have tea or drinks here, or just stop by to use the bathroom. Walk into the lobby, take the back elevator marked for the Terrace (Terrazza), and go up. Bathrooms are to your right. Then step onto the terrace and experience heaven on earth. Who could ask for anything more?

For reservations from the U.S., call © **800/221-2340**. Local phone 041/52-26-480. Fax 041/52-00-208. www.starwood.com/danieli.

HOTEL MONACO & GRAND CANAL
Calle Vallaresso, San Marco 1325 (ACTV: San Marco).

The hotel is not quite as grand as others, but it's not quite as expensive either . . . and the location can't be beat, nor can the story or the details. This is the hotel the Benetton family owns, and some of the public space is magazine perfect. Note the total renovation, which combines the old-fashioned Italian rococo with moderne, and don't miss the fabulous upstairs lobby for a drink or hot chocolate. Bathrooms (basement) are also grand; I really wanted to swipe the liquid soap. So chic.

Reservations from the U.S. are made through Prima Hotels (© **800/447-7462**). Local phone 041/52-00-211. Fax 041/52-00-501. mailbox@hotelmonaco.it.

SOFITEL VENEZIA L'ISOLA
Laguna di San Marco (ACTV: San Marco then private shuttle);
Mailing address: c/o Giardini Papadopoli.

Oh me oh my, o sole mio. I have seen many hotels in my time, but this is something else. Okay, first a little background. This hotel was created out of a hospital on a private island—the hospital, built by Mussolini, has that really neat 1930s architecture. The private island is directly across from San Marco; it is planted with zillions of trees and plants that give off oxygen because the hospital was for those with lung problems. And I am just warming up.

Now Sofitel has bought the place and totally redone and expanded it so that this is really a resort and conference space as well as a hotel. The theme is related to travel through the ages, and the style is slick and stunning; the details—such as the private boat landing (indoors)—will make you swoon. The rooms, most of which have terraces with views, are gorgeous but not stiffly decorated, so you get more of a relaxed feeling. And, yes, there is a chapel so you can pray . . . or have a wedding.

In most cities, I like to be in the action. However, because Venice gets so crowded, this hotel is the perfect solution. There is a private shuttle boat back and forth to San Marco. Prices begin around 272€ ($300). For reservations from the U.S., call © **800/221-4542**. Local phone 041/335-667-0918. www. sofitel.com. *Warning:* There is another Sofitel in Venice (see below); don't get the two mixed up.

Four-Star Finds

HOTEL BISANZIO
Calle della Pietà, Castello 3651 (ACTV: San Zaccaria).

I was just walking along past the Danieli on the way to my girlfriend's restaurant (Al Covo) and on the sidewalk was a sign for this hotel, so I followed it, and lo, a find. It's set back from

Riva degli Schiavoni, but it's brilliantly located and charming and real and funky and affordable. It's a Best Western Hotel with only 40 rooms.

For reservations from the U.S., call © **800/528-1234**. Local phone 041/42-03-100. Local fax 041/52-04-114. www.bisanzio. com.

HOTEL FLORA
San Marco 2283A (ACTV: San Marco).

In the heart of the shopping district, this hidden hotel of infinite charm will steal your heart, as will its location and price. Find the hotel through a tiny alley that leads to its courtyard. The hotel is small and charming, with a hint of funky elegance. You'll do best to book by calling and developing a personal relationship with the hotel itself—it is family owned. It's air-conditioned; breakfast is included in the room rate, as are taxes. A single room with bath costs about 164€ ($180); a twin room with bath is 182€ ($200). This hotel is technically rated with three stars, not four . . . but I give it four. Local phone © **041/ 52-05-844.** www.hotelflora.it

HOTEL SATURNIA
San Marco 2398 (ACTV: San Marco).

This hotel is not far from the Bauer (described above) and almost across the road from the Flora, but is far more visible. It's also a midpoint hotel between the two extremes: The Flora is less expensive and less formal than the Bauer. Rates at this hotel vary with the season—the least-expensive price for a double room is about 227€ ($250) and the high is about 364€ ($400), still making it a bargain by local standards. Breakfast buffet and taxes are included; there are demi-pensione and full-pensione prices depending on your needs. This hotel can be booked in the U.S. through SRS-Worldhotels (© **800/223-5652**; www. srs-worldhotels.com). Local phone 041/52-08-377. www.hotel saturnia.it.

SOFITEL VENEZIA
San Croce 245, Giardini Papadopoli (ACTV: Piazzale Roma).

First off, don't get this mixed up with the listing above—a very different Sofitel property. This is a lovely hotel, but it's not what I would call a drop-dead luxury hotel, nor is it a resort—although it is right on a garden. It's a bread-and-butter hotel for those who want luxury but are watching dollars. This hotel is located almost across the water from the train station, so it puts you into a totally different part of town—you do get tour groups and you don't get spoilt silly, but you are in a more "real" area of town and can walk or water taxi around.

I like the hotel and enjoyed staying here, but the visit was much more of a real-people experience than being in any of the palace hotels or being in the center of San Marco. The hotel has several giveaways that provide extra value—books on walking tours and hidden back-street historical finds. Also, because of the location, you wander round less touristy parts of Venice, which is yummy. Also, there are many promotional deals. Rooms begin at 275€ ($250) per night. To reserve a room from the U.S., call **800/221-4542.** Local phone 041/710-400. www.sofitel.com.

Snack & Shop

AL COVO
Campiello della Pescaria, Castello.

Okay, so this isn't on your ordinary list of legends and land-marks, but it's part of mine because Diane is from Texas and comes to me through my official foodie friends. Her husband is the chef, and he is getting increasingly famous and recognized by American authorities, so book now. The restaurant is on the far side of the Danieli, far enough away from the tourists to be pure and family-oriented. The food is fabulous (try Diane's wal-nut cake), and you will get the special treatment you crave from a great team. If you think I'm the only one onto this place, forget it. It came into my family of journalists because Marcella Hazan brought Faith Heller Willinger here, and Faith brought Patricia Schultz, and she told me, and . . . . For reservations, call © **041/52-23-812**. Note that Al Covo now sells its own products as well.

Caffè Florian
Piazza San Marco, San Marco.

So you sit there at sunset on the Piazza San Marco at a little table, drinking a strawberry version of the Bellini because it's strawberry season and Florian won't use canned peaches like they do at Harry's (tsk, tsk). There's a tiny band shell, and they play schmaltzy music and all you want to do is sing and dance and laugh and cry. And that's before you see the bill. Just once before you die. No wonder Napoléon said that San Marco was Europe's most elegant drawing room. Ah, yes, they sell the china, the dishes, and their own house brand of coffee and tea and even spumante. A fabulous gift to bring home for someone who knows Venice. © **041/520-5641.**

Harry's Bar
Calle Vallaresso, San Marco 1323.

There is a Harry's Bar, there is even a Harry (call him Arrigo), and no, Harry's Bar is not in the Gritti Palace, as many think. It is where Hemingway and the gang liked to hang out and is located halfway between San Marco and the Gritti. This is the home of the famous Bellini. I have sipped Bellinis at Harry's—it was swell, and, yes, I saw everyone I knew. I have wondered just why Harry's is so famous and later discovered that the thing to do is not sip Bellinis (this is for tourists) but to dine upstairs with a chef whom many consider one of the best in the world. Me? I sit downstairs and nibble on the croque-monsieur, which is fried to a crisp and makes a super lunch or snack. I also like their *latte macchiato:* milk stained with coffee. © **041/528-5777.**

HOSTARIA AL RUSTEGHI
San Bartolomio 5529.

This is an itty-bitty, teeny-weeny deli/sandwich shop that you won't find if you aren't looking for it or are headed to the public toilets near the Coin department store. I always stop here to pick up little sandwiches for the train ride back to Milan. It's open from 9:30am to 3pm, Monday through Saturday.

TERRAZZA DANIELI
Hotel Danieli, Riva degli Schiavoni, San Marco 4196.

The rooftop of the Hotel Danieli has a wonderful restaurant called the Terrace (Terrazza). The view is spectacular, and the food ain't bad. Ian and I always try to book a lunch here while in Venice, but I have also been known to make this my first stop after I arrive via train from Milan in the morning. A mere cup of coffee overlooking the Adriatic is enough to make your heart sing. You can afford coffee here, so don't miss it!

THE SHOPPING SCENE

Please understand the most basic law of shopping in Venice: Because of transportation, everything is essentially imported to Venice. That means higher prices than anywhere else in Italy. It means you'll pay top dollar for a Coca-Cola, a roll of film, or a pair of Italian designer shoes. Also, this isn't really a city for designer shopping, although you can buy most everything here.

Your best buys will always be locally made souvenir items, which are quite moderately priced. Also note that the tourist junk here is far more attractive than that found in any other major Italian city. There's also more than the usual number of hidden resources, since this is the kind of town where the best stuff is definitely hidden.

As for the souvenirs, I truly believe that at the beginning of each season the retailers in Venice have a meeting and peg the prices to exactly what the euro is trading at against the dollar.

The Best Buys in Venice

I have been known to go nuts for glass, handbags, paper goods, and local crafts—all can be best buys in Venice. More important, even if you've seen these items for less money elsewhere, they offer good value as items bought in Venice to be remembered as such and cherished. You don't want to buy your Carnevale mask in Rome just because you might get it cheaper there, do you? Marbleized paper items cost less in Florence, but only slightly less.

Glass   Murano is the glass capital of Italy, and Venice is the front door to the glass candy store. Even when it's expensive, glass usually costs less here than if bought in the U.S. Also in the glass category are mirrors and chandeliers. Art glass, a sub-category, is very expensive but more available than in any other city. If you buy, be sure you spring for shipping and insurance and know what to do if anything goes wrong. You do not want to hand-carry a one-of-a-kind glass masterpiece, no matter how stable you think your hands are.

Masks   Carnevale has its own rituals—mask-wearing among them. The city now sells scads of masks in every format, from cheap plastic ones to incredibly crafted ones made of leathers or feathers. For the best ones, get to the back streets and alleys and away from the TTs (tourist traps).

Silks   When you see the incredibly pleated teeny-tiny Fortuny silk baggies for jewelry or potpourri for 27€ ($30) at Stadium (Venetia Stvdivm, now expanded to six branches), you'll know why Marco Polo came home.

The Worst Buys in Venice

If you can help it, don't buy:

- Clothing. Not a good buy in Venice unless you need it or hit a sale or bargain.
- Designer items. Hermès is more expensive in Venice than in Milan.

- Film. Film is expensive everywhere in Europe; it costs about 14€ ($15) a roll in Venice. Besides, if you don't already have a digital camera, you should buy one instead of another pair of shoes.
- Fake designer handbags. Give me a break.

The San Marco Rule of Shopping

If you are looking for the best prices on the average tourist items—from souvenirs to snacks—my rule is simple: Avoid San Marco.

San Marco is the center of the tourist universe and therefore the center of the highest prices. The farther you go from San Marco, the more the prices drop. Shop on the island where the train station is and you'll find the best prices in town.

If you insist on TTs, hit the ones way past San Marco and the Hotel Danieli and on the way to the public gardens. You'll save as much as .90€ ($1) per item. You'll also avoid the most severe crowds.

The Gondoliers

I don't care how touristy you think it is—riding in a gondola is part of the Venetian experience and something you must do at least once. While you can be hustled by a gondolier, there are fixed prices for their services that vary from season to season. Even if you have to save up for the experience, this is one treat that you shouldn't miss. *Tip:* Take your gondola ride at high tide—at low tide you'll have a view of the scummy exposed sides of the canals.

When there aren't as many rich tourists around, prices drop. The winter price can be 60€ ($66); the spring price for the same service is 65€ ($72), but you can try to bargain. Night service, any time of the year, is 75€ ($83) beginning at 8pm. These are the prices for 50 minutes of sailing time with up to six persons in the boat. For each additional 25-minute period after your first 50 minutes, the flat rate is 35€ ($39). You are also expected to tip.

Aaron's Turn: The Gondoliers

It had been my romantic notion to take my girl for a gondola ride once we got to Venice. In fact, one of the reasons we went to Venice was to realize this dream. Ah well, live and learn.

We quoted a few gondoliers, and the standard price seemed to be 80€ ($88) for a 50- to 60-minute ride. At least that was the standard answer we got; the going rate is supposed to be much cheaper, according to a chart in a small tourist booklet they give you at your hotel, which quotes 65€ ($72) as the proper rate.

One gondolier in particular said that he would give us the short ride (30–40 min.) for 60€ ($66). (How anybody thinks that 40 min. on a gondola isn't enough for them truly eludes me.) We accepted his offer.

I kept hoping that the guy would start singing to us in Italian, so I kept humming "Volare" under my breath in the hopes that he might subconsciously have the urge to bust into it Dean Martin style. No such luck. He did, however, whistle some cheesy elevator-jazz song for 20 seconds before losing interest in the music and us.

Okay, that was the official line as taught to me by the city. In person, I find that knowing these prices is helpful, as is carrying around a copy of the freebie booklet *Un Ospite di Venezia*, which is given away at your hotel and has a section on gondola prices. You bargain fiercely or find someone you like and forget the money. Gondoliers do 45 minutes, not 50; they want far more than the guidelines say they should get; they are especially not friendly when there are lots of tourists around. Their idea of a great fare is a chump who says "yes" to the quoted price and then lays a tip on top.

The gondolier will sing to you—it's part of the deal—but if you ask him to stop the boat en route so that you can get out for a look-see while he waits, or to provide extra services (other than posing in your family snapshot), he will expect more money.

All things are negotiable, but try to have a handle on costs before you get in—nothing spoils the magic more than a fight about money after the fact.

I've seen as many as six people squished into a gondola, so the cost can be amortized into a reasonable expense. You have not seen Venice until you've seen it from a gondola—it is worth the money. If you want an update or inside fact, call the hot line: ✆ 041/528-50-75.

Shopping Hours

High season is March to October, and shops are open from 9am until 12:30 or 1pm, and then are open from about 3 or 3:30 to 7:30pm. If lunchtime closings bore you, remember that the shops on the nearby island of Murano do not close for lunch.

Off season, most Venice shops are closed on Monday until 3pm. During Carnevale weekends, many things are open no matter what day or what time of the day. For Sunday shopping tips, see below.

Sunday Shopping

Venice, because of its high tourist population, is one of the few cities in Italy that does not close up on Sunday. *Si, si,* **Emporio Armani**, **Trussardi**, and **Versace** and the like are open on Sunday afternoon. Just about everyone is open on Sundays—but closed on Mondays.

Sunday is also a good day to visit the islands; shops are open on both Murano and Burano. Check with your concierge for exact opening and closing times, but plan a day trip to Murano as early as you like—the fires are crackling at 9am, and shops are open nonstop until 4 or 5pm. On Burano, Sunday hours tend to be 10am to 1:30pm.

Holiday Hours

While Venice does have the most liberal of all the holiday hours, stores do close up early on Christmas Eve and New Year's Eve. Some stores are actually open on New Year's Day—but late in the day, after noon. If there are tourists, there are some stores open.

Street Vendors

One of the glories of Venice is the street action—not just the throngs of tourists, but the zillions of street vendors who make it possible for you to do very thorough shopping in Venice without ever setting foot inside a store.

The street vendors stay open until the light begins to fade, which in the height of summer can be quite late. There are illegal salespeople hawking wares from blankets all over town—they usually operate during lunch hours and after hours as there is less chance they will be arrested then. Louis Vuitton, anyone? Cartier perhaps? "This is real Chanel, lady."

Like other retailers, street vendors and cart dealers rig their prices according to the crowd. Therefore, the farther you walk from San Marco, the better the prices at kiosks and carts.

Fairs & Mercatini

San Moisè is the location of many outdoor fairs, from antiques markets to the regular Christmas market. Vendors set up booths and sell from 9am to 8pm.

Buying Venetian Glass

I confess that up until the minute I walked into Bergdorf Goodman one fateful day, I thought that only old ladies liked Venetian glass. Then I took one look at a bowl filled with hand-blown Murano glass in the form of colorful hard candies and flipped out. Such style, such finesse, such color. If this is the passion of little old ladies, sign me up. I've had a sweet tooth ever since. Bergdorf's gets about $12 per glass candy. In Venice you'll pay from .90€ to 4.50€ ($1–$5).

Once you get hooked on glass candies, a whole new world of glass design opens up. Fazzoletto (handkerchief vases) will surely be next. While you may not flip out for pink glass goblets with hand-painted roses and baroque gold doodads, you will gasp when you take in the designs made from the early 1920s right through the 1950s—all highly collectible works of art when they are signed by a big-name glass house. Even post-1950s glass is collectible: What you buy today (if you buy wisely) will be happily inherited by your children.

The colored strings of glass swirled into clear, white, or colored glass are called threads; the value of a piece—aside from the signature—is based on the composition of form, color, and threads or patterns; the way the piece reflects light should also be taken into account, although this is easy to look for in a vase and impossible to consider in a piece of candy. Smoked glass is hot now, as is glass matted with ash, and deco glass. Crizzled glass is crickly-crackled glass with a nice effect, but it won't last over the centuries and makes a bad investment.

The important names to remember are **Venini, Seguso, Brandolini, Poli, Barovier, Toso,** and **Pauly.** A vase from the 1940s went for $125,000 at auction at Christie's in Geneva in 1990; prices continue to rise. New pieces are not inexpensive as they are considered serious artwork.

Famous designers create styles for glass houses, just as they do for furniture firms. The designer's name associated with a famous glass house can make a piece even more valuable. Do check for signatures, labels, or accompanying materials that uphold the provenance of your piece. If you are buying older pieces of glass—even from the 1950s or so—check the condition carefully.

If you are trading up and browsing for some of the important stuff, here's a quick-fix dictionary to make you sound like a maven:

Vetro battute   Flat beaten glass with a scored surface.

Vetro sommerso   Glass in bubbled, lumpy form is layered over the glass item—the rage in the mid-1930s.

Vetro pennelato   No, it doesn't have pieces of penne pasta in it—this is painted glass with swirly streaks of dancing color that zip across the body of the item inside the glass.

Vetro pulegoso   This is bubbled glass with the tiny bubbles inside the glass—it will never be confused with sommerso when you see the two in person.

Vetro inciso   Flat beaten glass with scored lines all running in the same direction.

Vetro pezzato   Patchwork made of various pieces of colored glass almost in mosaic form; introduced in the early 1950s.

Vetro a retorti   Twisted glass with the threads swirled within the body of the work.

Murrina   Slices of colored glass rods encircled with gold and sold as charms or pendants.

I must take some time here to warn you about the hawkers who offer you free trips to Murano and act as guides, etc. They are dangerous, emotionally and physically, and should be avoided. They not only get a percentage of what you buy, but make their living by preying on tourists and telling half truths or lies that might convince you to buy something you weren't certain about.

If you want the free boat ride, ask your hotel concierge to book it. If you can afford to get there on your own, do so, and buy only from the houses of good repute. If you ship, be prepared to wait a very, very long time for your package to arrive.

While we are into warnings, I got a note from a reader who asked a glass shop about a specific address in Murano and was wrongly told that the shop had closed and was encouraged to do business where she was asking.

Shipping

Anyone seriously considering glass or mirrors or chandeliers is also thinking about shipping. Almost all the stores, even the TTs, will volunteer to ship for you. I am not big on shipping, especially expensive items, but I have noticed that things shipped from Venice do tend to reach their destination—eventually. I have had several nervous letters from readers who have waited many months in a state of panic. My basic advice is simple: Don't fall in love with anything you cannot carry yourself. Always buy from a reputable dealer and pay with a credit card that has a protection plan on it.

Shopping Neighborhoods

Most of the shops are found in the historical and artistic center, between **Ponte di Rialto** (the Rialto Bridge) and **Piazza San Marco**. A new area of mostly designer shops has been evolving at **San Moisè**.

Looking at a map can be very confusing because of the cobweb of interconnecting streets, bridges, and canals. Finding an address can be equally difficult, as many streets and shops show no numbers, or the numbers are clear, but the street they are on is not clear.

Merceria One main street will carry you from Piazza San Marco to the Rialto Bridge: Merceria. It hosts hundreds of shops. Many of the shopping streets branch off this one thoroughfare, or are very close. Merceria is not a water-bus stop (San Marco is), but if you get yourself to Piazza San Marco and stand at the clock tower with your back to the water, Merceria will be the little street jutting off the arcade right in front of you. If you still can't find it, walk into any shop and ask. You need not speak Italian.

Piazza San Marco The four rows of arcades that frame Piazza San Marco can be considered a neighborhood unto itself. Three of the arcades create a U shape around the square; the fourth is at a right angle to one of the ends of the U. There are easily a hundred shops here—a few of the shops are showrooms for glass firms and a few sell touristy knickknacks, but most are jewelry or glass shops (or cafes). Although many of these shops have been in business for years and some of them have extremely famous names, this is the high-rent part of Venice and isn't very funky. I was quite shocked at the high turnover I noticed on my last visit: Many old, reliable firms have packed up. One of the newer names to the area is **Michaela Frey,** a Viennese jeweler known for her enamel works who does a fabulous Saint Marks Square bangle bracelet for those who can handle a pricey souvenir.

Behind San Marco   Now, here's the tricky part. "Behind San Marco" is my name for the area that includes **San Moisè** and **San Giglio** (this way to the Hotel Bauer) and is best represented by the big-time shopping drag called **Via XXII Marzo.** This street comes off of Piazza San Marco from behind and forms an L with the square and Merceria. The farther you get from San Marco, the less commercial.

Frezzeria   This is the main shopping street also behind San Marco, but it goes off to your right if your back is to San Marco and you're facing the road to the Hotel Bauer and American Express. It's a small alley of a street that twists and turns more than most, and it's packed with small shops, many of which are artisan or crafts shops. There are also some designer stores woven into the texture of the landscape.

Giglio   This is a secret part of town tucked back and away from the tourist areas. It's also the home of the **Gritti Palace.** Unless a shop is actually on the piazza, it probably will have a San Moisè address, so you may get confused. Not to worry. Aside from the antiques shops, there's a good paper store and a little market for food for the train or a picnic. It's very civilized and quite divine back here.

Rialto Bridge   They might just as well have named it the "Retailo" Bridge—not only are there pushcarts and vendors in the walkway before the bridge, but there are also shops going all the way up and down the bridge itself. The stores are not

like the crumbling, charming, old shops that line the Ponte Vecchio in Florence; they are teeny-bopper shops, leather-goods
stores, and even sporting-goods stores. Despite the huge number of street vendors from Piazza San Marco to Campo San
Zaccaria, street vendors here sell things I've never seen before.
Most of it is extremely touristy junk.

Over the Bridge   Once across the Rialto, you'll hit a two-
pronged trading area. In the arcades behind the street vendors
to the left are established shops; in the streets and to your right
are greengrocers, food vendors, cheese stalls, and, in summer,
little men selling little pieces of melon. You can have a walking feast for lunch in any season.

Once you make it past the immediate arcades, bear left and
follow the shops and crowds toward **San Polo.** The shops here
are a little more of the real-people nature and a little less expensive. On the other hand, a fair number of them are smaller
branches of the big designer shops found on the big island.

Piazzale Roma   This is by no means a hot retailing area, but
it is where the bus station is and where you will get your
vaporetto if you come in from the airport, or if you come by
bus. (The train station is not here.) Where there are tourists,
there are shops. In the case of Venice, or Venice in summer,
where there are tourists, there are scads of street vendors selling everything from T-shirts like the one worn by your favorite
gondolier to plates of the Doge's Palace.

Shopping Murano

Two different experiences are to be had here on the island of
glassblowers—so watch out and don't blame me if you hate
it. It can be very touristy or very special—it depends on how
you organize your time, as well as what season you visit. Go
by vaporetto in season and it can be a zoo. Go by private boat,
tour a glass factory, wander town, and then take the vaporetto
back: It's easy, it's inexpensive, and it's fun. It can even be glorious depending on the weather, the crowds, and your appetite
for colored glass.

Jenny's Turn: From Mestre with Baci

Mestre: So, you have decided to stay in Mestre, but how do you get to Venice? There is a quick bus that will take you there for a mere .70€ (75¢). The tickets can be bought at the newsstand; they have to be validated once you are on the bus. Like other European cities, the transportation authority works on the honor system, so don't be surprised if your ticket isn't checked. Just make sure you get on the bus going the right way. We took the bus going in the wrong direction and didn't know until we were at the end of the line. We had to wait an hour on the off-bus and then another 40 minutes to ride the line all the way back to where we started and then to Venice. A trip that should have taken 10 minutes took us about 2½ hours.

Meanwhile, even though your main idea is to visit Venice, you aren't dead and there are a few places to see in Mestre. If you plan on staying in Mestre, Piazza Ferretto is the place to go for all your young, hip shopping needs. This charming square offers enchanting cafes and the latest trendy Euro-styles. Favorite shops right on the piazza include . . .

Capelletto   Mostly shoes and handbags, some clothing, all big-name Italian designers (Prada, Gucci, Valentino). Prices on shoes range from about 91€ to 545€ ($100–$600).

Nara Camice   Dress shirts and ties for men and women. Very hip, very young. Think rock star at the Grammys. Moderate prices.

Reds   For the trendiest of high-school girls. Very cheap, cute, and colorful designs. Prices are very low, but quality isn't wonderful.

Caberlotte   Italian specialty goods and gourmet food market. Great selection of candies, liqueurs, and oils. If the Italian cheeses and wines are too foreign for your distinguished American likes, fear not: They also sell brands like Duncan Hines and Campbell's.

On Sunday, most showrooms (and their adjoining shops) are open from 9am to 4pm. TTs open midday. Sunday on Murano can be heaven. Take no. 5 at San Zaccaria, in front of the Danieli. The visit to Murano can be combined with a trip to Burano (take no. 12), or you can turn around and come back home. It's a long day if you combine both islands.

Murano is also the perfect lunchtime adventure when stores in Venice might be closed. Do not bring small children or strollers with you.

If you want to take a private boat to the island, call one of the glass factories to come get you. Yes, you are obligated to tour the factory, but you aren't obligated to buy. Besides, the tour is fabulous. It's a perfect Sunday adventure; Sunday is a big day on Murano because they cannot close down the furnaces since the temperature must stay constant, but the workers don't work, so there are demonstrations and tours.

If you go by public transportation, you will arrive in the heart of Murano. When you get off the boat at Murano, you'll know it by the giant signs that say *fornace* (furnace). You have two choices, really: to work the area or to realize quickly that this is one of the biggest tourist traps known to humankind. Walk briskly toward the museum and then head for the lighthouse.

By the way, you can also get a free ride to the island by private boat if you go with a hawker, but you *don't* want to do this! He gets 30% of what you spend in a secret kickback, and you get a lot of pressure to buy. But if you can take the heat, you will be escorted to the *fornace*. And it may be hell, so beware!

Hawkers will automatically gravitate to you; you need not even look for them. It's better to ask your hotel concierge to contact someone from a proper factory for you.

Glass with Class

ARCHIMIDE SEGUSO
Fondamenta Serenella, Murano.

One of the masters of the glass universe. There's also a showroom in Venice.

BAROVIER & TOSO
Fondamenta Vetrai 28, Murano.

This is a very trendy showroom with the latest designs in hot colors and sophisticated styles. They will ship for you at moderate prices, but expect to pay several hundred dollars for a vase. This is serious art, folks, so if you're looking for cheap gifts to send home, forget it.

FOSCARINI
Fondamenta Serenella, Murano.

This is a real showroom for important lighting fixtures that look like they were imported from outer space.

SENT
Fondamenta Serenella, Murano.

This is a double showroom with jewelry and home furnishings. It's very modern and very chic.

VENINI
Fondamenta Serenella, Murano.

The showroom on Murano is open to the trade only, and then only by appointment. Drat. There's a showroom at San Marco for mere mortals.

Other Glass Resources

For good, traditional showrooms that have it all, try either of the resources below. To find these shops, walk from the main drag toward the lighthouse and you'll wander into a far less touristy world and a hidden street (Viale Garibaldi) of more glassblowers and shops. Once at the lighthouse, round the turn following the water (there's a sidewalk) to find several more glass showrooms. Both have boat service and will pick you up at your hotel in town and return you when you are ready to go back.

BERENGO GALLERY
Fondamente Vetrai 109A, Murano.

This listing came from a reader who bought a piece and loved the experience.

VETRERIA COLONNA FORNACE
Fondamenta Vetrai 10–11, Murano.

This is another huge firm that will pick you up at your hotel and let you tour their scads of rooms of stuff. For pickup, call ✆ 041/73-93-89. I have enjoyed hours shopping here.

VETRERIA FOSCARI
Fondamenta dei Battuti 5, Murano.

I asked the concierge at the Bauer to pick a source for me, curious to see what he would suggest, and was pleased to find that this was his choice. They sent a boat for me and picked me up at my hotel, then returned me there when I was ready to go home. I even got a Coke along the way. A true delight. I keep going back, even though the source has passed on to another family member and I don't always stay at the Bauer.

The showroom is made up of a series of salons, organized by category of goods and by price. One room is devoted to chandeliers, other rooms to glassware. You'll also find beads and just about anything else you can imagine.

To get them to pick you up, call ✆ 041/73-95-40 at least 1 day in advance.

Shopping Burano

Although Murano and Burano sound like twin cities, they are not. But if you visit the two in the same afternoon (take the water bus from the lighthouse on Murano to Burano; it runs hourly, but go there for the exact schedule so that you can plan your time accordingly), you can sightsee and do some shopping at the same time. Many stores in Burano are open on Sunday afternoon, so you can combine the two islands in a fabulous Sunday outing.

As touristy and crass as Murano can be, Burano is totally different—I don't happen to like it as much, but I can see the natural, homespun attraction. Certainly the colors of the houses are divine. The shopping is awfully touristy. I get the feeling that Murano is in the glass business, and Burano is in the tourist business; there's something in the subtext of the air in Burano that lacks wonder. The lace is rarely handmade; there are few really good shops. But if you like to see, to stroll, and to avoid the throngs of pushing people in San Marco, this is a wonderful side trip. Don't think of it as a shopping adventure; rather, take your artistic eye and just enjoy.

You may want to poke into the fish market, **Fondamenta Pescheria,** held daily in the morning only—not that you're going to buy much, but it's fun and picturesque.

The lace-making school is the **Scuola di Merletti,** Piazza Galuppi (© **041/73-00-34**). The school is closed on Monday, and open from 10am to 4pm on Sunday and from 9am to 6pm Tuesday through Saturday.

The boat to Burano from Murano is as big as the ferry that takes you to Nantucket, and you will have the same sense of adventure. Burano is the third stop, so don't have a breakdown wondering when and where to get off (the 1st stop is Mazzorbo; the 2nd is Torcello). And yes, it's a bit of a schlep, so you'll be on the boat for a while.

When you arrive you'll see a narrow street lined with shops and think you are in heaven. That's because you haven't been in the shops yet. Pretty soon, you'll think you are in Hong Kong.

Here's the story of the woman in Venice who was buying a lace tablecloth. She had it spread out around her and draped all over—she was oooohing and aaaahing over it, but I knew it was from Hong Kong (like most of the lace in Venice) and I didn't know if I should tell her or not. Well, I didn't say a word because I didn't want to ruin her experience, but readers, you should know the facts.

If you don't like the lace shops, never mind; just take a good look at the colors of the stucco houses and storefronts—they are just fabulous. And the lace school is incredible.

Not all of the shops in the "heart of town" are open on Sunday, but the TTs are. Get the boat schedule before you wander so that you know how long you have—an hour on Burano is probably all you need. Note that when you return to Venice, you will probably end up at a vaporetto stop other than San Marco and will have to buy a new ticket and transfer to get back to your hotel.

VENICE RESOURCES FROM A TO Z

Antiques

If you are the type (like me) who likes flea markets and junk and reasonable prices, Venice is not for you (unless you hit it for one of the triannual flea markets). There are also regular real-people flea markets, but they are on the "land" side.

The few antiques shops in Venice are charming and dear and sweet and—should I tell you, or can you guess?—outrageously expensive.

But wait, should you luck into the **Mercatino dell'Antiquariato,** held each April, September, and December, you'll have the giggle of your lifetime. This market is not large, but it's sweet and simple and the kind I like: heaps of stuff on tables laid out in a piazza, the very convenient Campo San Maurizio. The dates are established well in advance and set for each year so that you can call for the exact times (© 041/45-41-76). This is a 3-day event held on a Friday, Saturday, and Sunday; there is no admission charge.

Bath & Beauty

LUSH
San Polo 89 (Rialto Bridge, San Polo side);
Strada Nuova Cannaregio 3822 (Santa Felice).

The British cult fave for deli-style cosmetics, beauty treatments, bath bombs, and more has set up several stores in Venice, with more expected. The shop right near Rialto is in the most convenient location for tourists; the goodies are not inexpensive but they offer high novelty and are currently not available in the U.S. Visit the Italian website (www.lush.it) for insight on products that are specifically Italian—many differ from what's on hand in other countries.

Beads

LESLIE ANN GENNINGER DESIGN STUDIO
Calle del Traghetto, Dorsoduro 2793a (Piazza Contarini-Michel, near Ca'Rezzonico Museum).

Talk about living out your best dreams: Leslie is American, lives in Venice, makes beads, and sells them from a fabulous little shop where you can buy ready-made jewelry or individual beads. The beads are made according to medieval (and secret) recipes but are inlaid with silver, which sparkles through. Check out the website: www.genningerstudio.com. To get here by boat, take the no. 1 vaporetto to the Ca'Rezzonico stop, turn right, and voilà—it's on the corner.

Boutiques

ARBOR
Gran Viale Lido 10a, San Marco 4759.

There are several branches of this boutique on the big island as well as at the Lido beach. Arbor carries the hot names, such as Byblos and Genny. The men's shop sells that stylish Italian look that thin men love to wear.

ELYSÉE
Frezzeria, San Marco 1693.

ELYSÉE 2
Calle Goldoni, Castello 4485.

This is not one but two very sleek boutiques carrying Mani, Maud Frizon, Mario Valentino, and the Giorgio Armani ready-to-wear collection for men and women. Armani is here exclusively. This is also a good place to check out the cheaper versions of Valentino—those licensed by GFT. Each shop has its own selection, including some shoes.

La Coupole
Via XXII Marzo, San Marco 2366;
Frezzeria, San Marco 1674.

Once again, two boutiques carrying the same big names and many lines. A few of their makers include Byblos, Alaia, and the sort-of-local Malo cashmere; shoes from Moschino; and earrings from Sharra Pagano of Milan. Both shops are small and elegant; prices are high.

Crafts

Il Ballo del Doge
San Marco 1823.

Cooperative of 14 artisans.

La Bottega dei Mascareri
Ponte di Rialto, San Polo 80.

Located at the foot of the Rialto, this shop offers unusual papier-mâché masks that are a notch above the average fare. Elaborate masks begin at about 50€ ($55), but simple ones begin around 14€ ($15).

La Venexiana
Ponte Canonica, Castello 4322.

You'll find masks and other Carnevale items here as well as some of the most incredible crafts I have ever seen. Don't miss it.

Max Art Shop
Frezzeria, San Marco 1232.

This store is right around the corner from the Hotel Bauer and the San Moisè designer shopping area at the start of Frezzeria; it will beckon to you from the velvet-hung windows. Inside, choose from velvet pillows, clothes, Carnevale-inspired wonder, and old-world charm.

Designer Boutiques

ARMANI
Calle Goldoni, San Marco 4412.

ARMANI JEANS
Calle Goldoni, San Marco 4485.

BULGARI
Calle Larga XXII Marzo, San Marco 2282.

CARTIER
30124 Venezia, San Marco 606.

D&G DOLCE & GABANA
San Marco 1313.

EMPORIO ARMANI
Calle dei Fabbri, San Marco 989.

ERMENEGILDO ZEGNA
San Marco 1241.

FENDI
Salizzada San Moisè, San Marco 1474.

FOGAL
Calle Merceria dell'Orologio, San Marco 221.

FRETTE
Calle Larga XXII Marzo, San Marco 2070A.

GIANFRANCO FERRÉ
Calle Larga, San Marco 287.

GIANNI VERSACE
Campo San Moísè, San Marco 1462.

GUCCI
San Marco 1317.

HERMÈS
Piazza San Marco, San Marco 125.

ISTANTE
San Marco 2359.

KENZO
Frezzeria Angolo Ramo Fuseri, San Marco 1814.

LA PERLA
Campo San Salvador, San Marco 4828.

LAURA BIAGIOTTI
Via XXII Marzo, San Marco 2400.

LORO PIANA
Ascensione, San Marco 1290–1301.

MALO
Calle della Ostreghe, San Marco 2359.

MAX & CO.
San Marco 5028.

MAX MARA
Mercerie, San Marco 268.

MISSONI
Calle Vallaresso 1312.

MONT BLANC
San Marco 4610.

ROBERTO CAVALLI
San Marco, Calle Vallaresso 1316.

SALVATORE FERRAGAMO
Campo San Moisè, San Marco.

TRUSSARDI
Calle Spadaria, 695 and 670.

VALENTINO
Salizzada San Moisè, San Marco 1473.

VERSACE
San Moisè 1462.

VERSUS
San Marco 1725.

WOLFORD
Cannaregio 5666.

Fabrics

GAGGIA
San Stefano, San Marco 3441.

Traditional silks, velvets, pleats, block prints, and the to-die-for local look that is part costume and part local treasure. Fabrics by the meter, also clothes and styles for the home.

RUBELLI
Campo San Gallo, San Marco 3877.

This Italian house is actually a source to the trade for reproductions of stunningly exquisite silken brocades and formal fabrics of museum quality. They have swatches, and they work with individuals, even if your last name is not Rothschild. Okay, the fabric costs 909€ ($1,000) per meter, but it's actually worth it.

VALLI
San Marco 783.

Valli is a chain of fabric stores with locations in all major cities and factories in Como; its shop in Venice happens to be right along your path, so it's a good place to stop in. The specialty of the house is designer fabrics, straight from the factory as supplied to the design houses, so you can buy the fabric in the same season. It's not cheap, but you can save money. I spent

91€ ($100) on some Gianni Versace silk and made a sarong skirt that I could never afford to buy from Versace ready-made.

VENETIA STVDIVM
Calle Larga XXII Marzo, San Marco 2403;
Mercerie, San Marco 723.

Without doubt, these are Venice's most exciting stores, offering Fortuny-style wrinkled fabric (mostly silks) in medieval colors that are pure artistry. The chain is expanding, so look for stores wherever you wander. The look is fantasy meets fashion with a Fortuny twist—there are long Isadora Duncan–like scarves and little drawstring purses that make the perfect evening bag. Prices begin around 182€ ($200). There are velvets as well as silks, and you should consider bringing your toothbrush so you can just move in. Heaven on earth.

Note: The main store is near San Moisè, but there are other branches, and each one promotes a different look. Branch stores in less touristy parts of town tend to be more home-decor oriented.

Foodstuffs

AL COVO
Campiello della Pecaria, Castello.

On the back of your menu from Al Covo, note that there is an order form for all the products. You take them away with you. These include olive oil, balsamic vinegar, pasta, and polenta. Ask Diane for details when you are there.

DROGHERIA MASCARI
San Polo 381.

This is not a drugstore, as you might guess from the name, but the last remaining spice merchant in Venice. Located in a real-people part of town, you get there by walking over the Rialto Bridge and going on to San Polo.

Glass

You'll recognize the difference between quality glass and touristy junk in a matter of seconds. Make a trip to the glass museum on Murano if your eye needs a little training.

L'ISOLA
San Zulian, San Marco 723;
Campo San Moisè, San Marco 1468.

There are a few branches of this contemporary gallery around town. It is the best source in Venice for the newer names in big glassworks. The San Marco address is across from the Hotel Bauer.

PAULY & COMPANY
Ponte Consorzi, San Marco 4392.

They don't come much more famous than this house, which was established in 1866. Pauly & Company has worked for most of the royal houses of Europe. It will paint your custom-blown glass to match your china (but not while you wait).

SALVIATI
Campo San Angelo, San Marco 3831.

Among the most famous master glassmakers in Venice.

SEGUSO
San Marco 143.

You'll find bright colors and outstanding contemporary works here.

VENINI
Piazzetta dei Leoncini, San Marco 314.

Credited with beginning the second renaissance of glass-blowers in Venice (1920–60), Venini is among the best. Buy anything you can afford and hang onto it for dear life.

Zora
San Marco 2407.

This is the newer guy in town. The shop is very close to the main branch of Venetia Stvdivm, the best store for silks in town, so you will be here anyway. While Zora makes glass, its specialty is glass picture frames, which are sophisticated and stunning and 364€ ($400) each. There are also tassels, beaded flowers, and golden grape clusters. Even if you buy nothing, don't miss it. You go through a little gate into what looks like a private house, so push on.

Handbags & Leather Goods

Fendi
Salizzada San Moisè, San Marco 1474.

If you have no other chance to shop for Fendi, this store is bigger than the one in Milan, modern, and right in the heart of your stroll across town. It's even near the American Express office, if you run out of cash. It does have sales; prices are about the same all over Italy, so your purchase will not cost less in another city. The store is located behind San Marco on the way to San Giglio, almost across the lane from the Hotel Bauer.

Gucci
San Marco 258.

Although I find this Gucci small and rather boring, without the flair of shops in other cities, it still offers the same gorgeous merchandise—sometimes on sale. You'll pass it on the way to the Rialto Bridge, so pop in if you have no other chance for Gucci.

Vogini
Near Piazza San Marco, San Marco 1257a–1301.

This was once my favorite leather-goods store in Venice, and one of a few faves in all of Italy. Now the basic glam is the fact that it sells the new line of Roberta di Camerino handbags, which are stunning and have a cult following thanks to marketing by Barney's in New York.

Home Style

ANTICHITA E OGGETTI D'ARTE
Frezzeria, San Marco 1691.

Ignore the word *antique* here and concentrate on glam home style, cushions of gilded velvet and painted velvet, and velvet dreams with fringe and beads. Fabrics from centuries past will make you weep with their glory.

MARIO & PAOLA BEVILACQUA
Fondamenta Canonica, San Marco 337b;
Campo Santa Maria del Giglio 2520.

These are two different addresses; the San Marco one is the easiest for tourists. The shop is the size of a large closet and is filled with velvets, pillows, tapestries, and tassels. Even if you live in the Sunbelt, you will be tempted to do your home over in dark velvets.

RAIGATTIERI
San Marco 3562.

Located near San Stefano, this shop specializes in faience. It's a two-part shop: One part offers country dishes, and the other more traditional ceramics. A faience plate will cost about 23€ ($25), and the shop will pack it for travel.

Linen & Lace

FRETTE
Calle Larga XXII Marzo, San Marco.

Here you'll find gorgeous linens from one of Italy's most famous makers for bed, bath, and lounging.

JESURUM
Mercerie dei Capitello, San Marco 4857.

Yo—they moved. Jesurum has upheld and continued the tradition of Venetian lace making, which was all but lost in the early 1800s. Just before the art would have died out, two Venetians undertook to restore it. One of the two was Michelangelo Jesurum, who—along with restoring the industry and putting hundreds of lace makers to work—also started a school so that the art would not die.

When you enter the Jesurum lace factory and showrooms, be prepared to flip your wig. The old church has been left with all its beautiful inlaid arches and its vaulted ceiling. Beautiful lace and appliquéd table linens and placemats are displayed on tables throughout the room.

MARIA MAZZARON
Fondamenta dell'Osmarìn, Castello 4970.

This is a private dealer whom you must phone (© **041/522-13-92**) to make an appointment to see her museum-quality treasures. Serious collectors only.

MARTINUZZI
Piazza San Marco, San Marco 67.

This lace shop is almost as good as Jesurum, and it's located right on the piazza. This is the real thing: embroidered goods, appliquéd linens, very drop-dead fancy Italian bed gear. The atmosphere is more old-lady lace shop than church-goes-retail, but the goods are high quality.

Masks

If you saw the movie or play *Amadeus,* you are familiar with the type of mask worn at Carnevale time in Venice. Carnevale in Venice got so out of hand that it was outlawed in 1797. But it's back again, and with it, a renewed interest in masks. One of the most popular styles is a mask covered with bookbinding paper that you can find at a *legatoria,* or paper-goods store (see below). But there also are masks made of leather, papier-mâché, fabric, etc. If all this is more than you had in mind, not to worry—there are masks in plastic for 5.45€ ($6) that will satisfy your need to participate. After 3 days in Venice, you'll swear you'll die if you see another mask, so make your selection carefully. Many of them seem like trite tourist items.

For a more special item, try any (or all!) of these famous mask makers:

ADRIANO MIANI
Calle Grimani, San Marco 289b.

BRUNO RIZZATO
Ponte dei Barcoli 1831.

LABORATORIO ARTIGIANO MASCHIERE
Piazza San Marco, San Marco 282.

LE MASCHIERE DI DARIO USTINO
Ponte dei Dai 171.

MA BOUTIQUE
Calle Larga San Marco, San Marco 28.

Optical Goods

I bought pairs and pairs of eyeglass frames back in the days before LASIK. High style, fair prices.

DANILO CARRARO
Calle della Mandola, San Marco 3706.

I wish I could take credit for this source, but Patricia Schultz brought me here after a friend of hers brought her, and so the chain is passed on. Here you'll find local makers of chic and fabulous frames that retail for about 59€ ($65) per pair. All sorts of colors and many types of tortoise-y patterns. They also do a hot fashion color for a season and then never do it again.

Best of all, they have a website, so you can shop electronically (www.otticacarraro.it).

Paper Goods

Legatoria means bookbindery in Italian, and the famous designs are copies of bookbinding papers from hundreds of years ago. The best makers use the same old-fashioned methods that have been in the house for centuries. Many of the shops will make something to order for you, but ask up front if they will mail it for you; most won't. These papers have become so popular in the U.S. that the paper-goods business now is divided between those who are staying old-fashioned and those who are counting the tourist bucks and loving it. When you walk into the various shops, you can feel the difference. There are many 9€ ($10) gift items in these stores. A calendar-diary of the fanciest sort costs 45€ ($50).

Legatoria Piazzesi (Campiella della Feltrina, Santo Stéfano, San Marco) and **Il Papiro** (Calle del Piovan, San Marco 2764), the two most famous paper shops in Venice, are almost across the way from each other, right near Campo San Stéfano at Ponte San Maurizio. Piazzesi also sells old prints. Don't let the street address throw you; just keep walking and you'll see these two beauties. They are past the main tourist shopping but in a gorgeous part of town not far past the Gritti.

There's a relatively new chain of shops around town called **In Folio** that sells paper goods and books and gift items as well as sealing wax and wax seals. When I was a teenager, sealing wax was the rage in America; now it's got a nice medieval twist to it that tourists are scarfing up. There are five or six of these shops scattered around town: San Marco 55, San Marco 739, San Marco 2431, San Marco 4852, and Castello 4615.

Shoes

Check the "Handbags & Leather Goods" listing earlier in this chapter for other sources.

BRUNO MAGLI
Calle XXII Marzo 2288, San Marco 1302;
Calle Frezzeria, San Marco 1583.

As you can tell from the addresses above, Magli has two different shops in Venice, although I swear I saw more. Not only is there a Magli everyplace you look, but they display different models, forcing you to visit each, if only to drool.

CALLEGHER ROLLY SEGALIN
Calle dei Fuseri 4365.

An old-fashioned shoemaker who creates everything by hand and made to measure. Unbelievable stuff . . . ranging from the type of creative and crazy things you might expect Elton John to wear (shoes shaped like gondolas) to very simple, elegant court shoes. He'll create or copy anything, although the price is about 455€ ($500) a pair. Closed on Saturday.

RENÉ CAOVILLA
1296 San Marco.

The only shop owned by master shoemaker Caovilla, who owns the factories on the mainland where most designer shoes are made.

SONNENBLUME
Ponte di Rialto.

Okay, I am going to put this in perspective—I have big feet and can rarely find shoes that fit and I am on a tight budget. So excuse me if I rant and rave. This source makes old-fashioned espadrilles, sells them from the Rialto Bridge, and makes a fashion statement to boot—you should excuse the expression. Sizes go up to 43. Technically speaking, these are not espadrilles—a French shoe—but a creation made by Italians after World War II when supplies were scarce. The original shoe soles were made from tires. The uppers are made in silk, velvet, and linen in the most yummy fashion colors of the rainbow. You can custom order. Prices are about 36€ ($40) per pair. Order online at www. sonnenblume.it.

SUPERGA
Calle dei Fabbri, San Marco 4673.

This is one of the hottest casual shoe brands in Italy, with shoes for adults and for kids. Sizes, of course, are continental, so use the size chart in the front of this book, or ask them. I needed a lesson in kiddie sizes, which they happily gave me (the U.S. kids' size 12 = 30; 13 = 31½; 1 = 33; and 2 = 34). Prices were steep for kiddie shoes, and I decided not to splurge, but you will go nuts for their bold designs, great colors, and futuristic contours . . . all with comfy crepe soles.

Weddings

I can't tell you how many people tell me they want to be married in Venice or ask me how to go about it. "Samantha" is my only answer. For information on Samantha Durell, who can arrange a wedding or reaffirmation ceremony in Venice, call her directly at ℘ 041/523-23-79.

VENICE SHOPPER'S STROLL & TOUR
••

ALL-DAY TOUR: SAN MARCO TO SAN GIGLIO

1. Begin your day at the **Piazza San Marco;** hopefully it is January or February, and you can actually see the square and the architecture and even the pigeons—as opposed to the mobs of international tourists.

2. Walk completely around the piazza, under the covered portico. There are many old-fashioned glass showrooms here, a few lace shops, some jewelry shops and TTs, and a few

overpriced but still fun-to-splurge-on cafes. As you go around, get your bearings—look for the back way out of the square, which you'll want later on. Don't miss **Michaela Frey** and her fabulous lion-of-Venice bangle bracelets.

3. Closer to the basilica, find the **Merceria,** which is a street leading away from the piazza in a relatively straight line toward the Rialto Bridge. Use this street as your guiding point to wind your way toward the Rialto Bridge. If done well, this area alone will take you more than half the day. Once you reach Riva del Carbon, take a right, and you will be at the foot of the Rialto Bridge.

4. Cross the bridge, but don't shop yet! Enjoy all the fruits and vegetables at the market and the small shops tucked here and there. Visit **Coin Rialto** to see the architecture.

5. Walk back along **Ruga Rialto** and stop in any of the charming little boutiques that interest you.

6. Cross back over the bridge and buy what looks good. Now you'll know what you couldn't get for less on the other side.

7. Wind your way back to the Piazza San Marco along the Merceria. Believe it or not, you will notice things coming back that you didn't see going.

8. Now that you have returned to the point of origin, head to your right from Merceria and move across San Marco to the "back" gate of the piazza and shop your way to San Giglio. This is a relatively straight line including a small ghetto of fancy-schmancy designer boutiques, **Venetia Stvdivm** for Fortuny-style silks, antiques shops, and **Zora** (next door to Venetia Stvdivm) for Venetian-glass picture frames, which may make you weep from the power of their beauty . . . or the power of their price tags.

9. Finish up at the next plaza. Have a drink at the **Gritti** or enjoy a tiny market at San Moisè if you are lucky enough to find one. Or head back toward San Marco and spend your lounge time in the upstairs lobby of the **Hotel Monaco & Grand Canal,** newly renovated and drop-dead chic.

Chapter Eight

....

MILAN

WELCOME TO MILAN

Milan: The world's most beautiful ugly city.

Sure, you may find it simply ugly as a first-timer, but just wait. Milan grows on you. Milan worms its way into the soul of a shopper . . . and fills you with promise, even if it's just the promise of a new pair of shoes.

Milan is not a one-night stand. Milan is not the kind of place you fall in love with at a glance. Milan is not pretty on the surface. But there's more style per mile here than in just about any other city in the world . . . and the surrounding area is filled with factories and outlets and bargains galore. You can make day trips from Milan; you can rent cars from the Milan airport; you can do it all from northern Italy.

Milan's real strength is in the inspiration it provides, not only to the fashion world, but to visual and creative types of all sorts. Walk down the streets, press your nose to the windows, and you'll get *ideas*. There's no doubt that Milan is the real capital of Italian fashion. It's no secret that international *garmentos* comb the streets and markets to find the goods they will tote to Hong Kong to reproduce in inexpensive copies. A day on the prowl in Milan makes my heart beat faster, my pocketbook grow lighter, and my shoulder grow weary—from carrying all those shopping bags.

What you see in Milan today will be in style in America in a year. Even if you can't afford to buy, you will feel invigorated by the city's creative energy just by walking its streets and window-shopping. Milan is not a great tourist town; it's a business city, and one of its businesses just happens to be fashion. So what's not to like? There's surely no business like shoe business. Or fur business. Or ready-to-wear.

Metro Milan Area

Don't overlook Milan as more than just a single city: It's a total destination. From Milan you can easily get in and out of Venice and into other northern Italian cities. Milan is less than an hour from Como and not far from Turin. From Milan, you can get to Switzerland—or anywhere! Milan is the hub of northern Italy and a great hub city for those who will rent a car to drive around for a weekend, a week, or a lifetime.

ARRIVING IN MILAN

Because Milan is this hub, there are plenty of ways to get in and out of town. But there are a few tricks to learn. There's also a bit of bad news, so watch this space carefully and be sure to ask a lot of questions.

The news is simple: In 1998, local authorities decided to switch all international flights to Malpensa International Airport and to use the more user-friendly (and closer to town) Linate Airport for intra-Italian commuter flights. The hub has indeed been switched, despite a rough start. Meanwhile, several airlines have sued. Rulings keep changing with the courts and the times. This is, after all, Italy.

The division of labor did not work as planned, so one must watch flight designations carefully, as intra-Italian flights may go to either Linate or Malpensa. When I fly to Milan from Paris, I have my choice of airports depending on the airline and flight. It pays to investigate, especially if your time is limited or you are not on an expense account.

Remember: Linate is 15 minutes and 14€ ($15) away from downtown and is the answer to all your questions. Malpensa is 1 hour away, and the taxi or limo ride costs about 91€ ($100).

By Plane

Milan has two different international airports, as I just explained. In the old days you could save yourself a lot of time and money if you booked a flight that landed at Linate, which is much closer to downtown Milano than Malpensa. This may be less easy to do now.

Malpensa is changing rapidly; it has opened a new terminal and a new runway, and changes will continue in the next few years. Watch this space.

If you arrive at Malpensa International Airport, you better have a rich sugar daddy or be prepared to wait for the bus. The bus is easy to find and drops you right at the Centrale train station, where you can hop on the metro or get a taxi to your hotel. Of course, you may want to spring for a car and driver, which will cost under 91€ ($100), including the tip. (I use Europe Car Service, © 02/942-51-00; fax 02/94-24-01-40; ecs@ecs-car.it; Malpensa transfer is about 68€/$75 plus tip.)

There is a new airport express train for those who can manage their luggage. Naturally, I've never taken it. The train trip takes 40 minutes. Check it out via www.malpensa express.it.

Just when you thought I couldn't dis Malpensa enough, may I offer up some happy news: Malpensa is out there in the wide-open spaces in terms of getting out of town and hitting the road without going into Milan. It's also halfway to Como and the outlets, and yes, Switzerland.

For less than 9€ ($10), you can take the bus from Malpensa into downtown Milan; the bus runs regularly on the half-hour. Buy your ticket at the marked booth and then line up outside. There are two bus stops outside, so be sure you don't take the employee bus to the parking lot. The bus will deposit you at the Centrale train station in the heart of Milan.

Milan

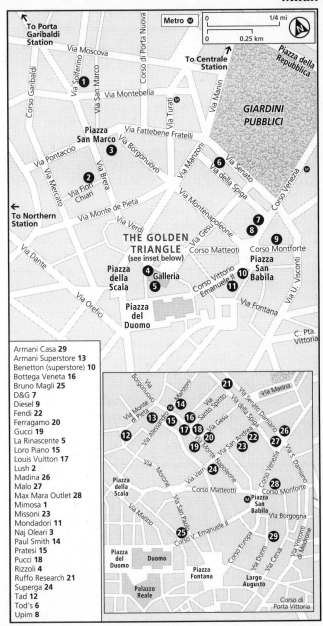

Armani Casa **29**
Armani Superstore **13**
Benetton (superstore) **10**
Bottega Veneta **16**
Bruno Magli **25**
D&G **7**
Diesel **9**
Fendi **22**
Ferragamo **20**
Gucci **19**
La Rinascente **5**
Loro Piano **15**
Louis Vuitton **17**
Lush **2**
Madina **26**
Malo **27**
Max Mara Outlet **28**
Mimosa **1**
Missoni **23**
Mondadori **11**
Naj Oleari **3**
Paul Smith **14**
Pratesi **15**
Pucci **18**
Rizzoli **4**
Ruffo Research **21**
Superga **24**
Tad **12**
Tod's **6**
Upim **8**

Jenny's Turn: Malpensa, To and Fro

So, you've just arrived in Milan. Just can't wait to get out there and see what all the hubbub is surrounding this infamous shopping city? Well, hold onto those traveler's checks; you're going to have to.

When arriving at the Malpensa airport in Milan, you are actually about an hour from the city center (and the shopping). So I should just hop in a cab, you ask? Not unless you want to shell out 70€ to 100€ ($77–$110) for the experience.

Instead, for a mere 5.50€ ($6), you can take the **Malpensa Bus Express**—a somewhat comfortable coach bus with some-what relaxing music to transport the weak and weary through the unpicturesque highways to their final destination of Milano Centrale. You do need to pay in euros, and you buy the ticket directly from the driver.

The bus pulls up outside the terminal on the street level, right near the arrivals portion of the airport. It's a little con-fusing to find, with no real signage, but it's very close to where you pick up your luggage. We knew the bus existed and were determined to take it, but an unenlightened traveler might wimp out.

Once on board, the next 75 minutes is your time to rest up and dream of your Milanese purchases in the not-so-dis-tant future. *Note:* You can get to the city by a train/subway deal to Milano Centrale, but it involves some transfers and confusion. We found it too daunting to try after a long flight.

Now then, this is a great service, and it's cheap, and it's fine and all that, but hey, you better be able to handle your lug-gage, 'cause *mamma mia,* when they drop you at the train sta-tion, they drop you at the side of the building, and the taxi rank is in the *front.* There are no luggage trolleys and no porters and no help whatsoever; go to the front for a trolley.

By Train

If you come by train, you will probably arrive at the **Centrale Station** in the heart of downtown. Pay attention as you exit because parts of this station have been changed and (if this is a return trip), the layout may not be as you remember it. Most important, there are no longer any porters. Nor is there an elevator. Oy!

They've reworked the escalators at the front of the station so that a luggage trolley can fit on them, sort of. I had some very frightening moments as I went down that very steep escalator, clinging for dear life to my trolley, hoping to balance it with enough counterweight so that we didn't go flying. There are pictograms on the trolleys and on the walls to show you how to get the trolley onto (and down) the escalator.

Arrivals and departures are now from the front of the Centrale Station. Centrale is connected to the metro if you can manage your luggage and prefer using public transportation rather than a taxi.

There are free trolleys, but they are usually at the entrances to the station: When you pop off the train, it's unlikely that you'll find a trolley when you need one. If you are traveling alone, good luck. You may want to pack your set of airline wheels with you, or invest in the kind of luggage that has rear wheels and a pull cord or handle.

Departure Tips

To catch a bus to either airport, take a taxi to the Centrale Station where the bus pickup is. You do not want to enter the main part of the station to catch the bus. The ticket window is to the side, right where you caught the taxi when you arrived. Beware of gypsies and beggars who may annoy you while you wait for the next bus. Last time I took a taxi to Centrale—to catch a train to Venice, actually—the driver asked me if I wanted the Pullman for the airport or a train, because he will drop you at two different places depending on which you want.

Getting Around

Milan happens to be a good walking city—most of the shops, museums, and other attractions are in areas that you can easily navigate by foot once you get yourself to a specific neighborhood. This is why it pays to pick a hotel in the center of the action and near a metro stop.

If you need a taxi, they can be found in ranks, hailed in the street, or called. Note that when you call a taxi, the meter starts once the driver heads toward your pickup location. Taxis in Milan are very expensive.

Getting around town on public transportation is not hard. The metro is great, but does not get you everywhere you want to go. However, it gets you to and from your hotel and the best shopping districts. Most of the luxury hotels are within a block of a metro station.

Tram and bus systems are very good. Between these three modes of transport, you'll do just great. Buy tram or bus tickets at a tobacco stand (marked with a T sign out front) before you get on the vehicle. Enter from the rear, and place your ticket in the little box to get it stamped. Keep it; you can use it again within 75 minutes.

Metro tickets can be purchased in the station; you will need coins to operate the ticket machines, but there are change machines. Magazine vendors inside stations will not give you change unless you buy something.

Milan's *metropolitana* has three main lines, each color-coded. Tourists will probably find the red line most convenient, as it goes to some of the major shopping areas and also stops at the Duomo. Look for the giant red M that indicates a station. Many guidebooks have a metro map printed inside them—and so does the brochure *A Guest in Milan,* which most hotels give away for free. Local telephone books come in two parts, both of which should be in your hotel room (look in the closet). One part is a phone book as you know it, and the other is a map and city directory with pages of information on how to use the city and surrounding provinces, including a metro map and a bus-route map.

You can take a regular train to nearby communities, such as Como or Bergamo, or even to Venice, for a day trip. There's a large commuter population that goes to Turin, mostly for business, but you can go there to shop or to see the Shroud.

If you are using a train pass, do not blow a day of travel on a local commuter ticket. The same ticket can get you to Paris or to Como. Save the rail pass for the important stuff. A first-class, round-trip train ticket to Como costs about 14€ ($15).

If you want to get to seriously out-of-the-way factory outlets, you'll have to rent a car or hire a car and driver. Hiring a car with driver is not outrageously expensive—about 182€ ($200) a day (this includes the tip) for 150km (93 miles), although there are half-day options. I use **Europe Car Service** (© 02/942-51-00; fax 02/94-24-01-40). Yes, I know there are more digits in one of the numbers; that's the way it is on the business card. The Web address is www.ecs-car.com.

Another possibility is to hire a taxi driver. I did the Como outlets that way. He drove me all over and waited for me while I shopped, and it cost about 23€ ($25) for a half-day.

More Information

There is a local version of the *Time Out* guide, *Time Out Milano*, but it is in Italian. Buy it at any news kiosk in Milan. The national newspaper *Repubblica* has a Milan section toward the rear of the daily paper that has local listings, weekend happenings, and some flea markets or specialty shopping events.

SLEEPING IN MILAN

Super Shopping Hotels

CARLTON HOTEL BAGLIONI
Via Senato 5.

This is a very small, chic hotel that is a member of Leading Hotels of the World, as well as part of the Baglioni chain, which is making huge strides into the luxury market all over Italy.

For reservations from the U.S., contact Leading Hotels of the World (© **800/223-6800**; www.lhw.com). Local phone 02/770-77. www.baglionihotels.com.

EXCELSIOR HOTEL GALLIA
Piazza Duca d'Aosta 9.

Where would you go if you wanted to sleep in the same beds used by Ernest Hemingway, Mikhail Gorbachev, and Madonna? Why, the Excelsior, of course. This is also one of the hotels used during Fashion Week, so it seems fitting (excuse the pun) to begin your own fashion forays here.

One step into this hotel and it becomes apparent why this is where the elite choose to sleep. The hotel lies in the center of Milan, just a few steps from Stazione Centrale Milano. It's easy to get to and a great starting-off point to anywhere in Milan and beyond.

It's difficult to miss the impressive Art Nouveau facade when exiting the train station: You sort of swan from Mussolini to masterpiece in a few steps. The hotel is perfect for pampered relaxation, yet it also caters to business needs with lines for a modem, fax, and PC in every room. There's a 24-hour small but up-to-the-minute business center. Other amenities include a fitness center, a small but luxurious shopping arcade, and a beauty center.

To reserve from the U.S., call © **800/225-5843**. Local phone 02/678-51. www.lemeridien-excelsiorgallia.com.

FOUR SEASONS HOTEL
Via del Gesù 8.

What would happen if the fashion angel came to Milan and decided to go into the hotel business? The Four Seasons, of course. You'll find this grand hotel discreetly located in the heart of the Montenapo shopping district. With up-to-date amenities and a posh atmosphere, it has a modern feel without seeming too rococo. For a shopper, it's simply the best location in town. As a result, it's become a fashion editor's hangout. There are two restaurants: Il Teatro (a Michelin one-star) and a more casual street-level cafe. It is the "in" place for visiting editors; a virtual zoo during Fashion Weeks . . . but a very chic zoo.

Note that the Four Seasons has not only extra lines for your computer, but 110-volt electrical outlets; getting online has never been easier in my life as from this hotel.

For an extra advantage, hit up the concierge desk for the hotel's slick magazine on shopping in Milan. For reservations from the U.S., call © **800/332-3442**. Local phone 02/770-88. www.fourseasons.com.

GRAND HOTEL ET DE MILAN
Via Manzoni 29.

This is a fancy-dancy hotel that's romantically small and dark, with a wonderful decorating style that takes you back in time. Yet there's a subway stop right alongside the hotel, so you get luxury and real life wrapped up in one. Shuttle service is available to airports and to the train station.

To reserve from the U.S., call **Leading Hotels of the World** at © **800/223-6800**. Local phone 02/72-31-41. Local fax 02/ 86-46-08-61. www.lhw.com/ghmilan.

Four-Star Finds

HILTON MILAN
Via Galvani 12.

Located near the main train station, this Hilton is not glam, but it does have various promotional rates. Watch it, though: The rates are most often per person, which may or may not cost out. Still, a winter promotion of 77€ ($85) per person, which includes breakfast, isn't bad. It's a bit of a schlep to the nearest metro. For reservations from the U.S, call © **800/ HILTONS**. Local phone 02/69-831. www.milan.hilton.com.

HOTEL MANIN
Via Manin 7.

This is a tiny hotel decorated like an ocean liner from the 1930s. It's right near the gardens and the fashion district and is considered a find by fashion editors and those looking for a good location and an affordable price. Call © **02/659-65-11.** www.hotelmanin.it.

JOLLY HOTEL PRESIDENT
Largo Augusto 10.

JOLLY HOTEL TOURING
Via Tarchetti 2.

You'll be jolly, too, when you learn about this hotel chain. There are two Jolly hotels in downtown Milan. The President is a business traveler's hotel, with small rooms of modern neo-Italian design. It's a great find because of its location. Largo Augusto is next door to Via Durini, designer shop row, and a block from the Duomo, which can be seen from your window.

The Jolly Hotel Touring is located near the Principe and the Palace and shares the same metro with them, but is a block closer to the shopping action. The rooms here are much nicer than those at the President. The hotel does cater to groups, but I was quite happy with my choice.

If you can handle a four-star rather than a five-star, this is a find. For reservations in the U.S., call © **800/247-1277.** Local phone numbers: Jolly Hotel President 02/77-461; Jolly Hotel Touring 02/63-35. www.jollyhotels.it.

Three-Star

HOTEL MANZONI
Via Santo Spirito 20.

I found this hotel by accident—it's small and well priced and in a great location near all the most expensive stores. There are only about 50 rooms and they go for between 136€ and

182€ ($150–$200) per night. With breakfast! Local phone
🕾 02/7600-5700. www.hotelmanzoni.com.

SNACK & SHOP

CAFÉ CORSO COMO
Corso Como 10 (metro: Garibaldi).

No that's not a typo; the name of the store is the address, and
this is the rather new cafe in part of the store. It's very chic; a
reservation in season is suggested, although when I got there
in winter, I had no trouble getting a seat. There's a bar to eat
at, as well as tables; the look is Italian-Zen with a menu of pasta,
salads, and sushi. Reservations 🕾 02/65-48-31; open from 11am
until midnight.

CAFFÈ ARMANI
Via Manzoni 31, Armani Superstore
(metro: Montenapoleone).

Because I frequently eat at the Caffè Armani in Paris, I thought
this would be a good place to test in Milan. Almost next door
to my hotel, it's in the heart of the truly great shopping
district, a few steps from a metro, and part of the Armani Superstore. All that said, the food was good and prices fair, but the
portions were so small I wanted to cry. I guess that's how to
stay small enough to wear Armani in the first place. Reservations 🕾 02/723-186-80.

COVA
Via Montenapoleone 8 (metro: Montenapoleone).

Cova is a lot like Sant' Ambroeus (see review later in this section), but more formal and touristy because it's on the list of
so many out-of-towners. It's a local legend and an "in" place
for tea, between-shopping breaks, and sweets. Come at 5pm
if you want to make the scene. The chocolates are a status-
symbol hostess gift in fall, the jellied fruit squares in summer.

Note the old Russian system for paying if you buy food to go: Make your choice at the counter, pay at the front desk, and return to the counter to pick up your choice. *Note:* There's a rumor going around town that the real estate that Cova sits on is worth about $25 million, so if it's sold out by the time you get there, well, you can't blame them! ✆ **02/600-0578.**

PECK
Via Spadari 9 (metro: Duomo).

This is possibly the most famous food store in Milan. Use it as your personal headquarters for picnic supplies. It also has a grill. The main food shop is on a side street on the far side of the Duomo, away from the Montenapoleone area but still convenient enough to be worthwhile. I always buy a picnic to take back on the airplane. Somehow, few airlines are able to provide food like Peck's. ✆ **02/876-774.**

SANT' AMBROEUS
Corso Matteotti 7 (metro: Babila).

I've fallen in love with this fancy space right off Montenapoleone. They have a bakery and candy shop for takeout orders, or you can stand at the bar or take a table. Sort of the Italian version of tea at the Ritz. They open at 8am if you prefer to breakfast here. I can eat their little *prosciutto crudo* sandwiches all day. ✆ **02/7600-0540.**

THE SHOPPING SCENE

Because Milan is the home of the fashion, fur, and furnishings businesses, you'll quickly find that it's a city that sells style and image. There aren't a lot of souvenirs. Near the Duomo, you can find the occasional piece, but the city lacks crass souvenirs and silly gift items. It's simply not a silly city. Milan is a city of big business: The souvenir stands are overflowing with an abundance of international magazines, not kitschy plastics. The big toy sold by street vendors? Plastic telephones for kids!

Although Milan was a medieval trading city, in its modern, post–World War II incarnation, Milan has sizzled and made its mark. The city hosts the international furniture salon every other year. There are fashion shows here twice a year, bringing a cadre of fashion reporters from all over the world to tell the fashion mavens just what Italy has to offer. Besides these, there are a zillion fairs and conventions and other business happenings, meaning Milan is always happening. Hmmmm, except in August.

Even if you aren't a fashion editor and don't plan your life around what comes trotting down the catwalk, you'll find that Milan's high-fashion stores offer a peek at what's to come. You'll also find that the markets and real-people shopping reflect the proximity of nearby factories . . . you'd be amazed at what can fall off a truck.

The best shopping in Milan is at these designer shops and showrooms, or at the discount houses, jobbers, and factory-outlet stores that sell designer clothing, overruns, and samples. If you really care about high fashion at an affordable price, plan to spend January of each year prowling the sales in Milan—not London.

The Best Buys in Milan

Alternative Retail   Mavens will give me the evil eye for mentioning this, but Milan is a good place for a bargain. There are good flea markets and street markets, and the buys in Como cannot be underestimated.

I hit a home run a few years ago at **Il Salvagente,** the famous Milan discounter where big-name clothes are marked down to reasonable prices during a January sale. My prize? A pink wool jacket from Mimmina—a big Italian name—for all of 123€ ($135). My girlfriend Mimi, an American fashion editor who covers the collections twice a year, regularly shops here and says that on her last trip, she "made out like a bandit." I got an e-mail from a radio show producer at NPR who said, "How did you find this place?" My last trip there? I found nuthin'. Who said life was fair?

Meanwhile, I cannot rave enough about Como. It's more than just a resort town; it's heaven for bargain shoppers who want high-quality silks. I'm talking about the biggest and best French and Italian couture names, and more. Mantero? Did we say it's time to buy **Mantero,** oh yes, *si, si, si.* Remind me to tell you about the scarf that cost 455€ ($500) in Munich and only 227€ ($250) in Italy. Of course I bought two—you needed to ask?

Designer Home Design   Again, maybe not a best buy in terms of price, but a best in terms of selection or unique opportunity. The hottest trend in Milan of late has been that all the big designers are doing home furnishings, from dishes and ashtrays to sheets, and then some. **Versace, Dolce & Gabbana, Missoni,** and **Ferragamo** are all into home design now. It's luxe, it's expensive, and it's gorgeous. Just press your nose to the **D&G Home** store; take one look at dark red silk brocade, leopard prints, and majolica; and know that when it works, it works! But wait, I now also shop for home design in the outlet store that **Lisa Corti** has in her workrooms—fabulous stuff and half the price of Saks.

Designer Selections   While designer merchandise is expensive, the selection and the possibility of a markdown or discovering a small, reasonably priced item is greater. **Etro** isn't a bargain resource and is available in other Italian cities, but it will please you to no end to buy here and to soak up the atmosphere of class, elegance, and northern Italian chic. The Etro outlet, right in town, will also please you to no end.

Fragrance, Makeup & Bath Products   I am calling special attention to this category because the more I research it, the more I am convinced you can make it work for you. Under normal circumstances, designer lines—especially French and American—are outrageously expensive in Italy.

However, **La Rinascente** has a policy for non-Italian passport holders that allows you to show your passport at the point of purchase and receive an immediate 10% discount at the cash register! This is good for perfumes, makeup, and even Italian bath bubbles and spa items.

Meanwhile, in the past year, Milan has gone makeup crazy, meaning that no longer are French and U.S. brands the must-haves they once were—there are possibly six new brands of makeup, all jazzy and affordably priced. See p. 257 to learn about designer makeup (Armani, Versace) as well as Madina, Kiko, and other new brands.

Young Fashions   Aaron and Jenny–our 20-something reporters—had a wonderful time exploring shoe, vintage, and fashion shops and found prices often fair. Some items were too high for them but fun to stare at; others were affordable and sensational. There are specific parts of town that cater to the young look and the young wallet—see "Shopping Neighbor-hoods," p. 228.

The Worst Buys in Milan

If you can help it, don't buy:

- Ceramics and faience. They're hard to find, and therefore expensive.
- Postcards. There's a bad selection.
- Important antiques. They're prohibitively expensive.
- Masks, marbleized paper goods, or traditional Italian souvenirs. These items are best bought where they're made.

Milan Style

In terms of clothing, Milanese style is much more conserva-tive, chic, and sophisticated than the more flamboyant south-ern Italian style. In Milan, if you don't buy from a trendy designer, you'll actually load up on basics—good cashmere sweaters and shawls, knits, shoes, handbags, and furs. That's right: furs! Northern Italy is one of the few places in the world where it's not only politically correct to wear fur, but part of the fashion scene. In Milan, attitude is part of fashion, so you can wear all black and be chic; it need not be expensive or laden with labels—you just need the look and a pair of great sunglasses.

Much of what is for sale in Milan is of the same design school as the English country look; this will interest Europeans far more than Americans who are looking for hot looks, not tweeds and V-necks. Also note that a large influence in Italian fashion these days is the American mail-order catalog look—Levi's, J. Crew, L.L.Bean, etc. I didn't come to Italy to buy things like this; you probably didn't either, and will someone spare me from Gap wannabes? Still, there's plenty of trendy stuff for the Ferrari in your soul.

Milan is a great place for spotting color trends. Yes, *fashionistas* always dress in black because it's easy, but Italian fashion highlights a few new, key colors each season. Even if you just window-shop, you'll soon see that almost all clothing in any given season, no matter which designer is presenting it, falls into a few color families. Each season will have one or two hot colors that define the season; each season will also have a wide selection of items in black because black is the staple of every Italian (and French) wardrobe. The best thing about these colors is that other designers and even mass retailers in America will pick up these same shades, so that what you buy in Italy will carry smoothly into the fashion front for several years.

Another aspect of Milanese style comes in furnishings, home decor, tabletop, and interior design. No matter what size you are or what age you are, you will see things to light your fire in this city of desire.

The Five Best Stores in Milan

In alphabetical order:

Corso Como 10
10 Corso Como (metro: Garibaldi).

This is one of the best stores in the world because of the way it constantly changes. It's owned by a woman who is a member of one of the most important fashion families in Italy and sells a little of everything, but all of it seemingly unique. See p. 1.

ETRO OUTLET
Via Spartaco 3 (no nearby metro; ask concierge about bus).

Great prices on quality items—accessories, yard goods, and clothes for men and women. You will go mad. See p. 262.

FREE
Centrale Milano train station (metro: Centrale).

I guess this just reveals the inner down-market part of my soul, but this grocery store sells a little of everything and most of it is unique and terrific. It's where I buy magic coffee, notebooks, flavored pastas, and all sorts of things. See p. 254.

LISA CORTI
Via Conchetta 6 (tram no. 15).

You will spend a lot for a taxi to get here, but to me it's worth it. Corti has shops in other Italian cities, but this is also the showroom and has the best prices. She makes home style and women's clothing in colorful prints, which are sold for double the price at Saks Fifth Avenue. See p. 86 for the Rome store. Call for directions at © 02/581-000-31. www.lisacorti.com.

MAX MARA OUTLET
Galleria San Carlo 6 (metro: Babila).

The official name of this store is **Diffusione Tessile,** but it is the Max Mara outlet and its smack dab in the center of everything, easy to get to, and easy to shop. See p. 263.

ALSO-RAN

LUSH
Via Fiori Chiari 6 (metro: Duomo).

If you haven't been to a Lush store in Italy, this is your chance. The store is on the way to the Brera district and offers an Italian version of the famous British bath products. See p. 238.

Shopping Hours

The big news in Milan is that shopping hours are not as strict here as elsewhere; nor are they as strict as they used to be. Furthermore, Milan now has stores that are open on Sunday!

Lunch Hours   Many of the big-name designer shops in Milan are open nonstop, which means that they do not close for lunch. If you don't want to take a lunch break, shop the Montenapo area.

Dime stores like **Standa** and **Upim** have always been open nonstop; **La Rinascente,** Milan's most complete department store, has always been open during lunch as well. Of course, most of the Standa stores in Milan have become **FNAC** stores, but those are open nonstop, too.

Monday Hours   Most stores in Milan are closed on Monday through the lunch hour (they open around 3:30 or 4pm). Note that La Rinascente does not open until 1:45pm on Monday. Most of Italy is dead from a retail perspective on Monday morning. But wait!

- Food shops are open.
- Factory stores are frequently open on Monday morning. If you are heading out to a certain factory or two, call ahead. Make no assumptions.
- Como factories are open on Monday morning!

Sunday Shopping

Laws have changed, and all of Italy's big cities have Sunday shopping now; mostly big department stores are open. If you want to shop on a Sunday, try for a flea market. Or go to Venice, which is wide, wide, wide open on Sunday. Milan is far more dead on Sunday than other communities, but you can get lucky—at certain times of the year, things are popping on Sunday. During Fashion Weeks, stores in the Montenapo district often open on Sunday; beginning in October and going on until Christmas, they also have specific Sundays when they open.

Some stores in the Navigli area are also open on Sunday.

The regular Sunday stores are **Corso Como 10** and **Virgin Megastore.** Sunday hours are most often noon to 5pm.

In season, Como (only 20 min. away) is wide open on Sunday, although you may want to call ahead to verify that your favorite factory shops will be open on the Sunday that you want to shop them. Some people go to Ancora for Sunday shopping.

But then I have left out my favorite thing: The **Aldo Coppola** (don't confuse with Peter Coppola in New York) hair salon at La Rinascente is open on Sundays from 10am until 8pm. Cool? For an appointment, call ✆ **02/890-597-12.** There used to be a cafe in this space overlooking the Duomo; Aldo is a local big name with a few salons in Italy. Blow me, baby.

Exceptional Shopping Hours

Summer Hours   Summer hours begin in the middle of July for some retail businesses; August is a total loss from a shopping point of view because most stores are closed. Sophisticated people wouldn't be caught dead in Milan in August; shoppers beware. When stores are open in August, they close at lunch on Saturday and do not reopen until 3:30 or 4pm on Monday.

Holiday Hours   The period between Christmas and New Year's Day can be tricky. Stores will close early a few days before a major holiday and use any excuse to stay closed during a holiday. Sales begin in the first week of January (usually after Epiphany), but store hours are erratic before then. There are weekend candy markets around the Duomo in the weeks before Lent.

Early January   The first week in January is also slow to slower—all factories are closed until after Epiphany, as are many stores. Others decide to close for inventory.

Night Hours   Stores usually close sometime between 7:30 and 8pm. Should you need an all-night pharmacy, there is one at Piazza Duomo and one at the Centrale train station.

Money Matters

An **American Express** travel office is at the corner of the Via Brera and the Via dell'Orso: It's Via Brera 3. This is in the thick of the shopping district, so you need not go out of your way to get here.

ATMs are easy to find.

Personal Needs

I needed shoelaces in Milan—sounds simple, huh? Forget it! Since **Upim** has gone upscale, it's become harder and harder to find the basics of real life. **Upim** used to be a lot like Woolworths. Now it's trying to be more like La Rinascente. It's unlikely you'll find everything you need in real life at an Italian department store, so try Upim as well as any number of pharmacies and grocery stores. P.S.: The shoelaces? **Foot Locker** on Victor Emmanuelle!

Look for a green neon cross if you want a pharmacy. There's a very good pharmacy in the Centrale train station, and they speak English. In fact, the train station has an excellent selection of shops selling basic items you may have left at home. Try **Free,** an enormous grocery store that sells everything from food and souvenirs to health and beauty aids—even condoms.

Shopping Neighborhoods

Golden Triangle/Montenapo   All of the big designers have gorgeous and prestigious shops here. You can easily explore this area in a day or 2, or even an hour or 2, depending on how much money or curiosity you have. Although the main shopping street is **Via Montenapoleone,** sometimes this area is referred to as Montenapo.

This is the chic part of town, where traditional European design flourishes along with Euro-Japanese styles and wild, hot Italian New Wave looks. It includes a couple of little streets that veer off the Via Montenapoleone in a beautiful little web of shopping heaven. This is where you'll find **Gucci,**

Ferré, Versace, Fendi, Ferragamo, and Krizia boutiques, as well as some very tony antiques shops.

There are furniture and fashion showrooms to the trade that are so fancy and secluded that you would never know they are there. There are also some reliable real-people shops, like sporting goods emporium **Brigatti,** that you'll enjoy.

The outermost borders of the neighborhood are **Via Manzoni** and **Corso Venezia,** two major commercial streets. Use them mostly for finding your way—although in the past year, Corso Venezia has become a hot address for designer bridge lines. Your real shopping streets will be **Via della Spiga, Via Sant' Andrea,** and, of course, **Via Montenapoleone.** But don't miss this little enclave's back streets, such as **Via Gesù** and **Via Borgospesso,** and also **Via Manzoni** (which is not a back street).

For anyone with limited time in Milan who wants to absorb a lot of the scene in just a few hours, this is the top-priority shopping district for looking around. You might not buy your souvenirs here, but you'll see the stuff that dreams are made of.

Duomo   The Duomo is the main landmark of Milan. It's an incredibly detailed and gorgeous cathedral; not a store. It is on the Piazza del Duomo and is happily surrounded by stores. You guessed it—there is even a **Virgin Megastore** to one side and the country's leading department store, **La Rinascente,** to another side.

Via Montenapoleone angles away from Corso Vittorio Emanuele II as you move away from the Duomo, so the Golden Triangle and Duomo neighborhoods sort of back up to each other. This connection makes it very easy to shop these two areas in the same afternoon. When you are finished with them, there are two other shopping neighborhoods, Brera and Largo Augusto, that you can connect with on the other side of the Duomo. You did come to Milan to shop, didn't you?

Corso Vittorio Emanuele II   This neighborhood is filled with big stores, little stores, and half a dozen galleries and mini-malls that house even more stores. The most maddening part about this area is that you can hardly find an address. Just wander in and out and around from the Duomo to **Piazza San Babila,** which is only 2 or 3 blocks.

At San Babila, turn left and you'll end up at Via Montenapoleone for entry into the Golden Triangle. Or you can do this in the reverse, of course. But don't forget to check out this intersection. Because the San Babila area is very important, you'll find everything from the new **Benetton** superstore to **Upim** to plastics mongers and fashion mavens. And the **Max Mara** outlet store (see p. 225 and 263) in the Galleria San Carlo.

At the front end of the Duomo, off the piazza, is a shopping center of historical and architectural landmark proportions, the **Galleria.** This is one of the most famous landmarks in Milan, and some tout it as the first mall in Europe. Other gallerias in Europe also make the same claim, but who cares? Take one look at the ceiling and you'll marvel. Then visit the **Prada** shop.

The Galleria has a vaulted ceiling and looks like a train station from another, grander, era. Inside there are restaurants and bistros where you can get coffee and sit and watch the parade of passersby. Several big-time shops are here besides **Prada**— don't miss **Rizzoli** for books in English. If you go out the back end, you will be at La Scala. Behind La Scala is the **Brera** area.

If you are at the piazza with the Duomo to your back and have not turned right to enter the Galleria, you can walk straight ahead toward the **Virgin Megastore** and yet more retail. The arcade across from the Duomo is filled with many old names of Milanese retailing and some newer shops, too, including a **Missoni** jeans store that sells the brand's sports line. **Galtruco** is a very famous fabric firm where you can buy every imaginable type of yard goods, including the designer fabrics from local mills.

Brera A fair (but not difficult) walk from the Duomo, Brera is one of the most famous shopping districts of Milan because it has slightly less expensive rents. It's the part of town where young designers can break into retailing and high style, and it has both designer shops and up-and-coming trendsetters.

The main stretch of Brera is rather commercial, with shops oriented toward teens, and quite a few jeans stores as well as very obvious branches of the famous international retailers, including **Laura Ashley, Shu Uemura,** and **Naj Oleari.** Behind all this, there are narrow and bewitching back streets closed to vehicular traffic that call out to you to explore them. Many of them host the most expensive antiques dealers in the city; some of them are the ateliers of new, hot designers.

There are designer shops in here also, including **Il Bisonte** (Via Madonnina 10) and **Angela Caputi** (Via Madonnina 11). Don't miss **Etro,** Via Pontaccio 17, at the corner of Vicolo Fiori. And while you're in this neck of the woods, don't forget that London's **Lush**—that adorable deli of bath bombs, face masks, and homemade soaps and suds first created in England—has opened up here at Via Fiori Chiari 6; the store is not identical to the English (or Canadian) versions, and therein lies its charm.

The best way to see Brera is during the **antiques street fair** (3rd Sat of each month), when vendors put out tables in the narrow streets and a well-heeled crowd browses. But any day is a good day. Carry on from Brera to Solferino (the street just changes names) and then over one to Garibaldi.

Largo Augusto/Durini   Another option is to move from the other side of the Duomo to Corso Vittorio Emanuele II, and over to **Via Durini.** Via Durini is only a block long, but it's a good-size block and it's crammed with fabulous stores. It veers off at an angle from San Babila and runs straight to Largo Augusto.

Via Durini has blossomed into an important Milanese fashion street: Mr. Armani offers three different **Emporio** shops; **Calvin Klein** has opened up shop; and there are designer showrooms, cute little clothing places, very chic fur salons, and furniture-design showrooms.

Please note that you can catch a bus to **Il Salvagente,** the discounter (p. 250), at Largo Augusto, or walk via the Corso

Porta Vittoria, and be there in 10 minutes. I usually walk because I enjoy window-shopping along the way.

Train Station/Ingrosso In the area between the Centrale train station and the Repubblica metro station, a grid system of flat streets makes up the *garmento* wholesale *(ingrosso)* and discount district of Milan. There are scads of stores here: You can browse and just go in and out—about half of them are closed for lunch, and all of them are closed on Saturday and Sunday. The area is trying to fashion itself as a fashion destination, calling itself **CMM** (Centro Moda Milano); it now has a printed brochure of the showrooms and has special hours for holiday shopping and during Fashion Weeks. Get the brochure for free at any showroom; CMM's fax number is 02/93-57-22-18.

If your time is limited and you crave high style and multiple marvels, this is not your destination. If you like a bargain and don't mind hit-or-miss shopping, step this way. I had a ball here last time I visited because I got lucky—cashmere twin sets for 227€ ($250; total price), stores that take credit cards and smile, **Tod's** boots for 182€ ($200) a pair, lots of brand names, and lots of selection.

For Euro visitors who specifically come to Milan to beat the high prices in other parts of Europe, this is your cup of tea.

Buenos Aires Don't cry for me, Buenos Aires, I've got my credit cards . . . and my Kleenex, as this area was so depressed last time I shopped it that I wanted to cry. Corso Buenos Aires is one of Milan's most "real" shopping streets—and it has been affected by the hard financial times.

It's also more of a street for teens and 'tweens and may not appeal to designer shoppers at all. The street is almost a mile long and features more than 300 shops: It is one of the most concentrated shopping areas in continental Europe. The best stores are located around the Lima station of the metro.

There are tons of bars, cute restaurants, markets, and fabric shops. This is also the place for jeans stores, unisex fashion stores, moderately priced shoe stores, and knock-offs of the latest Milanese designer goods. Avoid shopping on Saturday, because it's always mobbed. *Remember:* This is where

Aaron's Turn: Of Course, My Corso

The Corso Buenos Aires is a long street with an amazing number of stores. You might want to break this one up into 2 days unless you are really a die-hard shopper. If you can hack it, this street has something for everyone. My favorites were JDC (the "regular" and the "urban" stores), **Tanagra**, and Morgan.

The **JDC urban store** is called urban for a reason. The place is exactly like Urban Outfitters, from products to store lay-out and music selection. It had really cool sneakers, with a huge selection of **Chuck Taylors** and great jeans. Also a lot of baseball Ts and made-to-look-vintage T-shirts.

Morgan is one of the few skater shops I've ever seen abroad and is the only store in Italy I found that carried Etnies.

the real people shop, so few people will speak English. The clientele is not always chic; the scenery is neither cute nor charming.

Many of the shops have no numbers; often the number by a store represents the block rather than the store address (so many shops may be called "3"), but it's all easy once you're there. Just wander and enjoy—you can't miss the good stuff. Oh, yes, Standa is gone (the flagship **Benetton** is there now) but **Upim** is there, with a supermarket in the basement.

You can get there easily by taking the no. 65 streetcar from the Centrale train station and getting off at Corso Buenos Aires (about three stops). Or take the metro to Loreto and walk toward Venezia or vice versa.

Magenta   For the opposite type of experience, get to the Corso Magenta, a rich residential thoroughfare where the best bakeries, cafes, and shopping brands are located to serve those who live in this area; it's the equal to Paris's 16th or 17th arrondissement. From October to May, remember to wear your fur.

Navigli   South of the Porta Ticinese is the canal area of Milan. The canals have been mostly built over, so don't spend too much time looking for a lot of water (wait for Venice): There's just the one canal. Yet the Navigli is becoming a funky shopping neighborhood. You can wander around here for an hour or two if you like colorful junk shops, secondhand shops, artist's studios, and the feeling of getting in on the ground floor of up-and-coming Italian style. Cash only; no one speaks English.

The two streets running along the canal are called **Alzaia Naviglio Grande** and **Ripa di Porta Ticinese.** You can walk down one, cross a bridge, and walk back on the other side. There are some cute restaurants, and you can make an afternoon out of it if this is your kind of thing.

There is an **antiques market** held on the last Sunday of each month on both sides of the Naviglio Grande. Tell your taxi

Aaron's Turn: Corso di Porta Ticinese

This whole area feels a lot like Soho or Williamsburg (Brooklyn) to me: very hip clothing stores, a trendy new *gelateria,* and a charmingly snobbish record store all within a block of each other (just north of the river). The only difference is that much of the culture that was there before it was boutique-ified still remains.

Aside from vintage and outrageously priced denim, the street is home to a large variety of clothing stores. On Corso di Porta Ticinese, the Diesel clothing company has two spinoff stores: **55DSL** and **Diesel Style Lab.** Just like typical Diesel stores, these shops have hip and trendy clothes and are *really* expensive. Even if you don't buy anything, it's fun to look.

Porta Ticinese is also the home of a **Stussy** store and a **Carhartt** store. The Stussy store here was 10 times cooler than any of the ones I've seen in the U.S. It was the only store in Italy I saw that was hip to the new "trucker hat" fad, and they had some really fun novelty items. Unfortunately T-shirts were 36€ ($40) a pop (not outrageous by local standards). The Carhartt store was bigger and had more of a selection, but was still a bit too pricey.

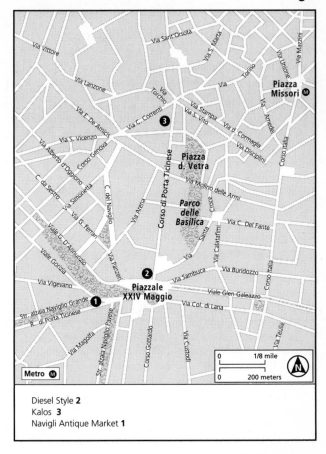

Metro Ⓜ

Diesel Style **2**
Kalos **3**
Navigli Antique Market **1**

driver either that you want *"mercatone dell'antiquariato"* or the name of the street, Ripa Ticinese, which is one of two streets hosting the market along the canal.

Every Tuesday and Saturday there is a regular **street market** along the Viale Papiniano. This is a great place for designer clothing that fell off trucks and all sorts of fun fashions and accessories. Plan to be there early—9 to 10am is fine. In addition to two lanes of stalls selling clothing and dry goods, part of the market is fruit and food.

Jenny's Turn: My Finds Milanese

CARPE DIEM
Viale Tunisia 1 (metro: Porta Venezia).

Need a frog-shaped toilet bowl or a toaster/CD player and don't know where to go? On Viale Tunisia, just off of the main shopping street of Corso Buenos Aires, lies this cute, kitschy tchotchke shop where the colors and odd interpretations of normal household items are as vivid and abstract as the imagination will allow. Stop in and pick up those much-needed monkey-shaped lighters or just to look at the marvels of modern nonsensicality.

KALOS
Corso di Porta Ticinese 50 (metro: Porta Genova).

Walking down Corso di Porta Ticinese, we stumbled upon a funky jewelry shop among the vintage clothing stores. I started gazing longingly at the handmade pieces innocently enough, as I often do when walking past a jewelry store. Then I noticed them. The prices. These gorgeous and unique pieces were priced very generously. What an invitation to shop.

I walked away with two necklaces and a pair of earrings for under 45€ ($50)—that's my kind of budget. The saleswoman (and jewelry designer) was very friendly, although she spoke little English, and gift-wrapped each box uniquely.

The jewelry items make perfect gifts for those at home who want a piece of Italian glamour, and at the same time are perfect for your wallet.

To save money, you can hop on the red line of the metro and get off at San Agostino and be right here.

Porta Vittoria   The Corso di Porta Vittoria begins shortly after the Duomo and changes its name to **Corso 22 Marzo.** Just use your feet. I like this walk because it takes you by **Il Salvagente,**

the discount designer store, and enables you to see something of middle-class Milan along the way.

The walk along Corso Porta Vittoria takes you through an upper-middle-class neighborhood where you'll find branches of many favorite stores, like **Max Mara** and **Bassetti.** This is where well-off locals shop; it's very nontouristy, not unlike the Corso Vercelli. There is a nice branch of **Coin.**

After the street name changes to 22 Marzo, you'll turn left on Via Fratelli Bronzetti to get to **Il Salvagente.** Hail a taxi to take you back to your hotel if you have too much loot.

Aprile & Beyond   Not for the average tourist, Aprile stands for the plaza (piazza) of the same name: XXV Aprile. It is an up-and-coming neighborhood that attracts design mavens and fashion editors because of a handful of important shops in the area, including **High Tech** and **Corso Como 10.** The few retailers who have set up shop here are inventive, creative, and exciting, so take a look if you want to be in with the in crowd. If you are more interested in sightseeing, and don't have much time in Milan, this area may not be for you.

Piazza XXV Aprile is between the Moscova and Garibaldi stops on the green line. After this plaza, Corso Garibaldi changes its name and becomes Corso Como.

MILAN RESOURCES FROM A TO Z

Antiques

Milan's antiques markets are great fun, but don't be afraid to get out of town to explore a few more. In Pavia and Brescia, there are antiques markets on the second Sunday of each month. In Carimate (Como), there's a flea market on the third Sunday. Begamo Alta also celebrates on the third Sunday, in Piazza Angelini. During April and October, many villages have antiques markets on certain Sundays. Ask your hotel concierge for details. For markets in Milan proper, see "Flea Markets," later in this chapter.

Antiques stores are located mostly in the Brera area, on or off Via Madonnina, with a few fancier ones in the Montenapo area. The Montenapo shops do not offer affordable items for mere mortals.

Serious dealers include **Legatoria Conti Borboni,** at Corso Magenta 31, for antique books; **Amabile,** at Via Brera 16, for carpets; and **Mauro Brucoli,** at Via della Spiga 46, for furniture. There's a tiny gallery of about 8 or 10 shops right near the Sheraton Luxury Hotels—the Palace Hotel and the Principe di Savoia—and the Jolly Hotel Touring. Take the Repubblica metro and walk or taxi to **La Piazzetta degli Antiquari** (at Via Turati 6).

Bath

LUSH
Via Fiori Chiari 6 (metro: Duomo).

I am assuming that most readers already know the Lush chain, either from visits in the U.K. or Canada or from the press. If you have no idea what I am talking about, this is going to be a must-do experience. For those who already know and may even be bored with the gimmick, snap out of it—what's brilliant here is that the concept has been adapted to local specialties, so you find things like limoncello shampoo, not sold in stores outside of Italy. While prices are not bargain basement, the novelty factor is high. This street is right off the Via Brera; there are now Lush stores all over Italy, so if you miss this one, you may still find another in your travels. Check out www.lush.it for more about the chain's Italian stores.

MIMOSA
Via Solferino 12 (metro: Duomo).

This small shop sells bath products from several international brands; what you want are the local brands. I've fallen for a line of mud products called Guam made by Lacote, which, despite either of these names, is indeed an Italian firm. Many of the products are made with algae, and then there's mud with algae—my fave. There are products for body, face, and bath. The shop's owner does speak English and will explain products and how to use them.

Books

There's a small international bookstore upstairs at the Armani Superstore (Via Manzoni 31) and another, larger one upstairs at 10 Corso Como.

MONDADORI
Corso Vittorio Emanuele II (metro: Duomo or Babila).

This is a big, modern bookstore with as much crammed downstairs as there is on the street level. It has an enormous selection in every category and a very good travel department. It offers some books in foreign languages, including English, and some gift items. There are now similar bookstores, sort of American-style superstores if you will, in the area and in other parts of Milan. It's a trend.

RIZZOLI
Galleria Vittorio Emanuele 79 (metro: Duomo).

This large bookstore has books in several languages and a travel department toward the front of the store, although it may not have the latest editions of guides. Open evenings and on Sunday.

Boutiques

FONTANA
Via della Spiga 33 (metro: Montenapoleone).

Modern Italian design of the most expensive and highest order. The interior is swank and very Milano, with lots of marble and sleek woods. The counters are suspended from thin wires and seem to hang in midair.

GIO MORETTI
Via della Spiga 4–6 (metro: Montenapoleone).

There are three different Gio Moretti stores: one for men, one
for women, and one for children (across the street). You'll see
all the big names here: For women, stock up on Sonia Rykiel,
Complice, and those designers who don't have their own free-
standing shops.

MICHELE MABELLE/MILANO MONAMOUR
Via della Spiga 36 (metro: Montenapoleone).

The name is enough to make you fall in love. Inside you'll find
Norma Kamali, Kansai, and Thierry Mugler, plus wild sequiny
T-shirts, a glitzy interior, and piped-in rock music.

RUFFO RESEARCH
Via della Spiga 48 (metro: Montenapoleone).

Two different stores, next door to each other, one for men and
one for women. It's leather, it's trendy, it's fairly priced considering how cool it is, and you will swoon at how leather can
be made to wrap, droop, flow, swing, and dance around the
body. The leather is so light and fine that it drapes like fabric.
Much of the work is created by Greek designer Sophia Kokos-
alaki, but the force behind the scenes is the president of the
firm, Giacomo Corsi, who insists on innovative style for both
the men's and women's lines. Hides come from Tuscany and
are worked on by the most famous Italian leather workers in
order to get them light enough to meet the requirements of the
design technology. The results are downright revolutionary.

Cashmere

One of the questions I am most frequently asked is about
cashmere—and Italian cashmere is of the highest quality
because of the way it is combed and milled. With so many factories in northern Italy, there's the chance to buy at outlets or
to check out what may have fallen off a truck and is being sold

at markets. I saw the best buys at the Tuesday/Saturday market.

DORIANI
Via Sant' Andrea 2 (metro: Montenapoleone).

More of a men's than women's source, more of an English than a cutting-edge look—but luxe beyond belief.

LORO PIANO
Via Montenapoleone 27 (metro: Montenapoleone).

This three-story temple to cashmere and luxe sells not only men's and women's things but items for the home. There are also interactive displays like videos and tests you can perform to see how the fabrics hold up, proving this is an art and a science.

MALO
Via della Spiga 7 (metro: Montenapoleone).

One of the most famous names in Italian quality cashmere, Malo has opened a shop that sells both men's and women's lines; in summer there are non-cashmere items, too. The factory outlet is located outside of Florence (see chapter 6).

MANRICO
Corso Magenta 11 (metro: Cardona).

The address says it all—this is a local source for those with money who are in the know. There's also a store in Aspen, so you get the idea.

Costume Jewelry

ANGELA PINTALDI
Via San Pietro All'Orto 9 (metro: Duomo).

This is very serious costume jewelry. Pintaldi's work is similar to Bulgari's, but funkier. For the last decade, Pintaldi has ruled as the in creator of creative and expressive jewelry, frequently made with semiprecious stones. She also works with ivory and other materials, based on color and texture—pure magic meets pure art.

Department Stores

ARMANI SUPERSTORE
Via Manzoni 31 (metro: Montenapoleone).

I don't know what to call this except a department store, although the word "showroom" comes to mind . . . as does "showcase," as does *"ohmigod."* I am horrified and delighted with the store and think all students of retail, marketing, and merchandising should rush here for a look-see. Everyone else, well, you are on your own.

The store is almost a city block long; it has three levels, some of which bleed through from one to the next to add height and drama. The giant video screen says it all—this is a store for people who don't know how to read (although there is a small bookstore upstairs). There's also a cafe, a branch of Nobu, a florist, and all the Armani lines, many of which have goods that are not sold elsewhere, such as the home-furnishings line, which looks like something designed by Terrence Conran. I am partial to the jeans line because the logo is AG, which are my son's initials. To me the best part of the store is the large makeup bar, because Armani makeup is great and relatively hard to find, even in Italy.

COIN
Piazza Giornate 5 (metro: Corso Vercelli);
Corso Vercelli 30–32 (metro: Corso Vercelli);
Piazzale Cantore (metro: Porta Romana);
Piazzale Loreto (metro: Loreto).

Pronounced "co-*een,*" Coin is not as convenient or as much fun as La Rinascente. But if you find yourself near one of the stores, by all means check it out. (There are four different locations in Milan.) I also find that Coin has more energy than La Rinascente and is more likely to have hot styles and designer copies. In fact, Coin specializes in designer-inspired looks at moderate prices; they have completely re-created themselves in the past 2 years and are far more upscale than ever before.

La Rinascente
Piazza del Duomo (metro: Duomo).

Being across the street from the Duomo and in the center of Milan makes this store seem more exciting than it is, although if I go in need of a design fix, I come away impressed.

There's a lot of merchandise in the store, and this is a good place to see a lot and absorb trends and makers quickly. The style of the store is in the American-Anglo model, so don't expect all goods to be Italian or to feel very Italian while shopping here.

Check out the handbag department for a good selection of low-to-moderately priced items. This is one of the few places in Italy where you can get a nice-looking 91€ ($100) bag. Other good departments are children's and active sportswear. The ski clothes are sensational, but expensive. I also like the basement housewares space, especially the small gourmet food market.

The big fashion names are not well represented in women's fashion, but there are lots of real-people clothes at fair (for Italy) prices. Here's the latest: the spa (7th floor) overlooks the spires of the Duomo.

The store does not close for lunch during the week, except on Monday, when the store opens late (1:45pm). The hours are extraordinary, especially for Italy: Monday though Saturday from 9am to 9pm. The store does have some special Sunday openings now.

Note that this is a full-service department store; along with the cafe there are hairdresser and beauty facilities, free alterations except on sale goods, banking facilities with an ATM, customer service, etc.

OVIESSE
Corso Buenos Aires (metro: Porta Venezia).

Technically this might be a lifestyle store, not a department store; it is the antithesis of the Armani Superstore. This is a temple to cheap thrills; the most exciting copies of fashions for the least amount of money you have ever seen . . . it is the Italian version of H&M and then some. I went nuts here and dream of going to all their other stores. Skirts for 18€ ($20). Knit polo shirts for 14€ ($15). You get my drift. Sizes up to 52, although the sizes run a little small.

UPIM
Corso Buenos Aires (metro: Porta Venezia);
Piazza San Babila (metro: Babila).

Bury my heart at the Piazza San Babila, because I will never forgive the Upim powers for what they have done to this store. Who takes a great dime store and turns it into Penney's, I ask you? It doesn't close for lunch; it may have inexpensive cashmere sweaters (if you come in the winter); and it is worth exploring, but, gosh, I liked the old Upim better. The Buenos Aires store is larger and also has a grocery store in the basement. The lower level at San Babila has trendy fashion and men's fashion, as well as lingerie; on the street level there's mostly women's fashion with some accessories and makeup, the reverse of what you'll find at the Corso Buenos Aires store.

Designer Boutiques

AMERICAN & CANADIAN BIG NAMES

Obviously you didn't go to Italy to buy American designs. Still, there is an American invasion beginning to take place in many different financial brackets. **Timberland** has three stores in town, **Foot Locker** is everywhere (try Corso Vittorio Emanuele II for convenience's sake), and **Guess** has opened quite a temple to teens, their second store in Italy, at Piazza San Babila. (The other is in Florence.)

Calvin Klein is in a large, sparse, very minimalist fancy-dancy space on the fashionable Via Durini. There is also a **CK** Milan store, and there are plans in the pipeline for a **CKCollection** store too.

Among the foreign-based arrivals is the makeup guru from Canada, by way of Estée Lauder: **MAC** is now in a very spiffy shop in the Brera district, having already moved off Via della Spiga.

CONTINENTAL & U.S. BIG NAMES

Use Montenapoleone metro for all listings, unless otherwise noted.

BODY SHOP
Via Brera 30 (metro: Duomo).

CARTIER
Via Montenapoleone 16.

CELINE
Via Montenapoleone 25.

CHANEL
Via Sant' Andrea 10.

CHRISTIAN DIOR
Via Montenapoleone 12.

ESCADA
Corso Matteotti 22 (metro: Babila).

FOGAL
Via Montenapoleone 1.

GAULTIER
Via della Spiga 20.

GIEVES & HAWKES
Via Manzoni 12.

HELMUT LANG
Via Sant' Andrea 14.

HERMÈS
Via Sant' Andrea 21.

HUGO BOSS
Corso Matteotti 11 (metro: Babila).

KENZO
Via Sant' Andrea 11.

LAURA ASHLEY
Via Brera 4 (metro: Duomo).

LOUIS VUITTON
Via Montenapoleone 2.

PAUL SMITH
Via Manzoni 30.

RENA LANGE
Via della Spiga 7.

SWATCH
Via della Spiga 1.

TIFFANY & CO.
Via della Spiga 19a.

TIMBERLAND
Galleria San Carlo 9 (metro: Babila).

UNGARO
Via Montenapoleone 27.

WOLFORD
Via Manzoni 16b.

YVES SAINT LAURENT (YSL RIVE GAUCHE)
Via Montenapoleone 27.

ITALIAN BIG NAMES

ALBERTA FERRETTI
Via Montenapoleone 21a.

ANTONIO FUSCO
Via Sant' Andrea 11.

ARMANI CASA
Via Durini 24 (metro: Babila).

ARMANI SUPERSTORE
Via Manzoni 31.

ATELIER VERSACE
Via Gesù 12.

BENETTON (SUPERSTORE)
Corso Vittorio Emanuele II (metro: Duomo or Babila).

BLUMARINE (ANNA MOLINARI)
Via della Spiga 42.

BOTTEGA VENETA
Via Montenapoleone 5.

BRIONI
Via Gesù 4.

BYBLOS
Via della Spiga 42.

CERRUTI 1881
Via della Spiga 20.

D&G
Corso Venezia 7.

DIESEL
Galleria San Carlo (metro: Babila).

DOLCE & GABBANA
Via della Spiga 26.

EMILIO PUCCI
Via Montenapoleone 14.

ERMENEGILDO ZEGNA
Via Verri 3.

ETRO
Via Montenapoleone 5.

FENDI
Via Sant' Andrea 16.

FERRAGAMO
Via Montenapoleone 3.

GIANFRANCO FERRÉ
Via Sant' Andrea 15.

GIANNI VERSACE
Via Montenapoleone 11.

GIORGIO ARMANI
Via Sant' Andrea 9.

GUCCI
Via Montenapoleone 7.

KRIZIA
Palazzo Krizia, Via Manin (metro: Turati).

LA PERLA
Via Montenapoleone 1.

LAURA BIAGIOTTI
Via Borgospesso 19.

LES COPAINS
Via Manzoni 21.

MARIELLA BURANI
Via Montenapoleone 3.

MARINA RINALDI
Corso Vittorio Emanuele II at Galleria Passarella 2 (metro: Babila).

MAX & CO.
Via Victor Hugo 1.

MAX MARA
Corso Genova 12.

MISSONI
Via Sant' Andrea 2.

MIUMIU
Corso Venezia 3 (metro: Babila).

MOSCHINO
Via della Spiga 30.

NAJ OLEARI
Via Brera 58 (metro: Duomo).

NAZARENO GABRIELLI
Via Montenapoleone 23.

PHILOSOPHY DI ALBERTA FERRETTI
Via Montenapoleone 19.

PRADA
Via Montenapoleone 8.

PRADA (LINGERIE)
Via della Spiga 5.

ROBERTO CAVALLI
Via della Spiga 42.

SAMSONITE
Corso Matteotti 12.

TOD'S
Via della Spiga 22.

VERSACE JEANS COUTURE
Via Carducci 38.

VERSUS
Via San Pietro all'Orto 10.

Discounters

Also see "Outlets (In Town)," later in this section.

D. MAGAZINE
Via Montenapoleone 26 (metro: Montenapoleone).

Considering the address and convenience, this store is a must-do: a discount store selling high-end fashion names right in the heart of the biggest fashion stores in town and not far from the metro station. Now then, I can't tell you I was knocked out by what I saw, but there were Lagerfeld shoes, MiuMiu clothes, and some Helmut Lang items. The names were in place; I just wasn't tempted, and the store wasn't nearly as much fun as Il Salvagente. Still, when in the neighborhood, take a quick look.

IL SALVAGENTE
Via Fratelli Bronzetti 16 (no nearby metro).

American and European styles from big-name designers in suits and dresses; even in larger sizes, but you just have to hit it right. Men's clothing is on the second floor. This looks like a prison; you enter through a gate, walk down the drive, and turn into the door, where you will be asked to use a locker for your bags and maybe even your handbag. During sales it is mobbed. Il Salvagente is the most famous designer discounter in Italy. This is an operation that makes Loehmann's look classy, but if you are strong enough, my God, can you find stuff here. Attention savvy shoppers.

While the labels are still on the clothes, the merchandise is not well organized, so you must be feeling very strong to go through it all. There's so much here that you have a good chance of finding something worthwhile, but you could strike out.

Clothes are located in several parts of the store and upstairs as well; there are dressing rooms. Not everything is new. Some have been seen on runways or are over one season old; not everything is in perfect condition.

On various visits, however, I've seen Krizia, Gianni Versace, Valentino, Guy Laroche, Trussardi, made-in-Italy Lacroix handbags (for 91€/$100 each!), and more. On my most recent visit, I was truly dizzy from all the choices. I once happened on the January sale when prices at the cash register were 30% less than the lowest ticketed price.

Remember: The atmosphere is drab; the display is zero. This place is for the strong and the hungry. Hours: 10am to 12:30pm and 3 to 7pm; closed Monday morning and July 15 to August 30. On Wednesday and Saturday the store does not close for lunch and is open nonstop from 10am till 7pm.

SALVAGENTE BIMBI
Via Balzaretti 28 (no nearby metro).

Il Salvagente has a separate shop for children's clothing called Salvagente Bimbi; the layout is similar to the mother shop, but the store is harder to find—take a taxi, of course. It is hard to find a taxi to get you home, so you may want to ask them to call you a cab. "Taxi" in Italian is *taxi.*

Note: I used a car and driver to get here, and my Milanese driver was lost. Still, if you are looking for expensive kids' clothing at affordable prices, this is the place.

SEVEN GROUP
Via San Gregorio 49 (metro: Centrale).

This was my favorite showroom when I hit the wholesale district near the train station last visit; it's a large, open space, not crammed and crowded like many jobbers. It's open to the public, takes plastic, and gives tax-back refunds! The staff doesn't speak a lot of English, but who cares? I bought my cashmere twin set here and was tempted by many of the fashions. The bad part is that prices are not clearly marked, and you feel like you're a big pain every time you ask a question. Still, the quality and styling are sublime.

VESTISTOCK
Viale Romagna 19;
Via Boscovich 17 (bus no. 60, 90, or 91).

This chain of discount shops can be found in various neighborhoods, including the very convenient Buenos Aires for Viale Romagna and the train station district for Via Boscovich. If you hit it lucky, you can chose from labels such as Les Copains, Moschino, Versace, and Montana. There are men's, women's, and kids' clothes as well as accessories, so go and have a ball. Take bus no. 60, 90, or 91 for the Buenos Aires area shop, or call © **02/749-05-02** for specific directions.

If you prefer the store between the train station and many major hotels, it's open nonstop, from 9:30am to 6:30pm, Monday through Friday. There were Tod's boots when I visited and plenty of men's clothing in large sizes.

Flea Markets

The following markets sell all manner of old and/or used things—what we Americans consider a flea market. The words the Italians use to describe such a market are *mercato di pulci.* Note that more and more flea markets are opening all over Italy, so ask your hotel concierge if there is a new market and check the pages of the monthly magazine *Dove* (pronounced do-*vay:* Italian for "where," not the flying bird) for fairs and flea markets in nearby communities.

BOLLATE ANTIQUE MARKET
Piazza Vittorio Veneto, Bollate (bus no. 90 or 91).

Take the bus or a taxi to this suburb on the north side of Milan, where there is a Sunday *mercato dell'usato,* or antiques market. Unlike most Sunday markets, which are held once a month, this market is held weekly. Most of the dealers sell English antiques, if you can believe that; silver is especially hot, as are old prints. There's not much in the way of bed linens, but there are some old hats and a fair amount of furniture. About 300 dealers.

Consider renting a car for this day in the country, or hop the bus (take the no. 90 or 91 to the **Piazza della Liberta** in Bollante). Open from 8am to 6pm.

BRERA ANTIQUE MARKET (MERCATONE DELL'ANTIQUARIATO)
Via Brera (metro: Duomo).

This flea market, held on the third Saturday of each month, is a local favorite. Because it takes place right in the heart of downtown Milan (in the shadow of La Scala, in fact), this is a drop-dead chic market to be seen prowling. About 50 antiques dealers set up stalls, and many artists and designers turn out. To find it, just head for Via Brera. Do wear your fur and walk your dog, if at all possible.

NAVIGLI ANTIQUE MARKET
Naviglio Grande (metro: Porta Genova).

If flea markets are your thing, be in Milan on the last Sunday of the month. Then you can spend late morning at this fabulous flea market, which stretches all the way from Porta Ticinese to Porta Genova and the Viale Papiniano. With approximately 400 dealers, some say it is the most stylish flea market in all of Europe.

While the market is open from 8am to 2pm, do remember this is Italy, not New York—things are most lively from 10am to noon. You'll find the usual antiques and wonderful junk, and the crowd is one of Milan's top see-and-be-seen. To get here, either ride the metro to the Porta Genova station or take the no. 19 tram to Ripa di Porta Ticinese.

Food & Wine

ARMANDOLA
Via della Spiga 50 (metro: Montenapoleone).

This is a teeny-weeny, tiny, itty-bitty deli with fresh foods, dried mushrooms, tuna in jars, and all sorts of fancy, expensive, and yummy things. In the Tuna Quests, I paid 14€ ($15) for a jar of tuna fish—the recipient said it was worth the price. Some-times I buy a ready-made picnic here; you can't beat the loca-tion for convenience.

ENTECA COTTI
Via Solferino 42 (metro: Duomo).

Considered one of the best wine stores in Milano. They also have serious olive oil, as is the custom at a good *enteca*.

FREE
Centrale train station (metro: Centrale).

Don't snicker; I do a lot of my gourmet-food shopping here because it's convenient. Buy magic coffee here as well as Ital-ian specialty food items for gifts and home use.

PECK
Via Spadari 9 (metro: Duomo).

You can eat in the restaurant or just do takeout from the deli, the most famous in town. Near the Duomo.

Home Style/Showrooms

ALCHIMA
Via Torino 68 (metro: Babila).

One of the longest-running shows in modern Italian design, Alchima started it all and continues to be top-notch for see-ing and believing. The very latest is always on display. Whether you buy or not, you must stop in.

ARFLEX
Via Borgognona 2 (metro: Montenapoleone).

One of the big names in design, Arflex's showroom is filled with all manner of wild, creative home furnishings. A lipstick-red leather sofa, anyone?

B&B ITALIA
Via Durini 14 (metro: Babila).

Almost a supermarket of design stuff; new to the area and another in a string of important style shops. Some smalls and accessories.

CASSINA
Via Durini 16 (metro: Babila or Duomo).

One of the long-standing big names in post–World War II design, Cassina makes mostly office furniture, but all of their pieces are quite avant-garde. Colors are bright, deep, and vibrant, and the design lines are beyond clean. I popped into this showroom recently to look at the leather chairs designed by Mario Bellini—which are the prototype for the plastic Bellini chairs that my friend Alan makes with Bellini (at a Target store near you). Even though I was just snooping, the people in the showroom could not have been more gracious.

LISA CORTI
Via Conchetta 6 (tram no. 15).

I don't even know how to describe this space or shopping situation—it is a showroom, but it's also different. First off, you should know or understand who Lisa Corti is—an artist and magician with color and textiles, whose work is sold at Saks and is best seen in the pages of the Saks home-furnishings catalogs, which always have at least one full page in color with stacks of her things.

Corti is best known for her home design for tables, beds, and sofas, but also makes clothes for women and children and other accessories, and at one time, dishes or ceramics. She is an artist and does it all; her work is her signature. Even her postcards are glorious (and free). Perhaps a look-see on the website might help: www.lisacorti.com.

The showroom is in the middle of nowhere; if you take a taxi, have the driver wait for you. There is a front door on the street, but I didn't find it and went in through the courtyard. I also called (© 02/58-10-00-31) from my mobile phone, as I thought I was lost.

The showroom inside is the real showroom and work-room; the shopping op is sort of like being in the factory out-let. The prices are not low, but are just a fraction of the U.S. price. I paid about 136€ ($150) for a quilt that I had paid 227€ ($250) for in the south of Italy and that costs $350 at Saks. The showroom does detax, and someone there does speak Eng-lish. You might want to call ahead before you make the trek; hours are 10am to 1pm and 3 to 7pm.

Linens & Lace

BASSETTI
Corso Vittorio Emanuele II 15 (metro: Duomo).

A famous name in linens for years, Bassetti makes the kind of linens that fall between ready-to-wear and couture—they're more affordable than the big-time expensive stuff and far nicer than anything you'd find at the low end. Although it does sell colors, its hot look is paisley fabrics in the Etro vein. There are branch stores in every major Italian city.

FRETTE
Via Montenapoleone 21 (metro: Montenapoleone).

This line has gone so far upscale that Frette now calls it "home couture," with items such as pajamas and robes and leisure clothing as well as sheets and bedding for sale. Naturally there is a business in custom-created bed linen as well. There is an outlet store near the Jolly Hotel President at Largo Augusto.

JESURUM
Via Verri 4 (metro: Duomo).

A branch of the Venetian linen house, famous for old lace bro-cades, really swanky stuff—with prices to match.

PRATESI
Via Montenapoleone 27 (metro: Montenapoleone).

The biggest and best shop for this family-held sheet and luxe group is the flagship space in Milan, where prices are 25% to 40% less than those in the U.S., and there's merchandise galore. But then, I am assuming you can't make it to the outlet store. Climb the stairs to the large showroom for the best selection of sheets, tablecloths, and other linens. Don't neglect the mezzanine level for children's sheets and other items appropriate for setting up a nursery.

Makeup

Don't look now, but there is a color war in Italy, centered in Milan, where everyone is suddenly doing makeup. This was probably instigated by the success of Versace makeup, which was actually launched a few months after the Versace murder and was obviously created before he died. With the success of makeup artist lines in the U.S., several Italian names have jumped into the fray. Most of the names are not familiar to Americans; some of them have pedigrees, however. And then there's Armani.

DIEGO DELLA PALMA
Via Madonnina 13 (metro: Duomo).

This is embarrassing, but here goes: I am forever getting Diego della Palma, a well-known local makeup artist, and Diego della Viale, the creator of Tod's shoes, mixed up. That said, Palma is an artist with connections to the Italian couture houses; he has a small shop that also sells his line, where you can make an appointment for lessons and a makeover. The address is adjacent to the Brera district on a great shopping street.

GIORGIO ARMANI
Via Manzoni 31 (metro: Montenapoleone).

As we go to press, Armani makeup did not have wide distribution in Italy or elsewhere in the world. This could be because the line is so new, and the intent is to keep it very exclusive. Regardless, you can see it all and play with it all at the Armani flagship (the line is also sold in Milan's La Rinascente). I have tested many of the products and adore the pearlized liquid foundation that really does add light to the face. Last time I bought a blush; it was presented to me in its own little Armani canvas tote bag.

KIKO
Corso Buenos Aires 43 (metro: Lima).

By the time I got to Kiko, a cute little shop in the best part of the trendy shopping (near metro stop Lima) on Buenos Aires, I could no longer tell one brand from the next. I can't quite tell how this line differs from Madina, although it is not as sophisticated in the packaging and marketing. Still, the line is well priced and is getting raves from local fashion editors.

MAC
Via Fiori Chiari 12 (metro: Duomo).

MAC, the professional color line from Canada, now owned by Estée Lauder, which has gone global, has a freestanding store in the Brera area. Aside from buying the products, you can get a makeup lesson or just play with the colors. The professional line is sold; all charitable promotions, such as products whose profits go to good causes, are continued in international stores.

MADINA
Corso Venezia 23 (metro: Babila).

With stores in Milan, Tokyo, and New York, Madina is the color story the press is in love with: Madina—sort of the Italian version of France's Terry de Gunzberg—used to do makeup for the opera at La Scala. She is married to the man who owns the most famous luxury cosmetics factory in Europe. The stores are small, but the packaging is very, very slick. Imprinted on the tablets of color are slogans in English—"color is seduction," "color is power," etc. Terry also does something like this, by the way.

There are hundreds of shades; the strength of the line is said to be in the intensity of the colors and their staying power. I tested several items, and while I like them, I don't find them any more extraordinary than other brands. Prices are moderate to low—a paint box of 12 shades of cream eye shadow for 14€ ($15) is a steal, and a great gift for anyone. There's also a wide selection of brushes and several styles of makeup bags. There is another store in Milan, Via Meravigli 17, which is on the corner of Corso Magenta, an upscale residential area with nice shopping.

NAJ OLEARI
Via Brera 28 (metro: Duomo).

Because this fabric designer is known for her bright colors, it makes sense that the firm would branch into color cosmetics, which are sold even in most big department stores. The line is so successful that now spa and treatment products have been added. Don't ask me: I don't make the news; I only report it.

PERLIER/KLEMATA
(ARMONIA NATURALI)
Corso Buenos Aires 25 (metro: Loreto).

You may remember Perlier as a French bath line; it was bought by the Italian Klemata family, who now has a chain of very spiffy bath and makeup stores all over Italy. There is probably a store coming to a mall near you in no time. This year the Klematas joined the color wars and added a color makeup line under the Perlier brand; it is sold only in their stores, which are named "Armonia Naturali." There are four other shops dotted around Milan.

Shu Uemura
Via Brera 2 (metro: Duomo).

Uemura is the king of color and the man who started it all over 20 years ago in Japan, where he brought professional makeup to the public. His products have a cult following, and he is clearly in a league above all others, as are his prices.

Markets

To a local, there's a big difference between a market and a flea market. A market sells fruits and vegetables and dry goods, and a flea market sells old junk. See "Flea Markets," p. 252.

San Agostino Market
Viale Papiniano (metro: San Agostino).

First, I must admit that no other guidebook calls this the San Agostino Market. I call it that because San Agostino is the name of the closest metro stop, and it helps me remember where this market is located on the Viale Papiniano.

This is a T-shaped market. The cross of the T is the fruit, food, and vegetable market; the long stroke is the dry-goods market. The dry-goods portion goes on for 2 blocks, so don't quit after the first block. Everything in the world is sold here, including a few designer items that seem to have fallen off the backs of trucks (but are carefully mixed in with less valuable items). For example, one dealer in the dry-goods market seems to specialize in bath articles, but also has a small selection of Missoni bathrobes.

You'll find everything here: the latest teen fashions, tapes and CDs, kitchen supplies, car supplies, pet supplies, aprons, and housedresses. There are also socks, towels, batteries, luggage, underwear, sewing thread, running shoes, designer shoes, lace curtains, and fabrics by the bolt. I saw the best cashmeres at the best prices here.

The market is open on Tuesday and Saturday.

Menswear

Boggi
Piazza San Babila 3 (metro: Babila).

Boggi specializes in the English look, the preppy look; whatever you call it, you'll find cable-knit sweaters and plaid hunting trousers. There are several shops; the main store is near Via Montenapoleone. It's not cheap here, but the quality is very high.

Cashmere Cotton and Silk
Via Madonnina 19 (metro: Duomo).

This is one of those fancy stores on the little side streets of Brera that is worth looking at, if only for its charm. Walk down a rather long corridor until you get into the store, which is modern with an old-fashioned feel. Inside, you'll find Milanese yuppies scurrying around, choosing among the shirts, sweaters, and suits made only of the three fibers in the store's name. Prices are very, very high, but the shopping experience makes you feel like royalty.

Dior Homme
Via Montenapoleone 24 (metro: Montenapoleone).

I am not sure which is more gorgeous, the architecture or the slim young things who shop here. They're all worth staring at in this new store, one of several men's stores created specifically to sell the work of Hedi Slimane. It's very stainless steel and art-gallery minimal; the dressing rooms have mirrors created by sensors that relay your image onto the wall.

Eddy Monetti
Piazza San Babila 4 (metro: Babila).

One of the leading sources for Anglo style in Milan, Monetti deals with rich gentlemen who want to look even richer. They hand-stitch suits and shirts but also sell off the rack. The Monetti customer likes special service and hates to shop; he wants to come here and be pampered and know that he'll walk out looking like a million euros.

ERMENEGILDO ZEGNA
Via Pietro Verri 3 (metro: Duomo).

For centuries, the Zegna family has excelled in the quality wool business. Until recently, the ready-to-wear was a small side-line, but now the world's richest men can buy the best suits that Italy ready-makes in a smattering of freestanding boutiques. There's one in Paris, one in Florence, and this shop in Milan, which is the closest to the mill in Biella and serves as the family flagship store. The shop is large and modern and sells classic tailoring to discriminating men. Although the house is famous for its wools, you can get other items, including cotton or silk dress shirts.

TINCATI
Piazza Oberdan 2
Via Verri 1 (metro: Montenapoleone).

An old-fashioned men's store, or haberdashery (as they used to be called), with fine woods on the walls and an upper mez-zanine filled with stock. Very good old-world reputation. Not for hotshots who want the Euro-Japanese look. Its shirts are famous because they come with a tab that passes between the legs (trust me on this) and an extra collar and two cuffs.

Outlets (In Town)

ETRO
Via Spartaco 3 (no nearby metro; ask concierge about bus).

This began life as an employee store in the firm's offices, but it's open to the public and is the kind of secret that every smart shopper in Milano knows about. It closes for lunch from 1:45 until 2:45pm. Saturday hours are 10am to 1:45pm. Closed Sunday. They take plastic. Now then, did I have fun? I get sweaty just remembering. The tiny shop has two levels;

the clothes are downstairs. There are bins of things; I got men's pocket squares for 23€ ($25) each; silk suspenders for 14€ ($15). There is fabric by the meter and everything else.

FRETTE HOTEL LINEN OUTLET
Via Visconti di Modrone 15 (metro: Babila).

In bed linen, Frette has two different consumer lines: an everyday, rather average line that I don't find particularly special, and an upscale line meant to compete with Pratesi. There is a third line, from the hotel division, which makes sheets for many of the world's five-star palace hotels (like the Ritz in Paris and the Four Seasons in New York). This division has an outlet store right in the heart of town; don't miss it if you enjoy the outlet rummage.

The outlet store is actually the employees' store right in the office building. You enter the building and then hang a left into the shop, where things are in boxes, on shelves, and on a few racks. As at all outlets, it's hit or miss. No one speaks English; no credit cards. Much of what you see has been made for the hotel business. Prices are excellent compared with the quality of the goods. Besides bed linen, there are bathrobes, etc.

The outlet shop is not far from the Jolly Hotel President and is worth the adventure, even though you may come up empty-handed.

There is another Frette outlet in the suburbs (Via Vittorio Veneto 45, Concerezzo; ✆ 02/606-93-90) that has everything and is not confined to the hotel line, as is this resource. For more on out-of-town outlets, see "Beyond Milan," at the end of this chapter.

LISA CORTI
See "Home Style/Showrooms," earlier in this chapter.

MAX MARA
Galleria San Carlo 6 (metro: Babila).

I can't stop to sing about this outlet as I am too busy getting there. It's large, it's clean, it looks like a normal store, it carries all of the Max Mara makes, including the Marina Rinaldi (large size) line. It has two levels, it has coats for 41€ ($45), and it takes plastic. *Note:* This location is in a mall. You will easily find the mall but may have trouble finding the actual store, as the mall has alleys. Ask.

Outlets (Out of Town)

See p. 152 for outlets in northern Italy.

FIDENZA VILLAGE
Autostrada A1.

This new outlet center is closer to Bologna but not all that far from Milan. Drive.

SERRAVALLE SCRIVIA
Serravalle Scrivia.

This is the oldest of the American-style outlet malls in Italy, meaning it's about 3 years old. It's closer to Genoa than Milan, although it's only an hour's drive from Milan. Don't try to do this on public transportation. I spent over an hour with my hotel concierge and his computer trying to route this, and with changing trains and all that stuff it was a nightmare not worth attempting.

Paper Goods

PINEIDER
Corso Manzoni 40 (metro: Montenapoleone).

Italy's most famous name in paper goods and old-fashioned, heavy-duty, richer-than-thou stationery is Pineider, with stores in every major city. The real news is that this old-timey brand has decided to perk itself up as other brands have done. Accordingly, it has hired the American designer Rebecca Moses, who lives in Milan, and has expanded beyond paper goods to gift items that are chic, sublime, and very expensive. There are now a few shops in Milan.

Perfume

For the most part, perfume is expensive in Italy, and you must be smart to catch a bargain, so buy it at the airport duty-free or in La Rinascente, where you get a 10% discount at the check-out counter if you show your passport. There are several branches of the enormous German chain **Douglas** dotted around the main shopping districts: You may want to ask about their Douglas Card, which can be used in any of the stores worldwide and will bring you extra perks.

If you are a fan of the scent **Acqua Di Parma,** note they have their first freestanding store, Via Gesù 3. If money is no object, pop into **Profumo,** Via Brera 6, where American and English imports are sold at higher prices than you are used to.

Secondhand Fashion

I spent a day touring many of Milan's tony secondhand shops because this form of alternate retail is so important in Paris and New York. I wish I could say this was great, that I bought stuff, or I think you'll want to. I am listing the best shops, but with the understanding that this kind of shopping is very hit or miss; you are on your own.

L' ARMADIO DI LAURA
Via Voghera 25 (metro: Genova).

This is by far the largest and the best, but it is a bit out of the way, although the woman working there (who speaks English perfectly) told me that most people come on the metro. The area is industrial; the building is frightening on first approach—only because everything is unfamiliar. You press the button on the console, enter the gate, cross the courtyard, and enter through a door slightly to your right, at maybe one o'clock on the clock system of direction-giving.

The store smells like used clothes; it's the same musty smell all of these stores have, but it's not a dirty-clothes smell. Designer clothes are packed into racks; there are some shoes and handbags and accessories. There are some sizes larger than 46 (thank God!). Hours are Tuesday through Saturday from 10am to 6pm; in summer the store is also open on Monday.

MERCATINI MICHELA
Corso Venezia 8 (metro: Babila).

I like this store because it's easy to get to and has very expensive clothes. I've never bought anything, but it's easy to pop up (the store is upstairs in an office building) and check. Sometimes you can find Pucci. They do a big business in wedding gowns.

Shoes & Leather Goods

Shoe shops obviously abound with shoes in just about all price ranges. The greatest problem with cheap shoes is that they wear out more quickly than well-made shoes. You can stick to brand-name shoes in Milan, or explore some of the low-cost no-names—it's all here. No-name shoes start at about 27€ ($30) a pair. Better no-name shoes cost 45€ ($50) a pair. Just wander the middle-class neighborhoods where real people shop.

In expensive shoes, there are two completely different schools of thought: English-style, conservative, country classics that you wear for 20 years, and high-fashion fluff bundles that will last only a season or two but will signal the world that you are a major player.

Please note that I have listed several of the big-name leather-goods firms under "Italian Big Names," earlier in this chapter, because they are more or less icons in the business and most of them also have clothing lines. The following names are not as famous in the U.S., but they deserve attention while you are studying the scene in Milan.

BOTTEGA VENETA
Via Montenapoleone 5 (metro: Montenapoleone).

BRUNO MAGLI
Corso Vittorio Emanuele (metro: Duomo).

CASADEI
Via Sant' Andrea 15b (metro: Babila).

COCCINELLE
Via Manzoni and Via Bigli (metro: Babila).

HOGAN
Via della Spiga 22 (metro: Montenapoleone).

SUPERGA
Via San Pietro all'Orto 11 (metro: Babila).

VALEXTRA
Piazza San Babila 1 (metro: Babila).

Sporting Goods

BRIGATTI
Corso Venezia 15 (metro: Babila).

Located on the edge of the Golden Triangle, Brigatti is a giant of a store, with floor-to-ceiling wood paneling, wide stairways, and stock-filled cabinets that are higher than three men. They carry all major brands, plus a wide selection of no-names. Tons of Fila. You really do not need another sportswear listing in Milan: This is where you find the colored gear you've seen on TV during Olympic telecasts.

PETER SPORT
Piazza Liberty 8 (metro: Duomo).

Around the corner from the Duomo, Peter Sport is my backup or control store for sporting goods and active sportswear. I prefer to load up at Brigatti, but I always check here to make sure I'm not missing out on anything. Peter Sport has three levels, a creaky elevator, and more stuff than you could ever dream of wearing, even if you are a professional athlete.

Tabletop & Gifts

HABITAT
Corso Vercelli 10;
Piazza Diaz, across from the Duomo (metro: Duomo);
Corso XXII Marzo 25, near Il Salvagente.

Habitat is what the locals consider a moderately priced store.
(We remind you that nothing in Italy is moderately priced.) Still,
you may find some gift items here, or at least be able to pick
up on the latest Italian design trends. Worth a visit for those
who are into design.

HIGH TECH
Piazza XXV Aprile 12 (metro: Garibaldi).

By Milan standards, High Tech is an enormous place. The second floor of this two-story selling space is completely devoted
to home furnishings, all with the look we've come to associate with the city of Milan. Begun by Aldo Cibic, formerly of
Memphis Milano fame.

IMMAGINAZIONE
Via Brera 16 (metro: Duomo).

As always, the Via Brera is a great place for finding new, hot
looks. This shop is no exception—it's crammed with weird but
wonderful stuff, including tableware, gift items, and cuff links.

LISA CORTI
See "Home Style/Showrooms," earlier in this chapter.

LORENZI
Via Montenapoleone 9 (metro: Montenapoleone).

After you finish with plastics, head to Milan's head cutlery store,
where you can also buy pipes and other gifts and gadgets
for men.

MORONIGOMMA
Via Braccio da Montone, at Via Giusti (metro: Babila).

This store has plastics from all over the world, so don't buy any of the expensive American products. Instead, get a load of Italian designer vinyl, car products, and household items.

With its affordable prices, this may be the only store in Milan where you can go wild and not be sorry the next day. It's conveniently located at the start of Via Montenapoleone, on the far side of the Piazza San Babila; there are many other wonderful design hangouts in the area.

SHED
Viale Umbria 42 (no nearby metro).

This former cheese factory has furniture designs from French big names as well as Italian and Japanese movers and shakers. A must-do for those with an eye for design—even if you don't buy a thing. Furthermore, the location is within walking distance of my trusty clothing discounter Il Salvagente.

TAD
Via di Croce Rossa 1 (metro: Montenapoleone).

Despite an unfamiliar-sounding address, this is in the heart of the Montenapo area and right near the metro station. (How else would I find it?) A multilevel shop selling candles, gifts, some home furnishings, and more, Tad is a store filled with ideas, so even if you don't buy anything, stop by and stare.

Teens

Teens need no specific addresses; just plop them onto Corso Buenos Aires. Or, try these specialty label stops.

DIESEL STORE
Galleria San Carlo (metro: Babila).

All the Diesel products (way beyond jeans) as well as a Style Lab; teen heaven.

ONYX
Corso Vittorio Emanuele 11 and 24 (metro: Duomo).

Cheap thrills and an amazing scene filled with technology and great clothes at great prices, sort of the local version of H&M.

MILAN ON A SCHEDULE

TOUR 1: MILANO PRONTO

No time to go shopping? Traveling with a man who paces in front of stores and makes you nuts? Between business meetings and have only an hour to yourself? For your Milan visit, may I suggest this spree:

1. Begin at the **Galleria** and walk briskly through it, pausing to look at the ceiling, to stare at the original Prada, and maybe to dash into **Rizzoli** for guidebooks in English . . . and maybe a hat for him at **Borsolino** . . . and something wonderful for you at **Prada**—the fur-lined sleeping bag, perhaps. Cut through the mall, heading to your right to La Scala, and hit the Via Verdi at a brisk pace: Now you are headed toward the Brera district.

2. After the Via Verdi changes names to become the Via Brera, begin window-shopping until you get to Via Fiori Chiari, which comes up on your left. You are now in the most charming neighborhood in Milan; it's so beautiful that you don't even need to go into the antiques shops. But you may. Just don't ignore the old buildings, the narrow doorways, the painted shutters, the flowers . . . then you get to **Lush** (no. 7): It's British, not Italian, but with an Italian accent, and so much fun you must indulge.

3. Stroll a few short blocks until you get to an alley on your right. Turn into it, then look left in the middle of the block and enter **Etro,** one of the seats of Italian luxury goods. The store's front is on the Via Pontaccio, which runs parallel to Fiori Chiari,

but the doors to get into this three-part store are on this side alley. They have a newer store on Via Montenapoleone, but the fragrance store is here, and this part is small, charming, and fabulous to sniff around.

4. When you leave Etro, backtrack and cross the Via Fiori Chiari and head on to Via Madonnina, continuing to window-shop. Merge onto Via Mercato, then veer toward the Duomo to the famous gourmet food store **Peck** (Via Spadari 9). Didn't Mother tell you the way to a man's heart was through his stomach? Buy something fattening and eat it while you walk, or buy a total picnic and take it to the Castle. Peck has several shops in the area, including a sit-down restaurant, **Peck Rosticceria** (Via Cantu 3), and a wine shop, **Bottega del Vino** (Victor Hugo 4). There are other food shops in this warren of streets, including a little supermarket.

5. Wander from here to the Duomo, about a block away, and light a candle that you got to go shopping at all. Didn't buy much? Well, maybe next time. If you didn't eat lunch at Peck or want to continue the tour, you can grab a bite at the cafe at **La Rinascente** and then shop this department store. You can then amble along the Corso Vittorio Emanuele II and grab hold of the tony Montenapo area (see the next section).

TOUR 2: BIG NAMES TO BARGAINS: ALL-DAY TOUR

This tour is best done as a walking trip, so wear comfortable shoes and carry your high heels in your tote bag, because you'll want them for trying on clothes when you get to the bargains. Of course, you may end up buying a new pair of shoes before you get to the bargains, but better safe than sorry. I bought three pair the last time I wandered around this part of town.

With a whole day at your disposal, you can see the best of two worlds: Milan's Golden Triangle of designer shops and Milan's best discounters, where you buy the clothes you saw in the Golden Triangle at better prices.

1. Begin your day in the high-fashion district of Via Monte-napoleone, lovingly called Montenapo, the main drag of the Golden Triangle where most of the major designers have boutiques that are downright amazing.

   Start with Montenapo itself, then hit the side streets. The streets to prowl are Via Sant' Andrea, Via Gesù, Via Santo Spirito, Via Borgospesso, and Via della Spiga. About half of the stores on these streets are internationally known designer-related shops; the others are small, but chic, local treasures devoted to jewelry, antiques, children's clothes, or leather goods. Concentrate on Italian names because the French ones are way too expensive. If you need a break, stop for coffee at the Four Seasons Hotel, which is in a convent on Via Gesù and has a small indoor cafe overlooking the garden.

2. When finished with the Montenapoleone area, walk toward San Babila and the outlet store owned by **Max Mara** (Galleria San Carlo 6) then maybe the resale shop **Michela** (Corso Venezia 8 at San Babila).

   Now head toward the Duomo on Corso Vittorio Emanuele II from San Babila. Be sure to stop at La Rinascente (located right at Piazza del Duomo).

3. Make sure you've already been to La Rinascente before you reach Via Durini, because you will be walking in the other direction later on. Okay, so you can skip La Rinascente and do this from San Babila or backtrack, as Via Durini is a back street that pokes right off of the circle at San Babila. It has many Armani shops and other designer headquarters on its 2-block length.

4. Then you head for the bargains at **Il Salvagente,** which is in walking distance but I'd rather you grabbed a cab (ask for Via Fratelli Bronzetti 16). Pass between the iron gates (yes, you are in the right spot), and go into the courtyard and through the doorway to your left. Shop till you drop—and then some. Call for a taxi to drive you back to your hotel; you should be too loaded down to walk. Way to go! Congrats!

MILANO MAGIC TOUR

As I've said, I've come to love Milan in a new way, and I know it's because of my adoration for the combination of the street market I call San Agostino (see "Markets," earlier in this chapter) and the bargains to be had in Como, which I do together in a Monday-Tuesday, one-two shopping punch.

When scheduling a trip, I arrange to be in Milan on a Sunday (my travel day) so that on Monday I can wake up ready to go to Como. Milan has little retail on Monday, and can be depressing, as can all of Italy on a Monday. The trip to Como is possibly the best Monday-morning activity you will find anywhere in Italy.

BEYOND MILAN

Lake Como Area

GETTING THERE

If you have a train pass, don't use it because it's a waste of money to use one of your travel days for the trip to Como. I bought myself a first-class round-trip ticket for about 14€ ($15). I bought it at the ticket counter in Milan's Centrale station; the transaction was in Italian, so I didn't get too much of what was happening. The ticket was marked "via Monza," and I panicked that I would have to make a connection in Monza—I did not. The ride was a simple 20 minutes on a commuter train—nothing to it. On my last trip, I booked a car and driver from Milan for half the day and 150km (93 miles). The cost was about 182€ ($200), which I thought was okay, except the driver kept getting lost. Consider arriving by train and then hiring a local taxi to drive and wait for you.

ARRIVING IN COMO

The train station (**Como San Giovanni**) is nice: There's a tourist-office window to answer questions, a map of the area posted in the hallway, and many free brochures. There's also a news agent and a bar.

Out front, you'll find a line of taxis and vans with, finally, some English-speaking help. I hired a taxi for the morning to take me around and wait for me. I was told that the flat fare from the train station to the **Ratti** outlet was a mere 6€ ($5.45). You can also get a taxi to drop you at Ratti and come pick you up at the agreed-upon time or when you call. Get your driver's radio number (or Ratti will get you a taxi).

The town proper is located below the train station, within walking distance. However, if you've come on a Monday, most of the town will be closed in the morning, so you might as well head first to your hotel (if you are staying) or the silk outlets.

THE SHOPPING SCENE

Como lies at the southern end of Lake Como, about 50km (31 miles) north of Milan, and offers all the charm you want in a teeny, old-fashioned village on the edge of a lake surrounded by forest and Switzerland. The town was the center of the medieval silk industry, although Como no longer has its own worms. For the most part, silk comes from elsewhere but is milled here.

The town caters to the wealthy landowners who live in the villas surrounding the lake, as well as to the merely rich and/or fashionable who stop by for the weekend (as Gianni Versace used to do). There are also loads of day-trippers and visitors, many of whom are visiting from Switzerland.

Best buys in the village shops are in clothes, silk scarves, and leather goods. While you'll find lots of antiques, most of them are fakes or reproductions. If you love it, and the price is right, who cares? Remember that U.S. Customs wants an item to be 100 years old or older for you to bring it back into the country duty-free.

If you love fabrics, you owe yourself a visit to **Seterie Moretti** (Via Garibaldi 69), located right on Como's main square, on the corner of Via Galio and Via Garibaldi. The shop was closed on Monday morning when I got there! They do open on Monday afternoon, however.

Seterie Moretti distributes signed fabrics to retail sources such as Galtrucco in Milan and Liberty in London. They retain the screens and rerun them without the designer name and with a slight variation in design. As a result, you get fabrics that look familiar, but are slightly different. There are five rooms of fabrics at Moretti, which has English-speaking staff and accepts credit cards.

Another silk maker is **Mantero,** with a showroom at Via Volta 68. The business was run by eight brothers about a hundred years ago—the firm actually produces wool, cotton, and silk. The silk comes from China (as does much Italian silk) but is screened in Italy; it's the ability of the craftspeople who work the screens that makes Italian silk so famous these days. Get a look at Mantero's silk scarves—you will go wild. I have recently begun buying them, about 227€ ($250) each (regular retail, not at the outlet) for the huge shawl size. Rumor has it this firm makes the silk screens for Hermès.

Not only are there house designs (nice botanical prints), but also goods that have been licensed by designers such as Chanel, Ferré, and Saint Laurent. Not bad, eh? I bought Richard a Ferré tie for 41€ ($45) that was so sophisticated I could have wept: whites and beiges and grays with seashells in a row. There was a scarf, the type I like, for about 182€ ($200), but it wasn't the one I wanted so I gave it up. Later I found what I wanted for only 45€ ($50) more in a regular retail store. Undoubtedly, this outlet has the most sophisticated merchandise, but the discounts are not huge, so don't panic if they don't have what you want.

These two stores are in the "downtown" Como area and are within walking distance. The downtown also has cute stores, although no big designer names. I was fond of the local branch of **Standa.**

The star of the area, however, is **Ratti** (Via Cernobbio, ✆ 031/23-32-62). The shop is at the base of the estate of an old villa that is not visible from the road. However, it is on the main road right off the lake, so it's not far at all.

Your taxi driver knows his way here blindfolded. If you are driving yourself, ask for directions—but this is a no-brainer (thank heavens). Even though no one here speaks English, you will have no trouble getting in; but having an Italian-speaking driver will make you feel less tense.

The Ratti outlet store has two rooms jam-packed with the goodies you want to buy—from men's ties and women's silk scarves to pillows, handbags, blouses, and even bolts of fabric. When I went, there were tons of Etro bathrobes, bolts of Versace fabrics, and enough ties to make you swoon. Now then, about prices: They are cheap, but not dirt-cheap. I paid 36€ ($40) for designer ties. I'm talking big-name designer ties, but, nonetheless, Filene's Basement frequently has the same names for 27€ ($30). I estimate that if you are a keen shopper, you could happily spend a couple of hours here.

MORE OUTLETS NEAR COMO

EMPORIO DELLA SETTA
Via Canturina 190, Como.

The Emporium of Silk sounds pretty good, huh? Many big designer names are represented in this clearinghouse for silk from the local mills. Discounts are in the 40% range. There are seasonal sales in January and July to add to your savings. Local phone ✆ **031/59-14-20.**

MANTERO
Via Volta 68, Como.

Note that this factory is closed Saturday and Sunday. Regular hours are 9:30am to 12:30pm and 2 to 6pm. They do take credit cards, showing just how sophisticated they are. Besides their own distinct line of silks and scarves and ties, there are big-name designer goods as well. This is the thrill of a lifetime. Local phone ✆ **031/27-98-61.**

SETERIE MARTINETTI
Via Torriani 41, Como.

By now you surely know that *seterie* means silk maker in Italian. This is rumored to be one of the best silk resources in the area, although there are so many good ones that it is hard to qualify them all. You'll find the usual scarves, ties, robes, and yummy items from the usual cast of international big-name designers. Closed on Monday morning. Local phone © 031/26-90-53.

PAST COMO

Not far from Como, you find yourself in Switzerland, headed toward Lugarno. But don't panic; you're also on the way to **FoxTown,** which is a 5-minute drive into Switzerland across the Italian border. So what? The good news: FoxTown is an outlet village with 130 stores (200 brands), a casino (for husbands, no doubt), and a cafe. There's quite a large number of big-name designer outlets here, including Yves Saint Laurent, Valentino, Bruno Magli, and Loro Piano. The bad news? Because you are in Switzerland, prices are not in euros but in Swiss Francs, which are always trading high. Even with a strong euro, you may not want to change money or incur CF charges on your credit cards.

For specific directions and information, call © **410/848-828-888** or go to www.foxtown.ch. FoxTown is open 7 days a week, 11am to 7pm nonstop. If you are driving, you want the Mendriso exit, which is 7km (4⅓ miles) from the Swiss-Italian border.

Parabiago

Parabiago is an industrial suburb of Milan, where many of the shoe factories and leather-accessories people have offices. Many consider it within the metro-Milano area, not a day trip, but no public transportation goes here, and when I asked my driving service about getting there, they made it clear they

Remember Armani

For those with cars and a spirit of adventure, head over to the new Armani outlet at the Intai factory, near Bregnano (which is between Milan and Como). Take the Autostrada/A9 to the Como exit and head for Bregnano; look for the factory at the crossroad of SS35. For more specific directions, call © 031/88-73-73. The shop, which accepts credit cards, is closed on Monday; otherwise, the hours are 10am to 1pm and 2 to 7pm.

considered it out of town. If you take a car, a taxi, or drive yourself, remember that even factory stores are closed at lunch.

CLAUDIO MORLACCHI
Via Castelnuovo 24, Parabiago.

While you're in Parabiago, stop by Claudio Morlacchi. The factory looks like a house, but don't be alarmed. Push the large wooden door and enter into a light, airy courtyard. To the right is a room with a small but wonderful display of all the shoes the Morlacchi people make. Among Morlacchi's clients are Lanvin and Guy Laroche.

FRATELLI ROSSETTI FACTORY
Via Cantù 24, Parabiago.

There is a Fratelli Rossetti boutique in Milan (Via Montenapoleone 1), but why shop there when you can go to the factory in Parabiago? The Rossetti factory has no ads and no markings; it kind of looks like a prison from the outside. The shop is in a separate building from the factory and houses a large selection of men's and women's shoes and boots in a big, open room with blue-rubber flooring. The shoes are displayed on L-shaped tables. The help does not speak English, but is very friendly. Men's shoes in traditional styles cost 59€ ($65) a pair;

more elaborate slip-ons cost 114€ ($125); boots range from 91€ ($100); high-heel pumps begin at 73€ ($80).

Biella

Biella is a mill town in northern Italy, famous because it is the headquarters of the **Zegna** woolen mills. It's also known for the **Fila** outlet store. Paola, from the Delta flight, gave me this info. There are other nearby outlets.

ERMENEGILDO ZEGNA
Via Roma 99, Centro Zegna, Trivero.

This is the one you've been looking for. This is the really big time of the big time. Of course, price tags—even at discount— can also be big time, but there is no finer or more famous name in Italian wool and cashmere. Trivero is near Biella. This place takes credit cards and is used to tourists and visitors; follow signs to **Centro Zegna.** Local phone ✆ **015/75-65-41.**

FILA
Via Cesare Battisti 28, Biella.

Here's an exception to factory stores being open on Monday morning—this factory store does open on Monday, but only at 3pm. It closes at noon, not 1pm, for lunch daily and reopens at 3pm. Needless to say, Fila is an enormously famous name internationally for sportswear. They are most famous in the U.S. for their tennis gear, but they make clothing and gear for all sports; their ski stuff is sublime. There are bargains for all members of the family, and the store is conveniently located near the cute part of the old city. Local phone ✆ **015/34-141.**

FRATELLI PIACENZA LANIFICIO
Biella.

Another cashmere mill. Wools as well; also mohair, which is big this year. There are bargains, but you are still looking at price tags over 4,545€ ($5,000) for a cashmere coat. Rumor

has it that Escada gets its goods here. Local phone © 015/
614-61. Call for an appointment and directions.

MAGLIFICIO DELLA ARTEMA
Strada Trossi 31, Verrone-Biella.

Located right outside Biella, this is yet another cashmere
resource from the famous mills; watch for Artema signs. Selling everything from underwear to outerwear, this outlet features the Zegna line as well as other Italian labels, including
some designer names from the big-name circuit. Open Tuesday to Saturday, from 9am to noon and 3 to 7pm; closed all
day on Monday. Local phone © 015/255-83-82.

Vercelli (Beyond Biella)

Vercelli is actually a province that includes the city of Biella.
It also includes a zillion mills, more known for their wool and
cashmere than for silk, but some silken luxuries can be found.
Vercelli is about a 2-hour drive from Milan, so I didn't go. Let
me know how it is if you get there.

SAMBONET
Via XXVI Aprile 62–64, Vercelli.

From the sublime to the ridiculous, guys, this one sells pots
and pans (big-name and stainless) and flatware and silver
plate, including seconds from Krupps and the Cordon Bleu lines.
Local phone © 0161/59-71.

Chapter Nine

....

NAPLES & THE AMALFI COAST

WELCOME TO NAPLES

Welcome to Naples, where the shopkeepers in some of the stores told me to take off my watches (yes, I do wear two), lest I attract a thief. Welcome to Naples, where the clerks at Ferragamo were not only rude but also refused to redo my tax-refund papers when I decided to buy *more*. Welcome to Naples, where I had the best pizza of my life, where I fell madly in love with the scarves at Rubinacci, and where you are less than an hour away from Capri . . . or Amalfi . . . and where life slows down to a pace worthy of days spent in the shadow of a volcano. Quick, my limoncello!

ARRIVING IN NAPLES

You can fly directly into Naples from large Euro-hub cities. The 2-hour flight from Paris to Naples, round-trip, costs about 300€ ($330) when bought 7 days in advance with a Saturday-night stay. I saw recent promotional deals for 168€ ($185).

You may want to fly into Rome—especially if you are doing this long-haul—and rent a car for the 2-hour drive to Naples; this gives you a car for driving along the Amalfi Coast as well. You can also take the train from Rome. The Naples train station is clean, modern, and not frightening.

If you arrive by cruise ship, the port (the Maritime Station) is next to the heart of town and well situated for your explorations and adventures. Note that the ferries and hydrofoils to the islands (Capri, Ischia, and so forth) use different piers in other parts of town, one alongside the Maritime Station and the other around the bay, about 2 miles away.

The Lay of the Land

Naples is an enormous city. On a day trip, you will probably only want to visit the nice shopping areas and the nice hotels, and have a look at the museums, the palm trees, my castle, and the sea. Watch your handbag.

If you think of the Grand Albergo Vesuvio hotel as the heart of the world, then the various areas to visit can be read as you tell time: As you face north, with the Bay of Naples behind you, the castle is at 6 o'clock, the Maritime Station is around 5 o'clock, the Via Constantinopoli and the National Museum are at 1 o'clock, the historic old town and Street of Angels are at 2 o'clock, and the fancy shopping is at 10 o'clock.

Warning

Please be sure to study a map of Naples before you go off on your own; also make sure the map is to scale. Learn where everything is in relationship to the main icons. The reason I knew I was being cheated by one of my taxi drivers was that he kept heading in the wrong direction, and I *knew* it was the wrong direction.

Getting Around

For cruisers, note there are taxis at the gates of the Maritime Station; do be clear with taxis about where you are going and vigilant about the meter; they may attempt to cheat you.

All hotels can get you a taxi; there are taxi ranks, usually at big squares, where you can usually find a cab when you are out and about. If the driver is honest and goes by the meter,

Naples

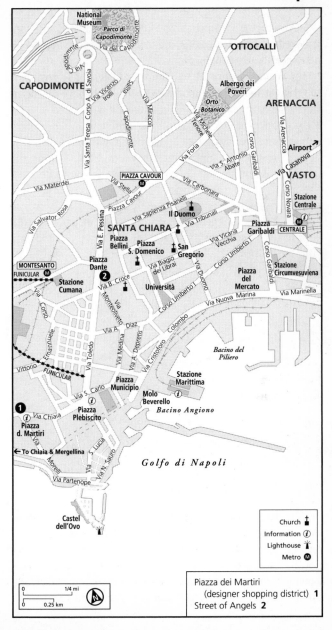

CAPODIMONTE

National Museum

Parco di Capodimonte

Via del Capodimonte

OTTOCALLI

Albergo dei Poveri

Orto Botanico

ARENACCIA

Via Arenaccia

Airport

Via Casanova

VASTO

Via Foria

Via S. Antonio Abate

Corso Novara

Stazione Centrale

Via Carbonara

CENTRALE M

Via Materdei

Via Salvator Rosa

Via Stella

PIAZZA CAVOUR M

Piazza Cavour

Via Sapienza Pisanelli

Il Duomo

Via Tribunali

Piazza Garibaldi

Via Vicaria Vecchia

Corso Garibaldi

SANTA CHIARA

Piazza Bellini

Piazza S. Domenico

San Gregorio

Via Biagio dei Librai

MONTESANTO
FUNICULAR M

Piazza Dante 2

Via B. Croce

Università

Corso Umberto I

Via Duomo

Piazza del Mercato

Stazione Cumana

Via Montevideo

Stazione Circumvesuviana

Via Marinella

Via Nuova Marina

Via A. Diaz

Via Cristoforo

Via A. Depretis

Colombo

Bacino del Piliero

Via Medina

Via Toledo

Vittorio Emannuele **FUNICULAR**

Piazza Municipio

Stazione Marittima

Molo Beverello

Bacino Angiono

Piazza S. Carlo

1

Via Chiaia

Piazza Plebiscito

Piazza d. Martiri

← To Chiaia & Mergellina

Via Morelli

Via S. Lucia

Via N. Sauro

Golfo di Napoli

Via Partenope

Castel dell'Ovo

Church	✝
Information	ⓘ
Lighthouse	🔆
Metro	M

0   1/4 mi
0   0.25 km

Piazza dei Martiri
(designer shopping district) **1**
Street of Angels **2**

round up the tab as a tip. To call a radio taxi, dial ✆ **3296.** Remember that traffic is fierce during rush hour and can run up the tab on the taximeter.

There is a metro, with two different lines. The metro is not of great use to a shopper, so listings below only have the metro stop when it actually makes sense to use it. I got tired of writing *no nearby metro*, so you get the idea. Also, when it's hot, you do not want to go into a hole in the ground.

For out-of-town trips, there are several train stations; the main one, Centrale, has trains that will take you to Pompeii and as far as Sorrento. There is a metro station at the main train station. On the waterfront, there are ferries that serve the islands. You cannot get to the waterfront by metro, however.

You may also want to book a car and driver for the day; your hotel can do this for you. If you rent a car to drive yourself (the concierge can do this for you or you can get one on arrival at the airport), don't try to drive in town. And remember, when driving the Amalfi Drive: no limoncello for you, *cara.*

SLEEPING IN NAPLES

EXCELSIOR HOTEL
Via Partenope 48.

Location, location, location—although this hotel is almost next door to the Vesuvio, it has a corner location, which means it has three-dimensional views. You owe it to yourself to venture to the roof garden for lunch at La Terrazza and a stare out at the deep blue. Cruise passengers enjoy lunch here—you can even see your ship.

The hotel is more ornate than the Vesuvio. Each room is different and is furnished with antiques. The hotel has been refurbished, so if you haven't been here for a few years, fret not. Rates vary but average about 250€ ($275). The hotel is a member of the Luxury Collection and is part of the Starwood family. Local phone ✆ **081/764-01-11.** www.excelsior.it.

GRAND ALBERGO VESUVIO
Via Partenope 45.

Although the hotel is more modern than you might be expecting, that means everything works. This is, after all, the leading hotel of the city, located right on the Bay of Naples with a view directly to heaven. That is my castle right over there, and nothing thrills me more than this view. Oh yeah, on a clear day you can see Vesuvius.

There's a new fitness center/spa, you can eat on the rooftop, and you are within walking distance of much of the fancy shopping. Do you need more? There are shopping packages as well as a Shopping Fidelity program in which you get a numbered personal card that entitles you to discounts, gifts, or privileges at the city's best shops. Rooms are about 295€ ($325). Since the hotel is a member of Leading Hotels of the World, you can book a room by calling © **800/233-6800** in the U.S. Local phone 081/764-00-44. www.lhw.com/vesuvio.

SHOP & SNACK

CANTA NAPOLI
Via Chiatamone 36.

This is one of my favorite pizza places and casual dining spots; it's great if you have kids with you, too. The walls are painted with the local scenery, the waiters are dressed in costumes, and the pizza is incredible. Located directly behind the hotels Vesuvio, Santa Lucia, and Excelsior. Local phone © **081/764-61-10.** It even has a website you can check out: www.cantanapoli.com.

THE SHOPPING SCENE

I can't say that anyone chooses to come to Naples for the designer shops, but you'll find plenty of places to drop a few dollars, have an ice cream, enjoy the day or the weekend or even the week, and make pleasant memories. Most important, you can buy **Perugina** chocolates and begin to get used to how much coral and fake coral and cameos can be yours.

Walking up and down and around the fancy shopping district in Naples is actually a treat. There are gorgeous antiques stores and great places for an afternoon gelato. It's a nice half-day shopping excursion, after which you can eat, quit, or move to secret sources or even museums (all with good gift shops). Note that it takes more than a weekend to have a bespoke suit made.

Shopping Hours

The stores are normally open from 9 or 9:30am to 1:30pm and from 4 or 4:30 to 8pm. Nothing is open on Sunday. On Monday, remember that you are in Italy. That means that nothing is open in the morning, and some things will open around 4 or 4:30pm.

On Saturday in summer, stores will close for the day at 1:30pm, but in winter they do reopen in the afternoon. If you need a pharmacy on a Sunday or during off-hours, there is a listing in the newspaper with the open stores, or your hotel concierge can guide you to an open pharmacy.

Even street markets get going late here—9am in fine weather. Don't get to a flea market before 9:30am.

Neighborhoods

Maritime Station & Hotel Heaven   Cruise passengers disembark at the clean, modern, safe Maritime Station, right in Naples near the Castel dell'Ovo, a 2,000-year-old fortress which is a monument; a nice touch, adding a little romance to a commercial seaport. There are several shops in the terminal. There's also a bank and a currency-exchange office. When a large ship comes to port, street vendors set up outside.

Castel dell'Ovo Located directly across the street from the Grand Albergo Vesuvio hotel, right near the Maritime Station, the Castel is on a small island, which also houses several adorable alleys for exploring (no shops, sorry) and many restaurants, bars, pizza places, and seafood eateries. It's adorable and great fun. *Note:* There's a tourist info stand here, too.

Luxury Shopping The main upscale shopping district is a few blocks from the strip of luxury hotels on the waterfront. Just walk along the water (with the castle to your rear) until you come to a clump of palm trees that represents the Piazza Vittorio, turn right, and head "up."

Now it gets slightly tricky, as this is a district and you don't want to miss all the parts—you can, and will, miss part of it if you don't look at a map.

The **Via Calabritto** is one of the main tony shopping streets (**Prada** at no. 9), with many of the big-name designers (but not all). It stretches from the Piazza Vittorio to the Piazza dei Martiri and the large **Ferragamo** shop. **Versace** is down the street from Ferragamo. You get the drift. There's a chunk of big names in a nugget right here.

There are a few side streets off the Piazza dei Martiri that will make you feel like you're in Italy; there are some antiques shops located down the Via Domenico Morelli.

The area is not without charm. Equally charming is the fact that you then easily segue to the Via dei Mille and Via Gaetano Filangieri, which have the rest of the luxury shops— **Bulgari, Zegna, Hermès, Frette,** etc.

Via Chiaia This is a real-people shopping street that's between the luxury shopping district and Via Roma. Use it to cross over from one neighborhood to the other or to get to Via dei Mille— it's all an easy walk. Shopping-wise, there's very little to distract you. Italy-wise, it's great fun.

Via Roma The Via Roma is the commercial heart of town; it is called Via Toledo lower down and becomes Via Roma near Piazza Dante. This street stretches for 2 miles from the Piazza del Plebiscito, right near the Maritime Station, through the center of town, passing the Piazza Carita on its way to the Piazza Dante and then ending near the National Museum.

La Pignasecca   This is foodie-land; just follow Via Pignasecca and Via Portmedina up and down, checking out all the tiny specialty shops. This is a central area in the real-people part of town.

Centro Antico   The core of the old town *(centro antico)* includes the famous Via San Gregorio Armend—this is the Street of Angels, where all the miniatures and *presepios* (crèches) are made. But don't look for Via San Gregorio Armend on your map, as it's a small area around the church of the same name. Instead, you want to find the rectangular area between the Piazza del Gesù and Piazza Dante, reaching over to the Duomo as its other border. The main streets for shopping, gawking, sight-seeing, and absorbing the soul of Naples are Via Croce and Via Tribunali. Via Croce will change its name a few times, so fret not. The area is part of a living history, outdoor-museum program that labels the buildings and tells you the path to walk (and shop).

Port Alba   Adjacent to the old town, you find the Port Alba, a medieval doorway that leads to a million bookstores. Just beyond this is the Via Constantinopoli, filled with antiques shops. Once a month there is an outdoor flea market on the weekend (except in Aug); see the next section, "Antiques & Flea Markets."

Antiques & Flea Markets

FIERA ANTIQUAIRA NAPOLETANA
Via Caracciolo.

This one is a little tricky, as there is often confusion about the dates; we were sent on the wrong weekend by knowledgeable people, and the listing in *Dove* magazine was equally unclear. Luckily, you can call the market offices directly and get the dates for the year (© 081/62-19-51). A weekend event, the fair is considered the best in southern Italy; it runs from 8am to 2pm.

MOSTRA MERCATO CONSTANTINOPOLI
Via Constantinopoli.

A weekend fair never held on the same weekend as the other fair, this is a more casual event in the street of antiques shops, with dealers set up on the sidewalk and under tents. Don't bother going if the weather is bad. For dates, call © **0347/486-37-15** or e-mail antiquario@tightrope.it.

Local Heroes

MARIANO RUBINACCI
Via dei Mille 1.

This shop is large, sells designer clothes, and offers a sort-of-Ralph Lauren–local-preppy look, complete with a series of silk scarves that would make Mr. Dumas-Hermès weep with envy. The scarves depict various scenes in Neapolitan history or geography or iconography and are sold in some hotel and museum gift shops as well. Prices vary depending on the difficulty of the silk screen and range from 136€ to 227€ ($150–$250). The best luxury souvenir in town.

MARINELLA'S
Riviera di Chiaia 287.

This itty-bitty tie shop is one of the most famous addresses in Naples. Come holiday season there are lines stretching down the street, no ties in stock, and shoppers are issued chits, which they gift wrap to present. The store creates custom ties, as long, short, wide, or thin as you want or need.

MAXI HO
Via Nisco 20 and 23;
Riviera di Chiaia;

Piazza dei Martiri;
Via dei Mille 32;
Via Cimarosa 85;
Via Luca Giordino 28.

Despite its silly-sounding name, this is one of the best stores in Naples. The various addresses are mostly in the luxury district and are not branches of the same store, but extensions of the store selling different looks. Each store sells a different group of designer brands geared for a certain look or age group.

Note: To get to the Via Cimarosa and Giordino shops, you must take the funicular from Piazza Amedeo to Piazza Fuga—a fun adventure.

UPIM
Via Nisco 11.

Upim is a chain of dime stores famous throughout Italy. There is a branch right in the heart of the fine shopping, a two-level store with tons of clothes, home fashions, and even underwear. I buy a lot of La Perla copies at Upim and love them. www.upim.it.

Shoppers Beware

Whether you are on your own or on a ship tour, you may be taken to "factories" to go shopping—be careful, they may or may not offer the real thing, or real deals. They certainly offer kickbacks to your guide.

CAPRI

Welcome to Capri

In Capri, I'm always too busy with the jewelry stores, the sandals, the latest incarnations of Tod's shoes and handbags, the cottons and the cashmeres, and even the lemons to get to the beach or to notice who's not wearing what. Capri is a shopping port . . . Capri is a shopping day trip . . . Capri is a spree. This is a town that has streets that are more like alleys, where you stroll in total contentment, remembering Jackie Kennedy . . . and you happily get lost and found in this maze.

You can research and buy lemon booze from a so-called lemon factory or two, ride in a convertible '57 Chevy stretch (with fins), buy plastic pens with your name on them in Italian, or sink deeply into **Gucci, Prada, Fendi, Hermès,** and all the better names of international and Italian fashion. In between, of course, you eat, sip, stare, and take a nap. The place to hang out? La Piazetta in the center of Capri.

Getting There

You may arrive by cruise ship (and tender ashore) or by hydrofoil from Naples, Amalfi, Sorrento, or another port or resort town. Regardless of how you actually arrive, you'll land near the funicular that takes you up to Capri proper. Sunglasses, please. If you have luggage, there are porters at the pier. They happen to be very honest, so don't fret.

Although I usually get to Capri via cruise ship, on my last visit I took the hydrofoil from Naples. The trip lasts about 45 minutes, costs about 11€ ($12) each way, and is most pleasant if you are on a larger vessel with space around you. There's a ferry or hydrofoil almost every hour; they all arrive at the same place in Capri but do depart from different stations in Naples depending on which line you book.

Secret Source

If you want a private boat to take you to Capri, contact **Gianni Chervatin** (© 081/837-68-95), famous former GM of the Grand Hotel Quisiana in Capri, who arranges jet-set details for the rich and famous. There is a public hydrofoil every half-hour in season.

The Lay of the Land

The island of Capri is rather big and has much more to it than just the resort town of Capri. From a serious shopping perspective, you can skip Anacapri, although it's fun visually.

In fact, I think you'll be surprised at the sprawl of downtown Capri. Best yet, a lot of it is hidden in back alleys, so take some time to look at a map. If you follow the main tourist trail, you'll miss the best stuff.

The Shopping Scene

As cruise ports go, Capri ain't bad. There are a lot of stores and a sprinkling of designer shops—small branches of **Prada, Gucci, Fendi, Ferragamo, Malo, Albertti Ferretti, Exte, Tod's, Hermès,** etc. As a beach town, Capri has become famous for its sandals, and there are scads of no-name shops selling the latest looks, as well as copies of the latest looks.

There are several *profumeri* (perfume shops). Each one carries several brands on an exclusive basis, but no single shop carries every brand. If you inquire about a brand a store doesn't carry, the clerk is likely to try to trade you over to the brand they sell, rather than tell you to walk down the street or around the corner. There is also lemon perfume.

The emphasis in Capri is on high-quality goods and cheap sandals; the resort fashions are very body revealing, in the southern Italian style. Note that the style of goods and the shopping experience is so totally different from Positano that there is virtually no overlap.

SHOPPING HOURS

Stores open around 9 to 9:30am and close at 1pm, although more and more are staying open during lunch. Those that close will reopen around 3:30pm and stay open until 7pm. Big names tend to be open nonstop. Stores are open on Sunday.

The TTs down by the port usually stay open during lunch and are often open until 8pm in the summer.

Note that the season begins March 15 and ends October 15; most stores are closed out of season. It's not unusual for the same owners to have a similar shop in Cortina or another Italian ski resort for the winter season.

The Best Buys in Capri

Cottons & Cashmeres   Despite the heat, cashmere is one of the leading lights of Capri. There are several specialty shops that sell premium cashmeres—some of them also sell cottons.

Jewelry   Until I visited Capri and saw its magnificent jewelry, I'd never been one for important (or even real) jewelry. Now, I've been converted. There's a good bit of latitude on price. If you have a few thousand dollars, you may be very happy.

Lemons   We're still in southern Italy, so there's lemon vodka galore. I also buy fresh lemons in the market down near the port.

Shoes   Capri has all sorts of shoe stores, from the fancy **Ferragamo** shop and little hole-in-the-wall stores that sell 27€ ($30) pairs of sandals to stores that sell **Tod's** and other designer brands.

Shopping Neighborhoods

Marina Grande   This is where your ship's tender or your ferry or hydrofoil comes to port; on the pier, there's a Customs office and a pushcart vendor selling fresh fruit in newspaper cones and ices. You'll also find several TTs teeming with Blue Grotto souvenirs, a liquor store, a minimart, and the funicular, which takes you up to Capri proper.

Main Street Capri   Capri has two main streets, Via Vittorio Emanuele and Via Camarelle. The former dead-ends to the latter when you hit the **Hotel Quisisana.** If you are facing the hotel from Via Vittorio Emanuele, bear left to explore Via Camarelle.

The island's toniest shops can be found here, selling everything from antiques and jewelry to expensive resortwear and affordable sandals.

Back Street Downtown   Hidden from view, but running parallel to Vittorio Emanuele, is a pedestrian alley—Via Fuorlovado—that is crammed with real-people shops. Don't miss the chance to prowl this street; it's far more charming than the main tourist thoroughfare.

Via Roma   The Via Roma in Capri is what the British call a high street; it's where the bus station is located and where you'll find the main thrust of the town's real-people shopping.

Finds

ALBERTO & LINA
Via Vittorio Emanuele 18.

This is one of the leading jewelers in town, part of a family that owns several jewelry shops. In case you haven't already guessed, Italian women define themselves and their success in life vis-à-vis their jewelry, which they buy in places like this and wear all of the time. Yes, even to the beach and right into the sea. That's how we all know it's real gold.

CARTHUSIA PROFUMI
Via Camarelle 10.

I am more amused by this store than serious about it, but I have met people who make this a ritual stop when they are in town. Before she had her own perfume line, Liz Taylor was supposed to have been a regular customer. Photo op with the tiles on the front of the store. This is a perfumer who makes a local scent that you can get only here; it's very lemony. Cute gifts.

LA COMPANNINA PIU
Via Fuorlovado 39i.

This is a very fancy gourmet food store, not at all funky. It sells all sorts of imported foods, so watch out for the English brands—but much to see, touch, and taste.

MARCELLO RUBINACCI
Via Camarelle 9.

This is my favorite shop in Capri—I come here first to stare at the colors, touch the cashmeres, sigh about the quality, and then buy a few T-shirts. Since the T-shirts are about 45€ ($50) each, this is my idea of extravagance. Hand-wash your cottons from this store; we had big-time shrinkage when we used the washer/dryer. This brand has expanded and has stores in Naples, Rome, etc.

SORRENTO

Most of you will probably arrive by car, train, or tour bus from Naples or Pompeii. A few lucky ones will arrive by cruise ship. However you come, you should stay long enough to see my favorite limoncello factory and to explore a good branch of **Standa,** the Italian dime store/grocery store, which, if you're on a cruise, may be your only opportunity to do a little real-people shopping and pick up a few affordable treasures. Dime stores are not plentiful in swanky resorts, believe me. Note that most of the Standas in Italy have been closed or turned into branches of FNAC, the French store for compact discs, books, etc. As we go to press, Standa is still open and is as described above.

Of course, Sorrento is more than a chance to shop at a dime store. When you see the little square and the carriages pulled by donkeys in fancy hats, the narrow alleys crammed with crates heaped with fruits and vegetables, and the faience spilling from stores; and when you stand at the overlook and peer down into the Bay of Naples; hmmmm, this is what we saved all that money for. This is what southern Italy is all about.

Sorrento is also the gateway to Positano and the rest of the Amalfi Coast. You can rent a car in Sorrento and drive yourself there. (If you're on a cruise, your ship will even arrange your car rental.) If you're feeling more adventurous, take a bus from the station in Sorrento. Even if Gore Vidal hasn't invited you to the villa for lunch, you're going to want to spend as much time as possible in these gorgeous, adorable, and ever-so-chic hill towns.

Getting There

You can take the train or a bus from Naples, drive, hire a car and driver, or take the ferry from Capri, a mere 8km (5 miles) away, or the hydrofoil from Naples.

If you are driving, forget all this hillside nonsense; you'll arrive right at town level and can ignore the port itself. If you're staying only a matter of hours, then head right to **Grand Hotel Ambasciatori** (Via Califano 18), which has parking on premises. Parking in town is difficult.

The Lay of the Land

Like many Italian resort cities, Sorrento is built on a hill above the harbor. You will come to port at Porto Marina Piccola, and then catch a shuttle bus up into the heart of town, Piazza Tasso. You can walk, but it's pretty far and very steep, and the road is curvy and dangerous.

Getting Around

If you arrive by car, park near the Via Fuonmura, in the heart of town, then walk. Cruise passengers can take the ship's shuttle bus. If you miss it, or need instant gratification, a taxi to and from town and the marina costs about 8€ ($9). Like the taxi drivers in Naples, they'll try to run up the meter. (For less than 1.80€/$2 each way, you can take a public bus.) Taxis in town congregate at the **Piazza Tasso,** lining up on Via Fuonmura.

Sleeping in Sorrento

HILTON SORRENTO PALACE
Via San Antonio 13.

Believe it or not, a Hilton has just opened up. It's outside of town, it's a rehab of an existing hotel, and it's not the last word, but it is a Hilton. To book a room, call ✆ **800/HILTONS** in the U.S., go to www.hilton.com, or send an e-mail to Sales_ Sorrento@hilton.com.

The Shopping Scene

Sorrento has a lot of charm to it, visually, emotionally, and even from a shopping perspective. There's no serious shopping, but there are several opportunities here that you won't find elsewhere.

While Sorrento has only one or two designer shops (there's an **Emporio Armani**), it does have a branch of **Standa,** one of the best dime stores in Italy, so you can have some serious fun here. Along with a main shopping street, there's a pedestrian back street that's shady and picturesque.

And there are lemons to buy. And where there are lemons, there's limoncello. Don't drink limoncello and drive, especially when we're talking about the Amalfi Drive!

SHOPPING HOURS

Stores open around 8:30 to 9am and close about 2pm for lunch. They reopen around 4pm. When there are ships in port, hours can be a little more flexible. The major TT department store in town, **A. Gargiulo & Jannuzzi,** Via Fuonmura, is open (nonstop, mind you) from 8am to 10pm in season.

Banks are open Monday to Friday 9am to 1:30pm and 3 to 4pm. This town is closed on Sunday.

Shopping Neighborhoods

Piazza Tasso   This is the proverbial town square: It's in the middle of everything, and many streets branch off in different directions, with each street offering different shopping opportunities. The donkey carts that you can rent for a trot about town are also here.

Corso Italia   This is the main real-people shopping street. It goes across the city and has two different personalities. The portion leading away from town and toward the Amalfi Highway has two designer shops (**Emporio Armani** and **Furla**), plus a branch of **Standa,** the dime store.

The portion that stretches to your right, if your back is to the sea and the donkeys are in front of you, is the main shopping street, with branches of **Lacoste** (very expensive!), the leather-goods and shoe store **Pollini,** and a few cafes.

Via Fuoro   This is everyone's favorite street because it's a pedestrian alley; no cars, just tourists. There are drug stores, grocery stores, ceramics shops—in sum, everything that's authentically Italian.

Via de Maio   This is the road that leads to the main square from the marina; the 2 blocks before you get to the square are filled with stores—some of which are quite nice. There are also two excellent pharmacies here.

Via Fuonmura   Leading away from town, this street has just a few stores on it and a hotel or two, but it's home to **A. Gargiulo & Jannuzzi,** the largest shop in town, which is frequented by cruise passengers. It is crowded, overpriced, touristy, and everything you can think of, but it also provides many services and is in cahoots with all the major cruise lines. And, it has good stuff—you just have to ask to see it.

Finds

A. GARGIULO & JANNUZZI
Via Fuonmura.

This is the largest department store in Sorrento, and it was designed for tourists. In business since 1853, it's open from 8am to 10pm nonstop. It's air-conditioned and accustomed to foreign visitors. (They speak English perfectly.) This is not a TT, but rather a sprawling space in several buildings with entire departments devoted to different crafts of the area. The section of the store farthest from the entrance is a ceramics shop. There's a linens department with exquisite work (some of it deservedly very, very expensive), a department that sells local inlaid wood marquetry, and some touristy souvenirs near the entrance.

CORIUM DI COPPOLA RAFFAELE
Via degli Archi 20.

London stringer Ruth found this small shoemaker shop and had several pairs of sandals made for about 45€ ($50) each. She was over the moon with her find and the quality of the work.

LIMONORO
Via Fuoro 22.

This is my favorite limoncello factory; it's pretty—lots of white tile—and has a great selection. There are many different sizes of products, gift packages, and beautiful lemon-laden wrapping paper.

STANDA
Corso Italia.

Standa is a chain of stores, with branches in virtually all major Italian cities; it's especially refreshing in Sorrento because it's not a tourist venue. It's a dime store. The store is not large, but it has a selection of Italian beauty products (try the Venus brand of skin care), linens, housewares, pots and pans, kids' toys, and even a grocery section.

POSITANO

The famed Amalfi Drive begins shortly after you bypass Sorrento and enter the kingdom of the curves, a twisty road that skirts the coast from above and often makes me queasy . . . and very grateful for my regular driver, Franco, who is always booked for me by the Hotel Le Sirenuse.

I never need go farther than Positano, but one can go all the way to Salerno, shopping as you go. Me? Bury my heart in Positano, where it simply can't get much better. And everyone speaks English.

Visitors say Positano; locals say Posi. So, while a day in Sorrento is a pleasant enough way to spend some time, if you're a do-everything kind of person on a cruise or a limited schedule, you can get through the pleasures of Sorrento (pleasurably) in 2 hours, and then be on your way to Posi, via the Amalfi Drive.

Cruise passengers can rent a car for the day or take a taxi. There's even a public bus from Sorrento for the truly determined (one-way fare is less than 1.80€/$2). There is water transportation directly from Naples, weather permitting.

Some of the stores in Posi close for lunch at 1pm and will not reopen until 3 or 3:30pm, so be sure to allow time for shopping before lunch. On the other hand, you can avoid the pressure by simply booking yourself into town and staying for a few days.

The Lay of the Land

Positano is one of the famed hill-clinging towns; it is literally dug into the side of a cliff and terraces itself from the beach to the top of a small mountain. There are some main streets, but most of the shopping is along pedestrian alleys and walkways. What I call "uptown" is the Via Colombo; what I call "downtown" is the Via Mulini. In this city, you are either up or down (or prone). Certainly the land lays between the black sands and Le Sirenuse; the crippled, infirm, short of step or breath, or simply lazy might want to reconsider. The lay of the land is vertical, not horizontal.

Snack & Shop

The best bet on a 1-day visit is to work your way up the steps and then, if you can afford the best, have lunch at **Le Sirenuse**, the posh villa-turned-hotel where you can eat on the terrace overlooking the sea. Lunch here is a tad pricey, but not over the top, especially if you have just a pasta or a simple lunch without going the whole route—23€ ($25) a person will make you feel like royalty.

If that's over your budget, **Chez Black** is down the hill, on Via del Brigantino (no number), where food starts at 9€ ($10) per person, and they serve pizza. *Note:* This restaurant is closer to the beach and catches the in-crowd in summer; a reservation is a must (© 089/87-50-36), and tell them I sent you, which won't help if they're busy. I ate lunch there with my girlfriend Abby; we had scampi on the grill and salads and desserts, and the bill was 64€ ($70) . . . so don't give up Le Sirenuse and then be shocked at Chez Black.

There are three or four other beach cafes in a row surrounding Chez Black.

Sleeping in Positano

L̶E̶ SIRENUSE
Via Colombo 30.

I would tell you maybe I am partial to this hotel because I have a long history of coming here and of visiting with my late husband, who adored it here. But since the hotel has been named the number-one best hotel in Europe by *Travel & Leisure*, well, I think the secret is out. Built into what was once a private villa, the hotel is drop-dead gorgeous in its perch on a hillside. You can sit by the pool and stare down at town or out to sea. You can also enjoy the new Aveda spa (built by Gae Aulenti, no less) or touch the antiques that are spread on the multilevel space and placed on the hand-painted ceramic green tiles. The hotel is open year-round; there are packages in the off season; rooms are about 273€ ($300). They always book my car and driver for me and do transfers to and from Naples airport, and anywhere on the Amalfi Coast.

The hotel is a member of Leading Hotels of the World, so you can book a room by calling ✆ **800/233-6800** in the U.S. Local phone 089/87-50-66. www.sirenuse.it.

The Shopping Scene

If you haven't already learned the International Rule of Inaccessibility, this is a good time to learn it. What makes a city into the kind of haven the rich and famous like to visit is its inaccessibility to the masses. All the great resort cities of the world, especially in the Mediterranean, are hard to get to.

This understood, you can understand that Positano is the center for the rich and famous along the Amalfi Coast. It is adorable, and its stores sell fun things. There are very few TTs and no branches of Gap. On the other hand, the selection gets to look uniform in short order; there are only a handful of stores that sell designer clothes or nonresort items that you might wear in the real world if you don't live in the U.S. sunbelt.

The scene is antithetical to what's happening on Capri. Here it's more laid back, and the look is sort of rich-hippie casual. It's a movie set, and stores display their wares to enchant . . . and sell. Flowers pour out of flowerpots, dishes are piled up on stairwells, cottons fly in the slight breeze, and lemons are dancing everywhere.

Dishes and pottery are a big thing; many stores sell them, and all stores seem to sell so much of the same thing that you soon get dizzy. There aren't as many jewelry shops as in Capri—the emphasis here is less on the body and more on comfort or home style. There are bathing-suit and clothing boutiques, but they sell funky fashions and comfortable things, even comfortably tiny bikinis. Many of the stores specialize in what I call Mamma Mia fashions: clothes made for short, wide women with a large bosom. I buy these clothes because they hide the waist and hips and allow for great comfort and eating space. Pass the pasta, please.

SHOPPING HOURS

Stores open at 9am and close for lunch around 1pm. They reopen at 3, 3:30, or 4pm, and stay open until 7 or 8pm. Many stores are closed off season, from mid-October until after March 15. Stores are open on Sunday and on Monday morning.

Finds

CERAMICA ASSUNTA
Via Colombo 97.

Just a few doors downhill and closer to town from Emporio de Sirenuse, this large shop (www.ceramicassunta.it) has a wide selection of local ceramics in assorted styles. Most of the ceramics shops sell more or less the same wares, but this store is large enough for you to see everything. The shop will pack and ship or deliver to your hotel.

DELIKATESSON
Via dei Mulini 5.

Just as the name implies, this is a deli, or minimart. I must admit to being outright shocked that they had sexually explicit–shaped

The Lay of the Clay

Maybe it has something to do with thousands of years of lava and ocean spray and shifting earth and great good luck, but the Amalfi area is home to fabulous clay and is therefore the place to buy dishes. Every other store in Positano sells dishes, but every town in the area has its share.

A few years ago there was a hand-painted look that caught on and every store sold. That theme is passé now, and solid rustic colors are in style, with a contrast raw border through which you can see some of the baked terra cotta.

For the most fun, head to the Vietri factory in the town of Vietri-sur-Mare, near Salerno. The entire town is filled with factories and stores, but Vietri itself (a popular brand with strong U.S. distribution) will allow you into the factory to buy or to design your own wares. For info in the U.S., call © 800/277-5933 or go to www.vietri.com. Tell them I sent you and you will receive directions and factory-store information. There is another firm that does much of the same—Solimene (go to www.solimene.com).

Remember when buying dishes: Prices may be low, but shipping isn't.

pasta, but I'm sure they will sell out before you get there. This is a tiny little place, but you can buy lemons (a great gift to take back home if you don't live in the U.S.), snacks, water, soft drinks, picnics, etc. Open Monday morning; closes on Sunday at 1pm.

EMPORIO DE SIRENUSE
Via Colombo 30, across the street from Le Sirenuse.

This is where I first discovered my idol, Lisa Corti, and where I first fell in love with my dear friend Carla, who buys for the shop and has the eye of a maven, whom I trust with all things Italian. The tiny shop is a mélange of gorgeous tiles set into the floors, hand-painted cabinets and armoires, and merchandise in gorgeous colors, all chosen to reflect the energy of the resort and the passion of the sea.

While perhaps 30% of the merchandise is from Lisa Corti (thank God), the clothes come from Missoni, Etro, and many smaller designers that Americans might not have heard of. Prices are fair, certainly no higher than elsewhere, despite this being a fancy resort. Although I had bought a mound of Corti things in Milan, I ended up with three more tablecloths—different designs I could not live without.

This is one of the best stores in Italy and is worth the trip to Posi if you love color and flair and the art of the unique. There is also a catalog and online business: www.emporio sirenuse.com.

MENA CINQUE
Via Mulini 30.

This is my favorite of the clothing stores because their linens have a lot of style and can be worn in the real world. I bought an electric-blue linen dress, very baggy but chic, for 100€ ($110). To dress it up, I wrap a tablecloth from Emporio Sirenuse (Lisa Corti) around my shoulders as a shawl.

Chapter Ten

....

MEDITERRANEAN DREAMS: ITALY'S PORT TOWNS FROM TOP TO TOE

COME SAIL WITH ME

In the past few years, the cruise business has added more and more ships and pushed cruises to the Mediterranean in grand, but affordable, style. Dubrovnik has been reopened, putting even more pressure on Italy, with Venice usually as the turn-around point for cruises that visit Slovenia and Croatia. Not to be left out, Rome's port city has spent the past few years tearing up the roads and making dust to pour money into its dreams of seafaring glory.

There are now several routes that give passengers a lot of Italy in a week or 10-day cruise: There's a northern Italian Rivi-era itinerary from Rome to Monaco, which may or may not include some French ports. A southern routing departs from either Venice or Athens and travels around the boot of Italy to Rome, with plenty of southern Italian destinations, includ-ing a possible sighting of Stromboli and the Dalmatian coast, which includes Slovenia and Croatia.

Genoa is reinventing itself to compete for cruise business on the Italian Riviera; several ships are calling there for the first time. Catania, which has been included as a destination for many years, is really going to town and taking on many designer shops that were near there before. A **CK Store**—yep, a Calvin Klein shop—opened.

Getting There

Depending on which parts of the Mediterranean coast you plan to explore, you have several transportation options. I am forever reminding people to look at a map and understand that the Nice Airport, which is technically in France, is really the gateway to northern Italy. If you are coming from a European hub city and are using regional aircraft, there are small airports that you can fly into—from Turin to Genoa to Pisa and on into that not-at-all-small airport in Rome. Of course, once you're in Rome, you're halfway down the coast.

If you're on a cruise ship, or joining a cruise ship, you will most likely board at Monaco, Rome, Venice, or Athens. Some cruise lines are testing Marseille and Genoa as turnaround points. I just saw one ship using Villefrance-sur-Mer, France.

In many cases, the destination cities are not on water. Your ship may bus you to a place of interest, you may sign up for a land tour, or you may be on your own to use public transportation.

Shopping Hours

Store hours in southern Italy are Mediterranean, which means that virtually everyone closes up for lunch and, possibly, for the rest of the afternoon, if it's hot enough. However, there is tremendous variety and no lack of creativity in the store hours in each port city, so ask when you arrive.

Note: If you buy a lot and decide to leave your packages at a store so you don't have to schlep them in the heat all day, you need to know exactly when the store will reopen after lunch so you can retrieve them before you leave town. I was once onboard a yacht that couldn't leave port because the big-time shoppers had left their haul behind closed doors that would not unlock until 5pm!

Getting Where?

Aaron and Jenny were meeting friends in **Cinque Terre** and attempted to get train tickets from France, but no one at the train station knew anything to help them. Furthermore, their friends did not have mobile phones or an address in Italy, and they were looking for Cinque Terre, the place. They did not know that Cinque Terre is a confederation of cities and not a destination.

Despite everything you have heard, there is no city named Cinque Terre, even if it is listed that way on a cruise map. Eventually Aaron and Jenny went to Genoa, where they met someone who told them to go to **La Spezia.** If you are looking for this much-talked-about part of Italy, do some serious research before you arrive.

PORTOFINO

Portofino is postcard perfect—indeed, anytime you see an ad about Italy, or a cruise through this part of Italy, there's always a full-page photo of the harbor at Portofino. Many cruise passengers pick a route that includes this destination simply because they have heard it is so glam.

The tiny harbor is surrounded by pastel stucco buildings, many of which are stores. There are itty-bitty **Hermès, Trussardi, Gucci, Armani, Stefanel,** and **Paul & Shark** boutiques as well as a few tourist traps (TTs) and street vendors who will happily take your cash.

Portofino is beautiful, but after about an hour or so you may be wondering what to do with yourself. Answer: Take the public bus to **Santa Margherita,** a town about 2 miles away. There's not a lot of shopping, but it's real and funky, and it's fun to walk around for an hour or 2.

In Santa Margherita, there is a street market with gorgeous vegetables; there are pasta shops, drug stores, ice-cream places, and, of course, shoe stores. But there's nothing that you really have to buy; no must-do stores. This is more the place for window-shopping, for strolling, and for feeling the power of the streets, the resorts, and the vibes of rich Italians. You don't have to spend a single euro to enjoy it. On the other hand, a reader wrote to say that a side street shop was filled with cashmere sweaters that not only had great prices, but would custom-make—and mail—two-sided cashmere jackets and shirts.

A Warning About Ventemille

Because I was going to be in Portofino on a Friday and I know that Friday is the day of the market in Ventemille on the France-Italy border (where they sell all the designer fakes), I thought it might be fun to head off on an adventure.

I was on a cruise at the time, with a limited amount of time in town, and I surely didn't want to miss the boat, so I discussed all the details with the concierge on the ship and the port agent. The agent warned me against going, saying that in summer the traffic from Portofino to Ventemille can make the drive 3 hours long (each way)! I heeded his advice. If you are driving, however, and want a small adventure, there is a market in Ventemille on Tuesday and Friday and in San Remo on Saturday. This is the market that is famous for the fake designer goods, where the Louis Vuitton fakes have been known to pass muster with the rich and famous.

CINQUE TERRE

....

As noted above, there are five towns here—none named Cinque Terre. This is the destination of choice for those who realize the jet set likes places that are hard to find. Many cruise ships offer a day here; backpackers and college kids are also onto the area.

La Spezia is the main transportation hub for those arriving by public transportation; many visitors walk from city to city to explore it all, although there are local trains that connect the towns. It's easier if you have a car, but the traffic is bad in season and finding parking can be like Dante's *Inferno*. Also note that all town centers are closed to cars.

Since there is so much walking and schlepping, shopping should be limited to small items. Prices are geared for the jet set and Eurotrash youths.

LIVORNO

If you're on a cruise and you come to port at Livorno, please note that this is neither a resort nor a tourist town. It's an industrial port not too far from Florence, which will be your destination for the day. No one driving the area would ever make the detour to Livorno. For Florence, see chapter 6. You may also want to contact Maria Teresa (p. 107), who does a lot of programs for cruise passengers coming into Livorno. True shoppers may want to skip Florence and head directly to the nearby factory outlets. You will need a car for this. Don't rule out other nearby—and less tourist-infested—cities, such as Lucca.

SARDINIA

Sardinia is a rather arid little island with not too much of anything except glamour—you come here to chill out at the drop-dead gorgeous resorts that overlook the sea. There are only one or two little funky villages, not much to tour, and only a little shopping. But what shopping it is!

Porto Cervo was built by the Aga Khan, as were many of the resort towns on Sardinia. If you remember my rule of inaccessibility and exclusivity, you get the drift here. Although this is a fake village, manufactured and built to be charming and cute, it's also pretty hard to get to. The proper arrival and departure point is the pier, as the Aga himself created this town to be reached by those visiting on private yachts.

Few Americans go to Porto Cervo unless they are on a cruise that makes a stopover here. The rest of the visitors are jet-setters from Europe and Arabia.

The good news about Porto Cervo is that it's a mall. The bad news about Porto Cervo is that it's a mall. But if you've come to this isolated-yet-glamorous island looking for something chic to do, you have found it. You can spend several hours shopping. The entire town is a tiered development that includes a gorgeous hotel and a lot of stores. At the back end is the parking lot for locals. At the front end is the marina, for those who come by yacht.

Built as a stucco village, with long terraces and piazzas and even views of the sea, the mall leaves plenty of space to stroll. There are stairs here and there that lead to other levels, so you can wander and explore a little without feeling boxed in. If you're thin and tan and love the good life, you may like it here. If you prefer the back streets of Brooklyn, this is not your kind of place.

There's a post office, a place to make phone calls, a few newsstands selling postcards, and two pharmacies. But mostly there are designer shops—**Gucci, Prada, Missoni, Nazareno Gabrielli,** and **Versace. Artigianato Sardegna,** one of the stores in the mall, sells local crafts.

My favorite store is actually in the rear of the mall: **Supermercato Sarma.** This is a large (by Italian resort standards) supermarket, which is air-conditioned and stocked with food and some dry goods and things for the beach.

SICILY

Sicily has become more and more chic in the past few years, not really because of cruise ships but because it is one of the last rare and raw spots in Italy that is still stylish. It's also the home island to many of the world's most famous designers and creative types, including Signor Dolce and Signor Gabbana, and even Signor Scorsese.

The main ports of call are Catania and Taormina. Most ships offer day trips to various historical sights, including Syracuse. For the most part, you do not come to Sicily to shop. But then, man cannot live on lemons alone.

If you really do want to shop, you may want to contact an American woman who, with her Sicilian husband, organizes all sorts of tours; you do not sleep with fishes. Go to www.rosy.sicilian.net or call © **091/866-5322**. Also offering tasting tours with some food shopping is a British tour organization called Tastes of Italy. Go to www.tastesofitaly.co.uk or call © **44-207-731-5885**.

CATANIA

This isn't the chicest place on earth, but it's got a really wonderful street market and is where I fell in love with the Olive Man. The best food markets in town are in Piazza Carlo Alberto and in the various streets running through Porta Uzeda. If your cruise ship has a shuttle bus, you will invariably be dropped off near the market.

Also note that one of the island's folk arts is bread made in shapes, usually produced for certain saints' days and religious holidays. In Catania, the feast of Saint Agatha is the day that bakeries sell sugared versions of her breasts.

TAORMINA

Taormina is a Sicilian coastal town located just south of the Straits of Messina—that's the narrow piece of water between the toe of the boot and the island of Sicily.

Although Taormina has plenty of TTs and can be crowded in season and unbearably hot in summer, there's something glamorous and a little bit funky about it that delights me.

Taormina is a town that has charm almost down perfectly; a town that mixes and mingles a variety of cultures—and has shopping souvenirs to go with it. Yes, this is the town where you can buy a Madonna set into a piece of lava from Mount Etna. But it's also where you can buy antiques (real and fake), faience, Sicilian folk crafts, a variety of foodstuffs (marzipan!), and a few pairs of shoes. That's not bad for an afternoon's work.

Taormina is a hillside village that overlooks the sea from its perch in the middle of coastal Sicily. The destination actually has two parts: upper (the town) and lower, which stretches around to include several spans of beach.

If you arrive by ship, there are two different ways to get to town: (1) by shuttle bus provided by cruise ships or (2) on a cable car, which departs from the other part of the beach that may not be convenient to where your ship comes in.

In town, there are two main shopping areas: the main street, a pedestrian-only thoroughfare called **Corso Umberto,** and the **Via Teatro.** The latter begins on your left as you enter town from the pier. It can be hard to find. Ask—it's worth doing.

INDEX